CHRISTMAS CAROLS

CHRISTMAS CAROLS
A Reference Guide

William E. Studwell

Indexes by
David A. Hamilton

GARLAND PUBLISHING, INC. • NEW YORK & LONDON
1985

Library of Congress Cataloging in Publication Data

Studwell, William E. (William Emmett), 1936–
  Christmas carols.

  Includes indexes.
  1. Carols—Dictionaries.   2. Carols—Indexes.
  3. Carols—Bibliography.   I. Title.
ML102.C3S9   1985   783.6'5   84-48240
ISBN 0-8240-8899-9 (alk. paper)

Printed on acid-free, 250-year-life paper
Manufactured in the United States of America

CONTENTS

ACKNOWLEDGMENTS

The author wishes to express his appreciation to the many organizations and persons who rendered assistance or encouraged the project. Among the organizations giving assistance were: Northern Illinois University, the University of Illinois at Urbana-Champaign, the University of Wisconsin-Madison, Northwestern University, Indiana University, the Library of Congress, New York Public Library, Mel Elliott Music of DeKalb, Illinois, and the First United Methodist Church of DeKalb, Illinois. Among the persons providing materials were: Mary Anderson, James Baker, Jitka Hurych, and Dorothy Jones of DeKalb, Illinois; and Lois Solberg of Sycamore, Illinois. Two persons who were particularly of assistance with their encouragement and patience were my associate John Berry of Sycamore, Illinois, and my wife Ann Stroia Studwell. Also, the competent preparation of camera-ready copy by Barbara Sherman of DeKalb, Illinois, should be noted.

PREFACE

This volume is the first reference book in the English language, and perhaps in any language, which broadly and comprehensively deals with Christmas carols. It would not be practical to treat all carols currently in print, for there are several thousand of them. This work, however, covers all of the more important and more popular English language and foreign carols and in addition provides a substantial selection of lesser-known carols based on interest, variety, availability, and relation to other carols being treated.

The book has four sections:

1. general background material on the carol;

2. a bibliography;

3. a historical dictionary which lists 789 carols, provides historical and other information about them, and in most cases locates them in one or more publications;

4. title, person and group, and place indexes to the historical dictionary.

The major section, the historical dictionary, will be more effectively used if the following information is clearly understood. First, the entry for each carol is a title in its vernacular (original) language. The carol may also have one or more variant vernacular titles, one or more titles translated into English, and/or one or more differing first lines. Since the carol may be listed under a title other than the one being searched for, and since there are many identical or similar titles in the historical dictionary, IT IS VERY IMPORTANT THAT THE TITLE INDEX BE CONSULTED BEFORE THE HISTORICAL DICTIONARY IS USED. Second, entries are always alphabetized under the initial article, with the exception of the English article, "The." Third, some elements of the dictionary require detailed explanations, as given below:

> *AUTHOR/COMPOSER*--if a carol is anonymous, the notation "folk" is always indicated unless there is some reason for believing the carol is mainstream (for example, use of Latin or association with the church).

DATE (LYRICS AND MUSIC)--sometimes the date of publication is
   indicated, sometimes the date of writing or creation is
   indicated, and sometimes both are indicated. DATES WITH
   QUESTION MARKS ARE SIMPLY BEST GUESSES AND ARE TO BE
   REGARDED AS SUGGESTIONS AND NOT NECESSARILY AS FACT!

FOUND--in most cases, three-letter symbols are given in this
   area. These symbols represent publications in which a
   text (both lyrics and music) of the particular carol is
   located. The full bibliographical information for the
   publication can be found in part A of the bibliography by
   searching under the three-letter code. If one to five
   locations were found, all such locations are given. If
   more than five but less than many were found, five locations are listed based on the importance, diversity, and
   availability of the texts. If many locations were found,
   the word "MANY" is indicated. When the only sources of
   information were reference works, sheet music, sound
   recordings, and similar sources, the "FOUND" category is
   deleted.

THE CHRISTMAS CAROL: DEFINITION, NATURE, CULTURAL IMPACT

The Christmas carol has been defined in various and differing
ways over the years. Some persons have limited its definition to
include only a group of songs written in the 15th and 16th centuries.
However, excluding songs like JOY TO THE WORLD!, ADESTE FIDELES, and
HARK! THE HERALD ANGELS SING is obviously totally unjustified. Other
persons have confined the definition to songs of religious content.
But most persons regard the completely secular song DECK THE HALLS
WITH BOUGHS OF HOLLY as a carol, and many also consider JINGLE BELLS
to be a carol. The only valid criterion in defining the carol is how
carol collectors/editors/publishers and carol singers/musicians/
listeners in everyday activity treat the carol. On that basis, the
Christmas carol may well be given the following broad definition:

> *A song used to celebrate Christmas and its adjacent*
> *events (including Advent, Epiphany, the New Year,*
> *and to some extent the winter season).*

One of the more important characteristics of the carol is its
long-term and widespread mass appeal. It is a phenomenon popular
with diverse and varied segments of society. Accordingly, the music
historian Arthur Jacobs has described the carol as a "song for use by
ordinary people"[1] and the OXFORD BOOK OF CAROLS has described the
carol as giving "voice to the common emotions of healthy people in
language that can be understood and music that can be shared by
all."[2] The carol is meant to be actively sung, played, and heard,
year after year, by all types of persons.

In addition to geographic influences, there are three considera-
tions which help shape the personality of each carol. The first is
age, whether the carol is traditional or recent. The second is content, whether the carol is religious or secular. The third is
authorship, whether the carol is from "mainstream" or folk sources.
Some famous persons are directly associated with carols, including
Martin Luther, Isaac Watts, Charles Wesley, Adolphe Adam, and
Benjamin Britten. But in general the carol is the domain of the
obscure. That is, most carols are either anonymous folk, anonymous
mainstream, the product of otherwise little-known persons, or the
incidental byproduct of persons who are primarily famous for other
reasons.

Carols can be any combination of these three factors to any
degree. An example of a carol which is in the middle ground of all
three categories is STILLE NACHT, HEILIGE NACHT (SILENT NIGHT, HOLY
NIGHT). Though generally regarded as "traditional," it was written
relatively recently (1818). It is mainstream because the authors of

both the lyrics and the music were educated persons whose identity
is known. Yet it has some folk characteristics because of its
simplicity and its origin in a rural church in Austria. And it
certainly is religious in content, but at the same time is not heavy
or theological in tone. In contrast, DECK THE HALLS WITH BOUGHS OF
HOLLY is a carol which is extreme in all three aspects. It is
clearly old, most likely created in the 16th century. It is defi-
nitely of folk origin. And it is decidedly secular, without the
smallest suggestion of religious content, and is in fact so jolly
and lively that it could easily (but wrongfully) be interpreted as
being detrimental to the religious spirit of Christmas.[3]

Perhaps the most significant feature of the Christmas carol is
its socio-cultural impact. Carols may be the most culturally in-
fluential single group of enduring songs in Western society. All
other types of enduring songs are generally confined by country/
region, group, language, and/or class. "Classical" songs by such
masters as Schubert and Mendelssohn are internationally appreciated
but have relatively limited audiences. Non-carol folk songs tend
to stay within national or regional borders and within social class
lines. Non-carol religious songs are to a large extent sectarian,
and even when shared by more than one religious group are limited to
the followers of the groups. National and patriotic songs have
little influence outside of the particular country or group. On
the other hand, everybody in Western society comes in contact with
the Christmas carol, no matter what their nationality, age, educa-
tion, class, beliefs, or lifestyle. (And the sphere of the carol
even transcends the predominantly Christian areas.) Furthermore,
because Christmas and its associated events (in their sacred and
secular manifestations) comprise by far our longest and most dominant
holiday period, the case for the strong cultural influence of the
Christmas carol becomes even more persuasive.[4]

---

[1]Arthur Jacobs, A NEW DICTIONARY OF MUSIC (Baltimore: Penguin
Books, 1958), p. 62.

[2]The OXFORD BOOK OF CAROLS (London: Oxford University Press,
1964), p. v.

[3]For further development of this theme, see William E. Studwell,
"The Role of the Jolly Secular Carol in a Religious Holiday: The
Case of DECK THE HALLS WITH BOUGHS OF HOLLY." (manuscript)

[4]For further development of this theme, see William E. Studwell,
"The Cultural Impact of the Christmas Carol," JOURNAL OF CHURCH
MUSIC (December 1982), pp. 13-14.

CAROL CHRONOLOGY

To 1400--relatively few carols were created, mainly Latin and Greek.

12th century--the oldest well-known carol, VENI, EMMANUEL (O COME, O
    COME, EMMANUEL), was probably created.

13th-14th centuries--some vernacular (national language) carols were
    created, including well-known ones such as W ZLOBIE LEZY
    (Poland), LA MARCHE DES ROIS (France), and IN DULCI JUBILO
    (a macaronic or combination Latin/vernacular carol from
    Germany).

15th century--although there were some songs called carols before
    1400, the carol really began to develop in the 15th century.
    Around 1400 in England, and somewhat earlier on the continent,
    the carol evolved as a popular dance form and soon flourished.
    (The word "carol" was probably derived from the Greek word
    "choros," meaning "dance.") This new type of song was a reac-
    tion to the strictness and puritanism of the Middle Ages, and
    was fostered by the more secular and humanistic spirit of the
    late Middle Ages and Renaissance. Among the carols created in
    this period were the English songs THE BOAR'S HEAD CAROL and
    COVENTRY CAROL.

16th century--the carol continued to flourish. In Great Britain,
    GOD REST YOU MERRY, GENTLEMEN and THE FIRST NOWELL were proba-
    bly created, and DECK THE HALLS WITH BOUGHS OF HOLLY was most
    likely created. In Germany, O TANNENBAUM (O CHRISTMAS TREE)
    was most likely created.

1535--the words for VOM HIMMEL HOCH, DA KOMM ICH HER (FROM HEAVEN
    ABOVE TO EARTH I COME) were published. (The music was pub-
    lished in 1539.) This was the first well-known carol by a
    famous person (Martin Luther).

1582--the first important collection of carols was published. Edited
    by Theodoric Petri of Finland, this collection, called PIAE
    CANTIONES, consisted of 73 Latin hymns and carols with tunes.
    Among the tunes was the one later used for GOOD KING WENCESLAS.

1640--the Puritans came to power in England. In 1644, Christmas was
    banned for several years. The carol began an almost two-
    century decline in England.

1641--around this date, the first-known carol in the Americas, JESUS
    AHATONHIA, was created in Ontario.

18th century--there was increased carol activity in the Americas. The first New World style Latin American carols were possibly created and the first carols of Black American origin were probably created. Toward the end of the century, United States mainstream carol writing began to flourish.

1719--the words for JOY TO THE WORLD! were published.

1739--the words for HARK! THE HERALD ANGELS SING were published.

1740--around this date, ADESTE FIDELES (O COME ALL YE FAITHFUL) was written.

1818--STILLE NACHT, HEILIGE NACHT (SILENT NIGHT, HOLY NIGHT), probably the best-known of all carols, was written.

1822--the first significant English language carol collection, Davies Gilbert's SOME ANCIENT CHRISTMAS CAROLS, was published. Starting with this, and continuing into the 20th century, folk carols were actively collected in England. In the United States, Clement Moore wrote 'TWAS THE NIGHT BEFORE CHRISTMAS, thus creating the modern myth of Santa Claus.

1833--William Sandys published an even more important English language carol collection, CHRISTMAS CAROLS, ANCIENT AND MODERN.

1839--the music for JOY TO THE WORLD! was published.

1840--the music for HARK! THE HERALD ANGELS SING was written.

1843--Charles Dickens published his classic story A CHRISTMAS CAROL and thereby revitalized the celebration of Christmas in England.

1847--CANTIQUE DE NOËL (O HOLY NIGHT), the best-known French carol, was written.

1849--the words for IT CAME UPON THE MIDNIGHT CLEAR were written. (The music was published the next year.) This was the first American carol of international repute.

1857--WE THREE KINGS OF ORIENT ARE was written. Also written was JINGLE BELLS, the first secular American carol of international repute.

1868--O LITTLE TOWN OF BETHLEHEM, the best known American carol, was written.

1871--CHRISTMAS CAROLS, NEW AND OLD, a collection edited by Henry Ramsden Bramley and John Stainer, was published. This was the first major collection of English language carols. A larger edition appeared around 1878.

1875--R. R. Chope's CAROLS FOR USE IN CHURCH, another historically important collection of English language carols and considerably larger than either of Bramley and Stainer's editions, was published. An even larger second edition was published in 1894.

1885--the words for AWAY IN A MANGER were published. The music was published in 1887.

1928--THE OXFORD BOOK OF CAROLS was published. (It was republished in 1964 with some changes.) This was the classic English language carol collection.

1942--WHITE CHRISTMAS was presented in the movie HOLIDAY INN. This became the most famous 20th century American Christmas song.

1949--RUDOLPH THE RED-NOSED REINDEER was published. The song introduced the first successful new Christmas character since Clement Moore's 1822 creation of Santa Claus, and also possibly encouraged a subsequent trend toward similar novelty songs.

1963--THE INTERNATIONAL BOOK OF CHRISTMAS CAROLS, the most important carol collection published in the United States, was issued.

BIBLIOGRAPHY

A. CAROL SOURCES CITED IN THE HISTORICAL DICTIONARY

ADU ADULT SCHOOL CAROLS (London: J. Curwen & Sons, [19--]).
     Small general collection.

ANS AMERICAN NEGRO SONGS: A COMPREHENSIVE COLLECTION OF
     RELIGIOUS AND SECULAR FOLK SONGS. Compiled and arranged by
     John W. Work (Philadelphia: Theodore Presser, 1940).
     Contains four carols.

APP THE APPLE TREE: CHRISTMAS MUSIC FROM THE CAMBRIDGE HYMNAL.
     Edited by David Holbrook and Elizabeth Poston (Cambridge:
     Cambridge University Press, 1976).
     Excellent, well-edited, medium-sized general collection.

BAE NOËL: THE JOAN BAEZ CHRISTMAS SONGBOOK. Edited by Maynard
     Solomon (New York: Ryerson Music Publishers, 1967).
     Small attractive collection.

BAP NEW BAPTIST HYMNAL (Valley Forge: Judson Press, 1926).
     Contains a number of carols.

BMC B.M. CO'S CHRISTMAS CAROL BOOK. Easy arrangements for
     playing and singing by Chester Wallis (Boston: Boston Music
     Co., 1944).
     Small general collection.

BOL Jans Bols, HONDERD OUDE VLAAMSCHE LIEDEREN (Buren, Nether-
     lands: Frits Knuf, 1979).
     Contains a number of Flemish carols.

BRI Benjamin Britten, A CEREMONY OF CAROLS (Oceanside, N.Y.:
     Boosey and Hawkes, 1956).
     Contains nine original tunes by Britten set to old
     carol lyrics.

BRO ENGLISH TRADITIONAL SONGS AND CAROLS. Collected and edited,
     with annotations and pianoforte accompaniments, by Lucy E.
     Broadwood (Totowa, N.J.: EP Publishing, 1974).
     Contains several carols.

BRU E. Bruning, HET NEDERLANDSE KERSTLIED VAN DE 14E TOT DE 20E
     EEUW (Tilburg: W. Bergmans, 1934).
     Medium-sized collection of Dutch carols.

BUD   DAS ALTE DEUTSCHE WEIHNACHTSLIED: EINE AUSWAHL MIT DEN
      WEISEN IN KLAVIERSASS. Herausgegeben von Karl Budde und
      Arnold Mendelssohn (Hamburg: Hanseatische Verlagsanstalt,
      1924).
      Large collection of older German carols.

BUR   THE ALFRED BURT CAROLS FOR CHILDREN. Lyrics by Wihla
      Hutson and Bates G. Burt. Music by Alfred Burt (Delaware
      Water Gap, Pa.: Shawnee Press, 1972).
      Eight carols.

CAN   CANCIONERO ([Madrid]: Departamento de Publicaciones de la
      Delegación Nacional del Frente de Juventudes, 1943).
      Excellent large collection of Spanish folk songs;
      contains many carols.

CAT   NEW CATHOLIC HYMNAL. Compiled and edited by Anthony Petti
      and Geoffrey Laycock (Full ed.; London: Faber Music, 1971).
      Contains a number of carols.

CAW   CHRISTMAS AROUND THE WORLD: A CAROL SERVICE (Minneapolis:
      Augsburg Publishing House, 1935).
      Contains ten carols.

CCB   THE CAMBRIDGE CAROL-BOOK. Edited by Charles Wood and George
      Ratcliffe Woodward (London: Society for Promoting Christian
      Knowledge, 1924).
      Medium-sized collection with a number of unique carols.

CCC   CHRISTMAS CAROLS AND CHORUSES (Chicago: Hall & McCreary,
      1933).
      Small to medium-sized general collection.

CCF   CAROLS FOR CHOIRS, 4. Edited and arranged by David Willcocks
      and John Rutter (London: Oxford University Press, 1980).
      Contains 50 carols.

CCM   CHRISTMAS CAROLS FROM MANY COUNTRIES. Arranged for unchanged
      voices by Satis N. Coleman and Elin K. Jörgensen (New York:
      G. Schirmer, 1934).
      Medium-sized general collection.

CCO   CAROLS FOR CHOIRS, 1. Edited and arranged by Reginald
      Jacques and David Willcocks (London: Oxford University
      Press, 1961).
      Contains 50 carols.

CCT   CAROLS FOR CHOIRS, 2. Edited and arranged by David Willcocks
      and John Rutter (London: Oxford University Press, 1970).
      Contains 50 carols.

CEI   OLD FRENCH AND CZECHO-SLOVAKIAN CHRISTMAS CAROLS. Arranged
      by Richard Donovan (London: Stainer & Bell, 1931).
      Publications of the Carol Society, v. 8; eight carols,
      with notes.

CEL SWISS, ENGLISH, AND SWEDISH CAROLS. Arranged by David
     Stanley Smith (London: Stainer & Bell, 1934).
     Publications of the Carol Society, v. 11; eight carols,
     with notes.

CET EIGHT FRENCH AND FLEMISH CAROLS. Arranged by Luther M. Noss
     (New York: Galaxy Music Corp., 1942).
     Publications of the Carol Society, vol. 18; eight carols,
     with notes.

CFF FLEMISH AND OTHER CHRISTMAS CAROLS. Arranged by David
     Stanley Smith (London: Stainer & Bell, 1938).
     Publications of the Carol Society, v. 15; eight carols,
     with notes.

CFI OLD CHRISTMAS CAROLS. Arranged by David Stanley Smith
     (London: Stainer & Bell, 1928).
     Publications of the Carol Society, v. 5; eight carols,
     with notes.

CFO OLD FRENCH AND GERMAN CAROLS. Arranged by David Stanley
     Smith (London: Stainer & Bell, 1927).
     Publications of the Carol Society, v. 4; eight carols,
     with notes.

CFS THE OXFORD BOOK OF CAROLS FOR SCHOOLS. A selection arranged
     for unison singing from The Oxford Book of Carols by Percy
     Dearmer, R. Vaughan Williams, Martin Shaw (London: Oxford
     University Press, 1956).
     Medium-sized general collection.

CHO R.R. Chope, CAROLS FOR USE IN CHURCH DURING CHRISTMAS AND
     EPIPHANY, EASTER, ASCENSION, AND HARVEST (London: William
     Clowes & Sons, 1894).
     Large general collection; this and the smaller 1875
     edition are among the first major English language carol
     collections.

CHT CHRISTMAS TIDE (Rev. ed.; New York: Paull-Pioneer Music
     Corp., 1932).
     Medium-sized general collection.

CHW CHRISTIAN WORSHIP: A HYMNAL (Valley Forge, Pa.: Judson
     Press, 1953).
     Contains a number of carols.

CNI TRADITIONAL BASQUE AND FLEMISH CHRISTMAS CAROLS. Arranged
     by David Stanley Smith (London: Stainer & Bell, 1932).
     Publications of the Carol Society, v. 9; eight carols,
     with notes.

CNT EIGHT BURGUNDIAN CAROLS. Arranged by Marshall Bartholomew
     (New York: Galaxy Music Corp., 1947).
     Publications of the Carol Society, v. 19; eight carols,
     with notes.

COE EIGHT TRADITIONAL FRENCH NOELS. Arranged by David Stanley
Smith (London: Stainer & Bell, 1924).
Publications of the Carol Society, v. 1; eight carols,
with notes.

COF THE COWLEY CAROL BOOK FOR CHRISTMAS, EASTER AND ASCENSION-
TIDE: FIRST SERIES. Compiled and arranged by George
Ratcliffe Woodward (Rev. and enlarged ed.; London: A.R.
Mowbray, 1933).
Medium-sized general collection emphasizing older carols.

COS THE COWLEY CAROL BOOK FOR CHRISTMAS, EASTER, AND ASCENSION-
TIDE: SECOND SERIES. Compiled and arranged by George
Woodward and Charles Wood (London: A.R. Mowbray, 1931).
Medium-sized general collection emphasizing older carols.

CSE OLD FRENCH AND POLISH CAROLS. Arranged by David Stanley
Smith (London: Stainer & Bell, 1930).
Publications of the Carol Society, v. 7; eight carols,
with notes.

CSI TRADITIONAL CHRISTMAS CAROLS. Arranged by David Stanley
Smith (London: Stainer & Bell, 1929).
Publications of the Carol Society, v. 6; eight carols,
with notes.

CST EIGHT SWISS AND FRENCH CAROLS. Arranged by Luther M. Noss
(New York: Galaxy Music Corp., 1941).
Publications of the Carol Society, v. 17; eight carols,
with notes.

CTE RUSSIAN, BASQUE AND FLEMISH CAROLS. Arranged by David
Stanley Smith (London: Stainer & Bell, 1933).
Publications of the Carol Society, v. 10; eight carols,
with notes.

CTH OLD FRENCH AND FRANCONIAN CAROLS. Arranged by David Stanley
Smith (London: Stainer & Bell, 1926).
Publications of the Carol Society, v. 3; eight carols,
with notes.

CTT EIGHT OLD CHRISTMAS CAROLS. Arranged by David Stanley Smith
(London: Stainer & Bell, 1936).
Publications of the Carol Society, v. 13; eight carols,
with notes.

CTW EIGHT TRADITIONAL CHRISTMAS CAROLS. Arranged by David
Stanley Smith (London: Stainer & Bell, 1925).
Publications of the Carol Society, v. 2; eight carols,
with notes.

DOR A COLLECTION OF DORSET CAROLS. Collected and arranged by
W.A. Pickard-Cambridge (London: A.W. Ridley, 1926).
Contains 42 carols.

DOU Aug. Doutrepont, LES NOËLS WALLONS (Liège: Société Liégeoise de Littérature Wallonne, 1909).
Study of carols from Belgium and France; includes 14 carols with music.

EAR EARLY ENGLISH CHRISTMAS CAROLS. Edited by Rossel Hope Robbins (New York: Columbia University Press, 1961).
Medium-sized collection.

ECF THE ENGLISH CAROL BOOK: FIRST SERIES. Music edited by Martin Shaw. Words edited by Percy Dearmer (London: A.R. Mowbray, 1931).
Contains 32 carols.

ECS THE ENGLISH CAROL BOOK: SECOND SERIES. Music edited by Martin Shaw. Words edited by Percy Dearmer (London: A.R. Mowbray, 1929).
Contains 22 carols.

ENG THE ENGLISH HYMNAL SERVICE BOOK (London: Oxford University Press, 1962).
Contains a number of carols.

ETE EIGHT TRADITIONAL ENGLISH CAROLS. Collected and arranged by R. Vaughan Williams (London: Stainer & Bell, [1919]).
Minor collection.

FCC FAVORITE CHRISTMAS CAROLS. Selected and arranged by... Charles J.F. Cofone (New York: Dover, 1975).
Medium-sized general collection.

FHS FOLKEHOJSKOLENS SANGBOG (Odense: Foreningens Forlag, 1964).
Very large collection of Scandinavian (mostly Danish) songs; contains a number of Danish carols.

FIN FINLAND SJUNGER: FINLAND I TON OCH BILD (Helsinki: Edition Fazer, 1952).
Medium-sized collection of Finnish songs; contains one carol.

FIR FIRESIDE BOOK OF FOLK SONGS. Selected and edited by Margaret Branford Boni. Arranged for the piano by Norman Lloyd (New York: Simon and Schuster, 1947).
Very good large collection; contains a number of carols.

FJE THE SHEPHERDS (LOS PASTORES): A SPANISH-AMERICAN CHRISTMAS FOR SA VOICES. Traditional melodies in settings by Helen Luvaas Fjerstad (Minneapolis: Schmitt, Hall & McCreary, 1972).
Ten carols with Spanish and English texts.

FYF William Wallace Fyfe, CHRISTMAS, ITS CUSTOMS AND CAROLS (London: J. Blackwood, [1860]).
Interesting book on Christmas; has some carol texts.

GAS GILBERT AND SANDYS' CHRISTMAS CAROLS: WITH SIX COLLATERAL
     TUNES. Edited by Richard R. Terry (London: Burns Oates &
     Washburne, [19--]).
        Republication of Gilbert's and Sandys' landmark collec-
        tions, with background information.

GIF Davies Gilbert, SOME ANCIENT CHRISTMAS CAROLS (London: John
     Nichols and Son, 1822).
        The first important English language carol collection;
        small collection of English folk carols.

GIS Davies Gilbert, SOME ANCIENT CHRISTMAS CAROLS (2nd ed.;
     London: John Nichols and Son, 1823).
        Enlarged edition of his 1822 book.

GLA GLADA JUL, HÄRLIGA JUL: 90 JULLEKAR, JULHYMNER OCH JULSÅNGER.
     Ny upplaga, reviderad och utökad av Kåge Dominique (Stock-
     holm: Carl Gehrmans Musikförlag, 1952).
        Medium-sized collection of Swedish carols.

GOL THE GOLDEN BOOK OF CAROLS. Edited by William L. Reed (New
     and rev. ed.; London: Blandford Press, 1967).
        Small general collection.

HAP HAPPINESS IS THE JOY OF CHRISTMAS MUSIC (New York: Big 3
     Music Corp., [197-?]).
        Large collection emphasizing recent American songs.

HAR THE HARVARD UNIVERSITY HYMN BOOK (Cambridge, Mass.: Harvard
     University Press, 1964).
        Contains a number of carols; very good historical notes.

HAW THE HAWTHORN BOOK OF CHRISTMAS CAROLS. Edited by Cyril
     Taylor (New York: Hawthorn Books, 1957).
        Medium-sized general collection.

HEL CHRISTMAS, ITS CAROLS, CUSTOMS AND LEGENDS. Compiled and
     arranged by Ruth Heller (Minneapolis: Hall & McCreary,
     1948).
        Good medium-sized general collection with information
        about Christmas in general.

HFW HAUSBÜCHLEIN FÜR WEIHNACHTEN. Herausgegeben von Ernst Hörler
     and Rudolf Schoch (Zürich: Musikverlag zum Pelikan, 1951).
        Contains 24 German carols.

HUS SONGS OF THE NATIVITY. Edited, with notes, by William Henry
     Husk (London: John Camden Hotten, [1855]).
        Contains many English-language carols, but only twelve
        tunes.

HUT CAROLS OLD AND CAROLS NEW. Collected from many sources and
     arranged by Charles L. Hutchins (Boston: Paris Choir, 1916).
        Huge general collection; contains many unique carols;
        perhaps the best collection prior to THE OXFORD BOOK OF
        CAROLS.

ICC   ITALIAN CHRISTMAS CAROLS: FROM "200 OLD CHRISTMAS CAROLS".
      Collected and edited by Richard R. Terry (London: Burns
      Oates & Washbourne, [193-?]).
      Ten carols reprinted from the editor's earlier work.

INT   THE INTERNATIONAL BOOK OF CHRISTMAS CAROLS. Musical arrange-
      ments by Walter Ehret. Translations and notes by George K.
      Evans (Englewood Cliffs, N.J.: Prentice-Hall, 1963).
      Excellent large collection with usually reliable notes;
      perhaps the best collection ever published in an English-
      speaking country; its chief virtues are its well-rounded
      coverage of many countries and its publication of the
      foreign text as well as the English translation.

JOH   FOLK SONGS OF CANADA. Edith Fulton Fowke, literary editor;
      Richard Johnston, music editor (Waterloo, Ont.: Waterloo
      Music Co., 1954).
      Excellent collection of Canadian folk songs; has a few
      carols.

JUL   JULENS MELODIBOK: 100 JULHYMNER, JULSÅNGER OCH JULDANSER.
      Utgivna av Otto Olsson (Stockholm: Nordiska Musikförlaget,
      1957).
      Large collection of Swedish carols.

KOL   KOLEDY POLSKIE ŚREDNIOWIECZE I WIEK XVI. Pod redakcja
      Juliusza Nowak-Dluzewskiego (Warszawa: Instytut Wydawniczy,
      1966).
      Huge, well-edited collection of Polish and Latin carols
      through the 16th century; two volumes.

LAN   THE SEASON FOR SINGING: AMERICAN CHRISTMAS SONGS AND CAROLS.
      Compiled by John Langstaff (Garden City, N.Y.: Doubleday,
      1974).
      Medium-sized collection with emphasis on folk carols.

LDS   HYMNS, CHURCH OF JESUS CHRIST OF LATTER-DAY SAINTS (Salt
      Lake City: Church of Jesus Christ of Latter-Day Saints,
      1948).
      Contains a number of carols.

LEA   TWELVE TRADITIONAL CAROLS FROM HEREFORDSHIRE. Collected,
      edited, and arranged by E. M. Leather and R. Vaughan
      Williams (London: Stainer & Bell, 1920).
      Useful collection of English carols.

LEI   James F. Leisy, THE FOLK SONG ABECEDARY (New York: Hawthorn,
      1966).
      Excellent large collection of folk songs from many
      nations; contains several carols.

LOM   Alan Lomax, THE FOLK SONGS OF NORTH AMERICA IN THE ENGLISH
      LANGUAGE (Garden City, N.Y.: Doubleday, 1960).
      Fine large collection of folk songs; has several carols.

LOP Francisco Lopez Cruz, EL AGUINALDO Y EL VILLANCICO EN EL
    FOLKLORE PUERTORRIQUEÑO ([San Juan]: Instituto de Cultura
    Puertorriqueño, 1956).
    This study of Puerto Rican carols contains twelve carols
    with both words and music.

LUC CANCIONES POPULARES. Música arreglada y editada por Allena
    Luce (Boston: Silver, Burdett, 1921).
    Medium-sized collection of Spanish language folk songs
    with a Puerto Rican emphasis; contains a number of carols.

LUT SERVICE BOOK AND HYMNAL (Minneapolis: Augsburg Publishing
    House, 1959).
    This hymnal of the Lutheran Church in America contains a
    number of carols.

MAL Don Malin, THE SYMBOLS OF CHRISTMAS: A MUSICAL PAGEANT (New
    York: B.F. Wood Music Co., 1962).
    Small collection of carols.

MAR CHRISTMAS CAROLS FOR TREBLE CHOIRS. Arranged and edited by
    Florence M. Martin (Chicago: Hall & McCreary, 1941).
    Small general collection.

MEC MEDIAEVAL CAROLS. Edited by John Stevens (London: Stainer &
    Bell, 1952).
    Fourth volume in the series MUSICA BRITANNICA; very large
    collection of 15th century English carols.

MED A MEDIEVAL CAROL BOOK. Edited by Richard R. Terry (London:
    Burns Oates and Washburne, [1931?]).
    Medium-sized collection of medieval English carols.

MEN THE MENNONITE HYMNAL (Newton, Kan.: Faith and Life Press,
    1969).
    Contains a number of carols.

MET THE METHODIST HYMNAL (Nashville: Methodist Publishing
    House, 1966).
    Contains a number of carols.

MON Juan Hidalgo Montoya, CANCIONERO DE NAVIDAD: VILLANCICOS
    POPULARES ESPAÑOLES (Madrid: A. Carmona, 1969).
    Excellent large collection of Spanish carols.

MOO Juan Hidalgo Montoya, FOLKLORE MUSICAL ESPAÑOL (Madrid:
    A. Carmona, 1974).
    Outstanding very large collection of Spanish folk songs;
    contains many carols.

NAT Lilia Giglioli, NATIVITÀ: SACRA FAMILIA E NINNE-NANNE NEL
    CANTO POPOLARE DI ALCUNE REGIONI ITALIANE (Firenze: Leo S.
    Olschki, 1972).
    This study of Italian carols contains a number of carols.

NHW NEUES HAUSBUCHLEIN FÜR WEIHNACHTEN. Herausgegeben von
     Ernst Hörler und Rudolf Schoch (Zürich: Musikverlag zum
     Pelikan, 1953).
          Contains 22 German carols.

NIL John Jacob Niles and Helen Louise Smith, FOLK CAROLS FOR
     YOUNG ACTORS (New York: Holt, Rinehart and Winston, 1962).
     Contains four American folk carols with background
     information.

NIN Joaquin Nin, DIX NOËLS ESPAGNOLS POUR CHANT ET PIANO
     (Paris: Editions Max Eschig, 1934).
          Ten traditional Spanish carols with music by Nin;
          Spanish texts with French translations.

NOB A ROUND OF CAROLS. Music arranged by T. Tertius Noble
     (New York: Henry Z. Walck, 1964).
          Medium-sized general collection.

NOR NORTH POLE, U.S.A. (New York: Your Music Store, [197-]).
          Medium-sized collection with emphasis on recent American
          carols.

NPF NOËLS POPULAIRES FRANÇAIS DE ROUSSILLON, GUYENNE, AUVERGE,
     LANGUEDOC, FLANDRE ET BOURGOGNE. Harmonisés par Joseph
     Canteloupe (Paris: Huegel, 1949).
          Six carols from French provinces, one from Belgium.

OBE Marx and Anne Oberndorfer, NOËLS, A NEW COLLECTION OF OLD
     CAROLS (Chicago: H.T. Fitzsimons, 1932).
          Medium-sized general collection.

OCC OLD CHRISTMAS CAROLS OF THE SOUTHERN COUNTIES. Collected
     and edited by Alice E. Gillington (London: J. Curwen &
     Sons, 1910).
          Contains 16 English folk carols.

ONS 170 CHRISTMAS SONGS AND CAROLS (New York: Big 3 Music Corp.,
     [197-]).
          Large collection emphasizing recent American songs.

ONT 120 CHRISTMAS SONGS (New York: Big 3 Music Corp., [197-?]).
          Large collection emphasizing recent American songs.

OWE A WREATH OF CAROLS. 47 Christmas songs selected and edited
     by Betty M. Owen and Mary E. MacEwen (New York: Four Winds
     Press, 1966).
          General collection.

OXF THE OXFORD BOOK OF CAROLS. [Edited by] Percy Dearmer, R.
     Vaughan Williams, Martin Shaw (London: Oxford University
     Press, 1964).
          This large collection is somewhat modified from the
          original (1928) edition; both editions are outstanding
          collections with excellent notes and other historical

material on the carol; although this is the classic of carol collections, its overly British emphasis makes it less comprehensive than some other collections.

PAZ   FAVORITE SPANISH FOLKSONGS: TRADITIONAL SONGS FROM SPAIN AND LATIN AMERICA. Compiled and edited by Elena Paz (New York: Oak Publications, 1965).
      Contains several Spanish language carols with English translations.

PEE   Flor Peeters, FOUR OLD FLEMISH CHRISTMAS CAROLS FOR MIXED VOICES AND INSTRUMENTS (New York: C.F. Peeters, 1967).
      Four carols arranged by Peeters.

PEN   THE PENGUIN BOOK OF CHRISTMAS CAROLS. Compiled and edited ...by Elizabeth Poston (Middlesex: Penguin Books, 1965).
      Well-edited medium-sized general collection.

PIL   THE PILGRIM HYMNAL (Boston: Pilgrim Press, 1935).
      Contains a number of carols.

POP   CHRISTMAS POPS (Hialeah, Fla.: Screen Gems-Columbia Publications, 1974).
      Medium-sized collection with emphasis on recent American songs.

PRA   PRAISE! OUR SONGS AND HYMNS. Compiled by John W. Peterson, Norman Johnson. Edited by Norman Johnson (Grand Rapids: Singspiration Music, 1979).
      Hymnbook with a number of carols.

PRE   CHRISTMAS IN SONG. Compiled and arranged...by Theo. Preuss (Chicago: Rubank, 1947).
      Medium-sized general collection.

PRS   THE PRESBYTERIAN HYMNAL (Richmond, Va.: John Knox Press, 1927).
      Contains a number of carols.

REB   SIX POLISH CHRISTMAS CAROLS. Arranged for piano by Louise Christine Rebe (New York: Schirmer, 1948).
      Useful small collection.

REE   THE TREASURY OF CHRISTMAS MUSIC. Edited by W. L. Reed (New York: Emerson Books, 1961).
      Medium-sized general collection with emphasis on 20th century carols.

REF   THE SECOND TREASURY OF CHRISTMAS MUSIC. Edited by W.L. Reed (New York: Emerson Books, 1968).
      Medium-sized general collection with emphasis on 20th century carols.

ROT   Alfred Röth, WEIHNACHTSLIEDER MIT NOTEN (Leipzig: Franz Schneider, 1933).
      Small collection of German language carols.

RSC   THE RSCM CAROL BOOK (Croydon: Royal School of Church Music,
      [197-?]).
         Contains ten carols.

RTW   ROUND-THE-WORLD CHRISTMAS ALBUM: A COLLECTION OF CHRISTMAS
      CAROLS AND SONGS FROM MANY NATIONS. Compiled and arranged
      by Felix Guenther. English adaptations by Olga Paul (New
      York: Edward B. Marks Music Corp., 1943).
         Very good medium-sized collection of international
      carols.

RUS   RUSSIAN FOLK-SONGS. Edited and compiled by Florence Hudson
      Botsford (New York: G. Schmirmer, 1929).
         Moderate-sized collection of folk songs from the Soviet
      Union; contains three carols.

SAN   William Sandys, CHRISTMAS CAROLS, ANCIENT AND MODERN
      (London: R. Beckley, 1833).
         The second important English language carol collection
      (the first was Davies Gilbert's 1822 collection);
      medium-sized collection of English and French carols.

SAO   William Sandys, CHRISTMASTIDE, ITS HISTORY, FESTIVITIES,
      AND CAROLS (London: John Russel Smith, [1852]).
         General book on Christmas containing 12 carols with music.

SCC   SEVEN CZECHOSLOVAK CAROLS. Arranged by Vilem Tauský and
      Sheila Lennox Robertson. English words by Mary Cochrane
      Vojácek (London: Schott & Co., 1942).
         Well-edited collection.

SEA   THE SEASON OF THE YEAR: FOLKSONGS OF CHRISTMAS AND THE NEW
      YEAR. Compiled and edited by Irwin Silber (New York: Oak
      Publications, 1971).
         Well-edited medium-sized general collection.

SEE   Ruth Crawford Seeger, AMERICAN FOLK SONGS FOR CHRISTMAS
      (New York: Doubleday, 1953).
         Very good medium-sized collection of American Christmas
      folk songs with a number of Black spirituals.

SEV   72 SUPER BLOCKBUSTERS FOR '72: THE NEW CHRISTMAS SONG BOOK
      (New York: Charles Hansen Music and Books, 1972).
         Medium-sized general collection with emphasis on recent
      American songs.

SHA   ENGLISH FOLK-CAROLS. Collected by Cecil J. Sharp (London:
      Novello, 1911).
         Contains 21 carols, with notes.

SHE   Haig and Regina Shekerjian, A BOOK OF CHRISTMAS CAROLS
      (New York: Harper and Row, 1963).
         Very good medium-sized general collection.

SIG   SING GLORIAS! CHORAL SETTINGS OF THE HYMNS AND CAROLS OF THE
      CHRISTMAS CYCLE IN WORSHIP SUPPLEMENT. Compiled and edited
      by Paul Thomas (St. Louis: Concordia Publishing House,
      1971).
         Medium-sized general collection.

SIM   Henry W. Simon, CHRISTMAS SONGS AND CAROLS (Boston: Houghton
      Mifflin, 1955).
         Excellent large general collection, with good notes.

SMI   J.R.H. deSmidt, LES NOËLS ET LA TRADITION POPULAIRE
      (Amsterdam: H.J. Paris, 1932).
         Very good study of the French carol; contains a number
         of carols.

SON   John LaMontaine, SONGS OF THE NATIVITY: CHRISTMAS ANTHEM
      (New York: H.W. Gray, 1954).
         LaMontaine provides music for five carol texts.

STA   CHRISTMAS CAROLS, NEW AND OLD. The words edited by Henry
      Ramsden Bramley. The music edited by John Stainer (London:
      Novello, Ewer and Co., [ca. 1878]).
         This is the 70-carol edition; the 1871 edition was
         considerably smaller, although it was the first major
         English language carol collection.

SWE   SWEDEN SINGS: BALLADS, FOLK-SONGS AND DANCES. Photographs
      and text by K.W. Gullers (Stockholm: Nordiska Musikforlaget,
      1955).
         Contains six carols.

TCC   TEN CHRISTMAS CAROLS FROM THE SOUTHERN APPALACHIAN MOUNTAINS.
      Compiled and simply arranged with accompaniment for piano by
      John Jacob Niles (New York: G. Schirmer, 1935).
         Very interesting collection.

THF   TWO HUNDRED FOLK CAROLS. Edited by Richard R. Terry (London:
      Burns Oates & Washbourne, 1933).
         By far the most valuable collection of folk carols;
         covers many areas of Europe.

TIE   NOËLS FRANÇAIS. Transcrits et harmonisés par Julien
      Tiersot (Paris: Heugel, 1901).
         Small collection of French carols.

TOM   TOM GLAZER'S TREASURY OF FOLK SONGS. Compiled by Tom Glazer
      (New York: Grosset & Dunlap, 1964).
         Very good large collection of folk songs; contains a
         number of carols.

TRA   THE TRAPP FAMILY BOOK OF CHRISTMAS SONGS. Selected and
      arranged by Franz Wasner (New York: Pantheon, 1950).
         Pleasant medium-sized general collection.

TRE A TREASURY OF HYMNS. Selected and edited by Maria Leiper
and Henry W. Simon (New York: Simon and Schuster, 1953).
Excellent large collection of hymns with many carols.

TWA Clement Clark Moore, 'TWAS THE NIGHT BEFORE CHRISTMAS.
Set to music by Ken Darby (Delaware Water Gap, Pa.: Shawnee
Press, 1971).
Moore's poem with one of its better-known musical
settings.

ULT CHRISTMAS, 100 SEASONAL FAVORITES (Winona, Minn.: Hal
Leonard Publishing Corp., 1982).
Very good collection with emphasis on recent American
songs; part of the publisher's "Ultimate series."

UNI UNIVERSITY CAROL BOOK: A COLLECTION OF CAROLS FROM MANY
LANDS, FOR ALL SEASONS. Edited by Erik Routley (London:
H. Freeman, 1961).
Very good large general collection.

VAN CHRISTMAS MUSIC FROM COLONIAL AMERICA. Compiled, edited
and arranged by Leonard Van Camp (New York: Galaxy Music
Corp., 1975).
Well-edited collection of ten carols.

WIL HARRY ROBERT WILSON PRESENTS CHRISTMAS CHEER (New York:
Consolidated Music Publishers, 1957).
Medium-sized general collection.

WON John LaMontaine, WONDER TIDINGS: A CYCLE OF CHRISTMAS CAROLS
FOR MIXED VOICES (New York: H.W. Gray, 1964).
LaMontaine provides music for nine carol texts.

WOR DAS GROSSE BUCH VOM DEUTSCHEN VOLKSLIED. Herausgegeben vom
Hans Christoph Worbs ([Hannover: Fackelträger Verlag,
1969]).
Large collection of German folk songs; contains a number
of carols.

YAL THE YALE CAROL BOOK. Edited by H. Frank Bozyan & Sidney
Lovett (Rev. ed.; [New Haven]: Yale University Press, 1950).
Medium-sized general collection.

YOU CAROLS FOR THE TWELVE DAYS. Compiled and arranged by Percy
Young (London: Dennis Dobson, 1966).
Medium-sized general collection.

ZPE ZPEVY BETLEMSKÉ: KOLEDY. Usporádal a harmonisoval Jan
Seidel (Praha: L. Mazác, 1943).
Large collection of carols from Czechoslovakia.

B. OTHER CAROL SOURCES OF INTEREST

In addition to the publications listed below, hymnals and folk
song collections typically contain some carols.

A NEW BOOK OF CHRISTMAS CAROLS. Compiled, edited, and arranged
by Ralph Dunstan (London: Reid Bros., 1923).
Medium-sized general collection.

A SECOND BOOK OF CAROLS. Compiled, edited, and arranged by
Ralph Dunstan (London: Reid Bros., 1925).
Medium-sized general collection.

AN ITALIAN CAROL BOOK. Edited by Charles Wood and George
Ratcliffe Woodward (London: Faith Press, 1920).
Medium-sized collection of Italian carols.

THE ANGLO-AMERICAN CAROL STUDY BOOK. Collected and arranged by
John Jacob Niles (New York: G. Schirmer, 1948).
Study, with texts, of several English folk carols and their
American counterparts.

AUTO DE NAVIDAD. Ordenado y compuesto por Jimena Menéndez-Paul
(Madrid: Aguilar, 1971).
Dramatic composition containing a number of old Spanish
Christmas songs.

Bela Bartok, RUMANIAN FOLK MUSIC: VOL. 4, CAROLS AND CHRISTMAS
SONGS (COLINDE). Edited by Benjamin Suchoff (The Hague: Nijhoff,
1975).
Very large, very hard to use collection of Romanian Christmas
carols and other songs; has English translations.

CÂNTICOS DO NATAL. Reünidos e anotados por Henriqueta Rosa
Fernandes Braga (Rio de Janeiro: Livraria Kosmos Editora, 1947).
Well-edited medium-sized collection of foreign carols
translated into Portuguese.

CAROLS FOR CHRISTMAS-TIDE. Set to ancient melodies, and harmonized for voices and pianoforte, by T. Helmore. The words
principally an imitation of the original by J.M. Neale (London:
Novello, 1853).
Historically significant collection of 12 carols derived from
the 1582 collection PIAE CANTIONES.

CAROLS OF TODAY: SEVENTEEN ORIGINAL SETTINGS FOR MIXED VOICES
(London: Music Department, Oxford University Press, 1965).
Old carols set to new music.

CHRISTMAS IN SONG, SKETCH AND STORY. Selected by J.P. McCaskey
(New York: Harper & Brothers, 1891).
Large imaginative older collection.

THE CHRISTMAS SONG BOOK. Compiled and edited by Adolf T. Hanser
(13th enlarged ed.; Buffalo, N.Y.: Sotarion Publishing Co., 1926).
Medium-sized general collection.

CHRISTMAS SONGS OF MANY NATIONS: A MUSICAL ENTERTAINMENT FOR
CHILDREN. Originated and compiled by Katherine Wallace Davis
(Chicago: Clayton F. Summy Co., [19--]).
Medium-sized general collection.

Livingston Gearhart, A CHRISTMAS SINGING BEE (Delaware Water
Gap, Pa.: Shawnee Press, 1962).
Medium-sized general collection.

GOTTSCHEER VOLKSLIEDER: BAND II, GEISTLICHE LEIDER. Herausgegeben von Rolf Wilh. Brednich und Wolfgang Suppan (Mainz: B.
Schott's Söhne, 1972).
Large collection of Yugoslav German folk songs; contains a
number of carols.

Robert B. Klymasz, THE UKRAINIAN WINTER FOLKSONG CYCLE IN CANADA
(Ottawa: Information Canada, 1970).
Very good medium-sized collection of Ukrainian carols
imported into Canada; has English translations.

KOLIADY (Oliphant, Pa.: Izdanie G. Pavlusis, 1912).
Collection of Russian carols.

99 POPULAR CHRISTMAS CAROLS (London: F. Pitman Hart & Co.,
[19--]).
General collection.

OLD CAROLS FOR CHRISTMAS. Arranged by David Stanley Smith
(London: Stainer & Bell, 1937).
Publications of the Carol Society, v. 14, eight carols, with
notes.

PROVENÇAL AND OTHER CHRISTMAS CAROLS. Arranged by David Stanley
Smith (London: Stainer & Bell, 1939).
Publications of the Carol Society, v. 16; eight carols, with
notes.

PROVENÇAL AND RUSSIAN CAROLS. Arranged by David Stanley Smith
(London: Stainer & Bell, 1935).
Publications of the Carol Society, v. 12; eight carols, with
notes.

Anna Sarlin, JOULULAULUJA (Helsinki: R.E. Westerlund, [19--]).
Medium-sized collection of Finnish carols; eight small
volumes.

SIX SEVENTEENTH-CENTURY CAROLS FROM THE NETHERLANDS: FOR MIXED
VOICES. Transcribed and edited by Frits Noske (London: Oxford
University Press, 1965).
Well-edited collection.

Robert Stevenson, CHRISTMAS MUSIC FROM BAROQUE MEXICO (Berkeley:
University of California Press, 1974).
Scholarly study containing 17 carols from Mexico and Spain.

THE WEXFORD CAROLS. Assembled and edited by Diarmaid Ó Muirithe
(Portlaoise, Ireland: Dolmen Press, 1982).
Contains a number of Irish carols, four with music.

C. REFERENCE SOURCES

The best sources of information about carols are the carol
collections themselves. Particularly valuable collections for
reference purposes are THE OXFORD BOOK OF CAROLS, THE INTER-
NATIONAL BOOK OF CHRISTMAS CAROLS, Henry Simon's CHRISTMAS SONGS
AND CAROLS, and the 19-volume series PUBLICATIONS OF THE CAROL
SOCIETY. These are all listed in parts A and B of the bibliography, with the Carol Society series entered under their individual
titles. When searching for publications other than carol
collections, generally avoid books featuring "stories of the
carols" or similar material, for they are frequently inaccurate.
Some books and periodical articles with significant reference
value are indicated below.

COMPANION TO THE HYMNAL: A HANDBOOK TO THE 1964 METHODIST HYMNAL
(Nashville: Abingdon Press, 1970).
Contains detailed and very accurate information on a number of
carols which are hymns.

Gerard and Patricia Del Re, THE CHRISTMAS ALMANACK (Garden City,
N.Y.: Doubleday, 1980).
General book on Christmas with much information about carols;
particularly useful for data on recent American Christmas
songs.

Edmondstone Duncan, THE STORY OF THE CAROL (London: Walter Scott
Publishing Co., 1911).
This general monograph on the history of the carol contains
much worthwhile information, but the material is not well
organized.

Armin Haeussler, THE STORY OF OUR HYMNS (Saint Louis: Eden
Publishing House, 1952).
Contains detailed and accurate information on a number of
carols which are hymns.

John Julian, A DICTIONARY OF HYMNOLOGY (New York: Dover, 1957).
This is the classic reference book on pre-20th century hymns;
provides accurate information, frequently brief, on carols
which are hymns; although this is the most comprehensive work
on hymns, many hymn-carols are not in this work; two volumes.

Erik Routley, THE ENGLISH CAROL (London: Herbert Jenkins, 1958).
Best book on the carol; not only covers the English carol, but
has much good information on the carol in general.

William E. Studwell, A series of articles on Christmas carols in
the December issues of THE JOURNAL OF CHURCH MUSIC (1976,
1978-   ).
    Particularly see "The cultural impact of the Christmas carol"
(December 1982).

HISTORICAL DICTIONARY

1. A BABE IS BORN

    Lyrics: AUTHOR--folk.
                PLACE--England.
                DATE--probably created 14th century.
                VARIANT VERNACULAR TITLE--A BABE IS BORN, ALL OF A
                                        MAID.
                DIFFERING FIRST LINE--A BABE IS BORN, ALL OF A MAY.
    Music: COMPOSER--folk.
                PLACE--England.
                DATE--probably created 14th century.
                VARIANT TUNES--a tune by Gustav Holst (1874-1934); a
                            later form (probably 17th century) of
                            the 15th century hymn tune HERR JESU
                            CHRIST, MEIN'S LEBENS LICHT.
    Found: THF, REF, OXF, SIM, ECS
    Notes: It is reported that the carol exists on a manuscript
                slightly predating Geoffrey Chaucer (ca. 1340-1400).

2. A BABE IS BORN I WYS

    Lyrics: AUTHOR--folk.
                PLACE--England.
                DATE--possibly created 15th or 16th century.
    Music: COMPOSER--F. Bainton.
                PLACE--England.
                DATE--written 20th century.
    Found: CCT, UNI

3. A CAROLING WE GO

    Lyrics: AUTHOR--John D. Marks (1909-   ).
                PLACE--United States.
                DATE--published 1966.
                DIFFERING FIRST LINE--A CAROLING, A CAROLING.
    Music: COMPOSER--John D. Marks (1909-   ).
                PLACE--United States.
                DATE--published 1966.
    Found: ULT, ONS, ONT

4. A CHILD MY CHOICE

    Lyrics: AUTHOR--Robert Southwell (ca. 1561-1595).
                PLACE--England.
                DATE--written late 16th century.
                DIFFERING FIRST LINE--LET FOLLY PRAISE WHAT FANCY
                                    LOVES.
    Music: COMPOSER--folk.
                PLACE--England.
                DATE--possibly created 15th-17th century?
    Found: THF, UNI
    Notes: The tune is also used for the carol THE HOLY WELL.

5. A CHILD THIS DAY IS BORN

   Lyrics: AUTHOR--folk.
              PLACE--probably West country, England.
              DATE--probably created 16th or 17th century.
              VARIANT VERNACULAR TITLES--A CHILD THIS DAY; NOVELS.
   Music: COMPOSER--folk.
              PLACE--probably West country, England.
              DATE--probably created 16th or 17th century.
   Found: OXF, SIM, HAW, ENG, THF

6. A CHINESE CHRISTMAS CRADLE SONG

   Lyrics: AUTHOR--Frances Roots Hadden (1910-   ).
              PLACE--United States.
              DATE--written 1966.
              DIFFERING FIRST LINE--GREEN, GREEN THE RIVERSIDE
                                    GRASSES.
   Music: COMPOSER--folk.
              PLACE--China.
              DATE--possibly created pre-modern era?
   Found: REF
   Notes: The lyrics were inspired by an anonymous 2nd century
              Chinese poem; the song is also known as SHIAO BAO-BAO.

7. A CHRISTMAS CAROL

   Lyrics: AUTHOR--folk.
              PLACE--probably United States.
              DATE--probably created 19th century.
              DIFFERING FIRST LINE--LITTLE STAR OF BETHLEHEM!
   Music: COMPOSER--Charles Ives (1874-1954).
              PLACE--United States.
              DATE--possibly first published 1935.
   Found: OWE

8. A CHRISTMAS CAROL

   Lyrics: AUTHOR--Clement Francis Rogers (1866-1949).
              PLACE--England.
              DATE--written late 19th or early 20th century.
              DIFFERING FIRST LINE--ALL MEN DRAW NEAR, CHRISTMAS IS
                                    HERE.
   Music: COMPOSER--folk.
              PLACE--Hungary.
              DATE--possibly created 17th-19th century?
   Found: CCO

9. A CHRISTMAS SPIRITUAL

   Lyrics: AUTHOR--Muriel Smith.
              PLACE--United States.

DATE--published 1967.
DIFFERING FIRST LINE--CARRY ON, SISTER.
Music: COMPOSER--Muriel Smith.
PLACE--United States.
DATE--published 1967.
Found: REF

10. A CRADLE SONG OF THE BLESSED VIRGIN

Lyrics: AUTHOR--Henry Ramsden Bramley (1833-1917).
PLACE--England.
DATE--published 1871.
VARIANT VERNACULAR TITLE--THE VIRGIN STILLS THE
CRYING.
Music: COMPOSER--Joseph Barnby (1838-1896).
PLACE--England.
DATE--published 1871.
Found: OBE, HUT, STA, MAR
Notes: The words are a translation of Latin lyrics; the tune
has also been attributed to John Stainer (1840-1901).

11. A DAY, A DAY OF GLORY!

Lyrics: AUTHOR--John Mason Neale (1818-1866).
PLACE--England.
DATE--written mid-19th century.
Music: COMPOSER--folk.
PLACE--France.
DATE--probably created 15th century.
Found: COF, HUT
Notes: The tune is also used for the carols NOUS VOICI DANS
LA VILLE, CÉLÉBRONS LA NAISSANCE, ADAM E SA COUMPAGNO,
and CHANTONS! JE VOUS EN PRIE.

12. A ESTA PUERTA LLAMA UN NIÑO

Lyrics: AUTHOR--folk.
PLACE--Galicia, Spain.
DATE--possibly created 16th-18th century?
ENGLISH TITLE--AT THE DOOR A BABE IS KNOCKING
(translated by John Morrison).
Music: COMPOSER: folk.
PLACE: Galicia, Spain.
DATE--possibly created 16th-18th century?
Found: MON, CAN, REF
Notes: The lyrics are somewhat similar to those for the
carols EL MINO JESUS and MADRE, EN LA PUERTO HAY UN
NIÑO, but the tunes are different.

13. A HOLLY JOLLY CHRISTMAS

    Lyrics: AUTHOR--John D. Marks (1909-   ).
               PLACE--United States.
               DATE--published 1962.
               DIFFERING FIRST LINE--HAVE A HOLLY JOLLY CHRISTMAS.
    Music: COMPOSER--John D. Marks (1909-   ).
               PLACE--United States.
               DATE--published 1962.
    Found: NOR, POP, ULT, ONS, ONT

14. A JOYFUL CHRISTMAS SONG

    Lyrics: AUTHOR--M.L. Hohman.
               PLACE--United States.
               DATE--published 1947.
               DIFFERING FIRST LINE--YONDER IN THE CRIB.
    Music: COMPOSER--François Auguste Gevaert (1828-1908).
               PLACE--Belgium.
               DATE--probably written second half of 19th century.
    Found: PRE

15. A LA MEDIA NOCHE

    Lyrics: AUTHOR--folk.
               PLACE--Puerto Rico.
               DATE--possibly created 18th or 19th century?
               ENGLISH TITLES--AT THE HOUR OF MIDNIGHT (translated
                               by George K. Evans); ON THAT HOLY
                               MIDNIGHT.
    Music: COMPOSER--folk.
               PLACE--Puerto Rico.
               DATE--possibly created 18th or 19th century?
               VARIANT TUNE--another folk tune from Puerto Rico.
    Found: INT, OWE

16. A LA NANITA NANA

    Lyrics: AUTHOR--folk.
               PLACE--Spain.
               DATE--possibly created 16th-18th century?
               ENGLISH TITLES--SLEEP, SLEEP MY LITTLE JESUS (trans-
                               lated by Norman Luboff); MY JESUS, HE
                               IS SLEEPING; ROCK A BYE, BABY.
    Music: COMPOSER--folk.
               PLACE--Spain.
               DATE--possibly created 16th-18th century?
    Found: INT, TRA, PAZ

17. A LUTE LULLABY

   Lyrics: AUTHOR--folk.
           PLACE--England.
           DATE--created 16th century.
           DIFFERING FIRST LINE--LULLAY MY BABE, LIE STILL AND
                        SLEEP.
   Music: COMPOSER--John Dowland (1562-1626).
           PLACE--England.
           DATE--written late 16th or early 17th century.
   Found: UNI

18. A MARSHMALLOW WORLD

   Lyrics: AUTHOR--Carl Sigman (1909-   ).
           PLACE--United States.
           DATE--written 1949.
           DIFFERING FIRST LINE--IT'S A MARSHMALLOW WORLD IN THE
                        WINTER.
   Music: COMPOSER--Peter DeRose (1900-1953).
           PLACE--United States.
           DATE--written 1949.
   Found: POP, ULT

19. A MERRY MERRY CHRISTMAS TO YOU

   Lyrics: AUTHOR--John D. Marks (1909-   ).
           PLACE--United States.
           DATE--published 1958.
           DIFFERING FIRST LINES--MERRY MERRY MERRY MERRY MERRY
                        CHRISTMAS TO YOU; JOYEUX NOEL,
                        BUONNE NATALE, FELIZE NAVIDAD.
   Music: COMPOSER--John D. Marks (1909-   ).
           PLACE--United States.
           DATE--published 1958.
   Found: POP, ULT

20. A MINCE PIE OR A PUDDING

   Lyrics: AUTHOR--Shaker community.
           PLACE--New York State.
           DATE--probably created late 18th or 19th century.
           VARIANT VERNACULAR TITLE--WELCOME HERE!
           DIFFERING FIRST LINE--WELCOME HERE, WELCOME HERE.
   Music: COMPOSER--Shaker community.
           PLACE--New York State.
           DATE--probably created late 18th or 19th century.
   Found: SHE, SEE, LAN

21. A NEW YEAR CAROL

    Lyrics: AUTHOR--folk.
             PLACE--England.
             DATE--possibly created 17th-19th century?
             DIFFERING FIRST LINE--HERE WE BRING NEW WATER FROM
                               THE WELL SO CLEAR.
    Music: COMPOSER--Benjamin Britten (1913-1976).
             PLACE--England.
             DATE--published 1936.
    Found: CCT, CCF, APP

22. A NEW YEAR CAROL

    Lyrics: AUTHOR--Ian Sciortino.
             PLACE--United States.
             DATE--published 1966.
             DIFFERING FIRST LINE--TELL ONCE MORE THE ANCIENT
                               STORY.
    Music: COMPOSER--Frances Roots Hadden (1910-   ).
             PLACE--United States.
             DATE--published 1966.
    Found: REF

23. A-ROCKIN' ALL NIGHT

    Lyrics: AUTHOR--folk (Black spiritual).
             PLACE--probably North Carolina.
             DATE--probably created 18th or 19th century.
             DIFFERING FIRST LINES--NOW AIN'T THAT A ROCKING ALL
                              NIGHT; MARY AND THE LITTLE
                              BABY.
    Music: COMPOSER--folk (Black spiritual).
             PLACE--probably North Carolina.
             DATE--probably created 18th or 19th century.
    Found: WIL
    Notes: For a carol with similar lyrics but a different tune,
             see AIN'T THAT A ROCKING ALL NIGHT.

24. A SCOTCH LULLABY

    Lyrics: AUTHOR--John James Moment (1875-   ).
             PLACE--United States.
             DATE--probably written first half of 20th century.
             DIFFERING FIRST LINE--WEE LAMB IN THE HEATHER, ALONE
                              AND ACOLD.
    Music: COMPOSER--folk.
             PLACE--Scotland.
             DATE--possibly created 16th-18th century?
    Found: OWE

25. A SHEPHERD BAND THEIR FLOCKS ARE KEEPING

Lyrics: AUTHOR--anonymous.
PLACE--England or United States.
DATE--probably written second half of 19th century.
VARIANT VERNACULAR TITLE--A SHEPHERD BAND THEIR
FLOCKS.
Music: COMPOSER--Michael Praetorius (1571-1621).
PLACE--Germany.
DATE--published 1609.
VARIANT TUNE--tune by Samuel Parkman Tuckerman (1819-
1890).
Found: OBE, HUT

26. A SOLIS ORTUS CARDINE

Lyrics: AUTHOR--Sedulius.
PLACE--possibly Italy.
DATE--written around 450.
ENGLISH TITLE--FROM EAST TO WEST (translated by John
Ellerton [1826-1893]).
DIFFERING FIRST LINE--FROM EAST TO WEST, FROM SHORE
TO SHORE.
Music: COMPOSER--anonymous.
PLACE--probably Germany.
DATE--created medieval period.
VARIANT TUNES--two other anonymous tunes.
Found: LUT, ONS, ONT, CAT, SIG

27. A VIRGIN MOST PURE

Lyrics: AUTHOR--folk.
PLACE--England (possibly Gloucestershire).
DATE--possibly created 17th century; possibly first
published 1734.
VARIANT VERNACULAR TITLES--A VIRGIN UNSPOTTED; A
VIRGIN MOST BLESSED.
Music: COMPOSER--folk.
PLACE--England (possibly Gloucestershire).
DATE--possibly created 18th century; possibly first
published 1822.
VARIANT TUNES--tune by William Billings (1746-1800),
a United States composer; other tunes.
Found: OXF, INT, LAN, THF, VAN
Notes: A derivative of this carol was created in the
Appalachian region.

28. ABREME LA PUERTA

Lyrics: AUTHOR--folk.
PLACE--Dominican Republic
DATE--possibly created 18th or 19th century?

ENGLISH TITLE--LET ME CROSS YOUR THRESHOLD
                    (translated by Olga Paul).
Music: COMPOSER--folk.
           PLACE--Dominican Republic.
           DATE--possibly created 18th or 19th century?
Found: RTW

29. ADAM E SA COUMPAGNO

    Lyrics: AUTHOR--folk.
                PLACE--Provence, France.
                DATE--possibly created 16th-18th century?
                ENGLISH TITLES--ADAM AND HIS HELPMATE (translated by
                            K.W. Simpson); WITHIN THE VALE OF EDEN
                            (translated by Anthony G. Petti).
                DIFFERING FIRST LINE--WITHIN A LOVELY GARDEN.
    Music: COMPOSER--folk.
                PLACE--France.
                DATE--probably created 15th century.
    Found: THF, UNI, CAT
    Notes: The tune is also used for the carols NOUS VOICI DANS
                LA VILLE, A DAY, A DAY OF GLORY!, CÉLÉBRONS LA
                NAISSANCE, and CHANTONS! JE VOUS EN PRIE.

30. ADAM LAY YBOUNDEN

    Lyrics: AUTHOR--folk.
                PLACE--England.
                DATE--probably created 15th century.
                VARIANT VERNACULAR TITLE--DEO GRACIAS.
                DIFFERING FIRST LINE--ADAM LAY IBOUNDEN.
    Music: COMPOSER--Boris Ord.
                PLACE--England.
                DATE--published 1957.
                VARIANT TUNES--tunes by Benjamin Britten (1913-1976),
                            Norman Fulton (1909-   ), Peter War-
                            lock (1894-1930), and John Ireland
                            (1879-1962).
    Found: CCT, APP, OXF, UNI, BRI

31. ADESTE FIDELES

    Lyrics: AUTHOR--John Francis Wade (1711-1786).
                PLACE--probably Douai, France.
                DATE--probably written between 1740-1743; first
                            published 1760.
                ENGLISH TITLES--O COME ALL YE FAITHFUL (translated by
                            Frederick Oakeley [1802-1880]); BE
                            PRESENT, YE FAITHFUL; others.
    Music: COMPOSER--John Francis Wade (1711-1786).
                PLACE--probably Douai, France.
                DATE--probably written between 1740-1743; first
                            published 1782.

Found: MANY
Notes: Oakeley's 1841 translation originally began "Ye faithful, approach ye," but was changed to its familiar
form when first published in 1852; the tune has been
wrongly attributed to John Reading (d. 1692); also,
the carol has been regarded as an old anonymous Latin
hymn and, because of its use in the chapel of the
Portuguese Embassy in London late in the 18th century,
as a hymn from Portugal.

32. ADORAMUS TE

Lyrics: AUTHOR--anonymous.
PLACE--Europe.
DATE--probably created medieval period.
ENGLISH TITLES--WE DO WORSHIP THEE (translated by
Theo. Preuss); ADORAMUS TE.
DIFFERING FIRST LINES--ADORAMUS TE, CHRISTE; WE DO
WORSHIP THEE, JESUS; WE ADORE
THEE, CHRIST OUR LORD.
Music: COMPOSER--Giovanni Pierluigi da Palestrina
(1525-1594).
PLACE--Rome, Italy.
DATE--published 1581.
Found: OWE, PRE, WIL

33. AGUINALDO

Lyrics: AUTHOR--folk.
PLACE--Puerto Rico.
DATE--possibly created 18th or 19th century?
ENGLISH TITLE--"MARY," SAID SAINT JOSEPH (translated
by Seymour Barab [1921-   ]).
DIFFERING FIRST LINE--SAN JOSÉ Y MARÍA.
Music: COMPOSER--folk.
PLACE--Puerto Rico.
DATE--possibly created 18th or 19th century?
Found: LAN

34. AH, BLEAK AND CHILL THE WINTRY WIND

Lyrics: AUTHOR--Bates Gilbert Burt (1878-1948).
PLACE--United States.
DATE--published 1954.
Music: COMPOSER--Alfred Burt (1919 or 1920-1954).
PLACE--United States.
DATE--published 1954.
Found: BUR

35. AIN'T THAT A ROCKING ALL NIGHT

Lyrics: AUTHOR--folk (Black spiritual).
             PLACE--probably South Carolina.
             DATE--probably created 18th or 19th century.
             DIFFERING FIRST LINE--MARY HAD THE LITTLE BABY.
Music: COMPOSER--folk (Black spiritual).
             PLACE--probably South Carolina.
             DATE--probably created 18th or 19th century.
Found: SEE
Notes: For a carol with similar lyrics but a different tune,
             see A-ROCKIN' ALL NIGHT.

36. ALEGRÍA

Lyrics: AUTHOR--folk.
             PLACE--Puerto Rico.
             DATE--possibly created 18th or 19th century?
             ENGLISH TITLE--HAPPILY SINGING (translated by George
                            K. Evans).
             DIFFERING FIRST LINES--HACIA BELÉN SE ENCAMINAN; ON
                                    THE ROADWAY TO THE CITY.
Music: COMPOSER--folk.
             PLACE--Puerto Rico.
             DATE--possibly created 18th or 19th century?
Found: INT

37. ALL AND SOME

Lyrics: AUTHOR--anonymous.
             PLACE--England.
             DATE--probably written 15th century.
             VARIANT VERNACULAR TITLES--NOWEL SING WE NOW ALL AND
                                        SOME; NOWELL, NOWELL,
                                        NOWELL; NOWEL SING WE BOTH
                                        ALL AND SOME; NOEL SING WE;
                                        NOWELL SING WE.
             DIFFERING FIRST LINES--NOWELL SING WE, BOTH ALL AND
                                    SOME; NOEL SING WE, BOTH ALL
                                    AND SOME.
Music: COMPOSER--anonymous.
             PLACE--England.
             DATE--probably written 15th century.
             VARIANT TUNE--tune by Elizabeth Maconchy (1907-   ).
Found: OXF, THF, MED, EAR, APP
Notes: The first known text of the carol (words and music)
             was written around 1450; there are two main varia-
             tions of this carol, both with the same tune and very
             similar refrains, but with completely different
             verses; the more common version begins "Exortum est
             in love and lysse," and the other version begins "In
             Bethlem in that fair city."

38. ALL BELLS IN PARADISE

    Lyrics: AUTHOR--folk.
            PLACE--England.
            DATE--possibly created 15th century.
            DIFFERING FIRST LINE--OVER YONDER'S A PARK, WHICH IS
                            NEWLY BEGUN.
    Music: COMPOSER--Martin Shaw (1875-1958).
            PLACE--England.
            DATE--probably written early 20th century.
    Found: OXF
    Notes: For a carol with similar lyrics but a different tune,
            see DOWN IN YON FOREST.

39. ALL HAIL TO THE DAYS THAT MERIT MORE PRAISE

    Lyrics: AUTHOR--Tom Durfey (1653-1723) and others.
            PLACE--England.
            DATE--written late 17th or early 18th century;
                Durfey's verses, published 1719.
            VARIANT VERNACULAR TITLES--THE PRAISE OF CHRISTMAS;
                       ALL HAIL TO THE DAYS.
    Music: COMPOSER--folk.
            PLACE--England.
            DATE--probably created 17th century.
    Found: OXF, YAL, NOB, CTW, ECF

40. ALL HAIL TO THE MORNING

    Lyrics: AUTHOR--Samuel Wakefield (1799-1895).
            PLACE--probably Pennsylvania.
            DATE--written 19th century.
            DIFFERING FIRST LINE--ALL HAIL TO THE MORNING THAT
                        BIDS US REJOICE!
    Music: COMPOSER--anonymous.
            PLACE--probably Pennsylvania.
            DATE--published 1840.
    Found: LAN

41. ALL I WANT FOR CHRISTMAS IS MY TWO FRONT TEETH

    Lyrics: AUTHOR--Donald Yetter Gardner (1913-   ).
            PLACE--United States.
            DATE--written 1946.
            DIFFERING FIRST LINE--EV'RYBODY STOPS AND STARES AT
                        ME.
    Music: COMPOSER--Donald Yetter Gardner (1913-   ).
            PLACE--United States.
            DATE--written 1946.

42. ALL IN THE MORNING

      Lyrics: AUTHOR--folk.
               PLACE--probably Derbyshire, England.
               DATE--possibly created 16th-18th century?
               VARIANT VERNACULAR TITLES--IT WAS ON CHRISTMAS DAY;
                                AND ALL IN THE MORNING.
      Music: COMPOSER--folk.
               PLACE--probably Derbyshire, England.
               DATE--possibly created 16th-18th century?
      Found: OXF, SEA, ETE
      Notes: Only the first part of the song is concerned with
               Christmas; the second part is concerned with Easter.

43. ALL ON A CHRISTMAS MORNING

      Lyrics: AUTHOR--Bates Gilbert Burt (1878-1948).
               PLACE--United States.
               DATE--published 1954.
               DIFFERING FIRST LINE--OH, WHO ARE THESE THAT THRONG
                                  THE WAY.
      Music: COMPOSER--Alfred Burt (1919 or 1920-1954).
               PLACE--United States.
               DATE--published 1954.
      Found: BUR

44. ALL THIS TIME

      Lyrics: AUTHOR--folk.
               PLACE--England.
               DATE--created 16th century.
               DIFFERING FIRST LINE--ALL THIS TIME THIS SONG IS BEST.
      Music: COMPOSER--William Walton (1902-1983).
               PLACE--England.
               DATE--published 1970.
      Found: CCT

45. ALL YOU THAT IN THIS HOUSE BE HERE

      Lyrics: AUTHOR--folk.
               PLACE--England.
               DATE--probably created 17th century; possibly first
                    published 1661.
      Music: COMPOSER--folk.
               PLACE--England.
               DATE--possibly created 16th-18th century?
      Found: HUS, CTT

46. ALLE GIOIE PASTORI

      Lyrics: AUTHOR--folk.
               PLACE--Italy.

DATE--probably created 16th or 17th century.
ENGLISH TITLE--SLEEP NO MORE, THE GLAD HEAVENS ARE
BLAZING! (translated by K.W. Simpson).
Music: COMPOSER--folk.
PLACE--Italy.
DATE--probably created 16th or 17th century.
Found: THF, ICC
Notes: The words and melody were possibly first published in
1674; the tune is the melody VIRGINELLE, FIDE ANCELLE.

47. ALLE JAHRE WIEDER

Lyrics: AUTHOR--Wilhelm Hey (1789-1854).
PLACE--Germany.
DATE--published 1837.
ENGLISH TITLES--AS EACH HAPPY CHRISTMAS; EVERY YEAR
AT CHRISTMAS (translated by Anne Shaw
Faulkner Oberndorfer [1877-   ]).
Music: COMPOSER--Ernst Gebhard Anschütz (1800-1861).
PLACE--Germany.
DATE--written 19th century.
Found: TRA, ROT, OBE, WOR

48. ALLELUIA, PRO VIRGINE MARIA

Lyrics: AUTHOR--anonymous.
PLACE--England.
DATE--created 15th century.
VARIANT VERNACULAR TITLES--ALLELUYA PRO VIRGINE MARIA;
ALLELUIA: DIVA NATALICIA.
ENGLISH TITLE--ALLELUYA. THE JOY OF VIRGIN MARY
(translated by John O'Connor [1870-
1952]).
DIFFERING FIRST LINES--DIVA NATALICIA; JOY DIVINE OF
CHRISTMAS DAY.
Music: COMPOSER--anonymous.
PLACE--England.
DATE--created 15th century.
VARIANT TUNE--another 15th century English tune.
Found: MEC, MED, THF

49. ALMA REDEMPTORIS MATER

Lyrics: AUTHOR--anonymous.
PLACE--England.
DATE--created 15th century.
DIFFERING FIRST LINE--AS I LAY UPON A NIGHT.
Music: COMPOSER--anonymous.
PLACE--England.
DATE--created 15th century.
VARIANT TUNES--two other 15th century English tunes.
Found: MED, MEC, THF, EAR

Notes: Although the first line of the first verse of this
           song is the same as that for the carol AS I LAY UPON
           A NIGHT, the two songs have no relation.

50. ALMOST DAY

   Lyrics: AUTHOR--probably Huddie Ledbetter (1885-1949).
              PLACE--United States.
              DATE--published 1951, but probably written much
                  earlier.
              VARIANT VERNACULAR TITLE--IT'S ALMOST DAY.
              DIFFERING FIRST LINES--CHICKENS A-CROWIN' FOR MID-
                                NIGHT; CHICKEN CROWING FOR
                                MIDNIGHT.
   Music: COMPOSER--probably Huddie Ledbetter (1885-1949).
              PLACE--United States.
              DATE--published 1951, but probably written much
                  earlier.
   Found: ULT, SEA, SEE, HAP, ONS

51. ALS ICH BEI MEINEN SCHAFEN WACHT

   Lyrics: AUTHOR--folk.
              PLACE--Germany.
              DATE--probably created 16th century.
              ENGLISH TITLES--WHILE BY MY SHEEP, WHILE BY OUR SHEEP,
                         WHILE BY MY SHEEP I WATCHED AT NIGHT,
                         and ECHO CAROL (four titles for the
                         same translation by Theodore Baker
                         [1851-1934]); WATCHING MY SHEEP
                         (translated by Jessie Epps); ECHO
                         CAROL (translated by Ruth Heller
                         [1920-   ]).
              DIFFERING FIRST LINES--WATCHING MY SHEEP I FEARED
                                NAUGHT; WHILE BY OUR SHEEP WE
                                WATCHED AT NIGHT; WHILE I MY
                                SHEEP DID WATCH ONE NIGHT.
   Music: COMPOSER--folk.
              PLACE--Germany.
              DATE--probably created 16th century.
   Found: INT, SIM, WOR, PRA, UNI
   Notes: The song was probably first published in 1623; the
              tune is also used for the carol WHAT SWEETER MUSIC.

52. AM WEIHNACHTSBAUM DIE LICHTER BRENNEN

   Lyrics: AUTHOR--probably Gustav Hermann Kletke (1813-1886).
              PLACE--Germany.
              DATE--probably written 19th century.
              ENGLISH TITLES--'TIS THE EVE OF CHRISTMAS (translated
                         by Ruth Heller [1920-   ]); THE
                         CHRISTMAS TREE WITH ITS CANDLES
                         GLEAMING (translated by George K. Evans).

DIFFERING FIRST LINE--O FESTIVE NIGHT, 'TIS THE EVE
OF CHRISTMAS.
Music: COMPOSER--folk.
PLACE--Germany.
DATE--possibly created 17th-19th century?
Found: INT, ROT, HEL

53. AN HEAVENLY SONG

Lyrics: AUTHOR--folk.
PLACE--England.
DATE--created 15th century.
DIFFERING FIRST LINES--AN HEAVENLY SONG I DARE WELL
SAY; THIS IS THE SONG THAT YE
SHALL HEAR.
Music: COMPOSER--folk.
PLACE--England.
DATE--created 15th century.
VARIANT TUNE--another 15th century English folk tune.
Found: MEC, MED, THF

54. ANG PASKO AY SUMAPIT

Lyrics: AUTHOR--Levi Celerio.
PLACE--Philippines.
DATE--published 1947.
ENGLISH TITLE--PHILIPPINE CAROL (translated by John
Morrison).
DIFFERING FIRST LINE--O MERRY CHRISTMAS SEASON.
Music: COMPOSER--Levi Celerio.
PLACE--Philippines.
DATE--published 1947.
Found: REF

55. THE ANGEL BAND

Lyrics: AUTHOR--folk (Black spiritual).
PLACE--probably South Carolina.
DATE--probably created 18th or 19th century.
DIFFERING FIRST LINE--THERE WAS ONE, THERE WAS TWO,
THERE WAS THREE LITTLE ANGELS.
Music: COMPOSER--folk (Black spiritual).
PLACE--probably South Carolina.
DATE--probably created 18th or 19th century.
Found: SEE

56. THE ANGEL GABRIEL

Lyrics: AUTHOR--folk.
PLACE--England (possibly Devonshire).
DATE--possibly created 15th or 16th century; probably
first published 1833.

DIFFERING FIRST LINE--THE ANGEL GABRIEL FROM GOD.
Music: COMPOSER--folk.
PLACE--England (possibly Devonshire).
DATE--possibly created 15th or 16th century.
OXF, OBE, SIM, CFS, YOU

57. ANGELS FROM THE REALMS OF GLORY

Lyrics: AUTHOR--James Montgomery (1771-1854).
PLACE--probably Sheffield, England.
DATE--published Dec. 24, 1816.
VARIANT VERNACULAR TITLE--ANGELS, FROM THE REALMS.
Music: COMPOSER--Henry Thomas Smart (1813-1879).
PLACE--probably London, England.
DATE--published 1867.
VARIANT TUNES--tune used for LES ANGES DANS NOS
                    CAMPAGNES; tune by G. Hirst.
Found: MANY
Montgomery based his lyrics on the above-mentioned
French song, and that tune was used with Montgomery's
lyrics until displaced in large part by Smart's tune;
the French tune is still dominant in Great Britain.

58. ANGELUS AD VIRGINEM

Lyrics: AUTHOR--anonymous.
PLACE--probably England, possibly Ireland.
DATE--created 13th or 14th century.
ENGLISH TITLES--GABRIEL TO MARY WENT (translated by
                    John O'Connor [1870-1952]); THE ANGEL
                    UNTO MARY (translated by Elizabeth
                    Poston [1905-   ]); ANGELUS AD
                    VIRGINEM (translated by William Adair
                    Pickard-Cambridge [1879-   ]).
DIFFERING FIRST LINES--GABRIEL TO MARY CAME; GABRIEL
                    TO THE VIRGIN CAME; CAME TH'
                    ARCHANGEL TO THE MAID.
Music: COMPOSER--anonymous.
PLACE--probably England, possibly Ireland.
DATE--created 13th or 14th century.
Found: OXF, THF, PEN, UNI, MED

59. ANGELUS EMITTITUR

Lyrics: AUTHOR--anonymous.
PLACE--Europe.
DATE--possibly created 14th-16th century?
ENGLISH TITLES--GABRIEL FROM HEAVEN HAS FLOWN (trans-
                    lated by John O'Connor [1870-1952]);
                    GABRIEL'S MESSAGE (translated by John
                    Mason Neale [1818-1866]).
DIFFERING FIRST LINE--GABRIEL'S MESSAGE DOES AWAY.

Music: COMPOSER--anonymous.
            PLACE--Europe.
            DATE--possibly created 14th-16th century?
Found: THF, COF, OXF, UNI
Notes: The song was possibly first published in 1582.

60. AO MENINO DEUS

Lyrics: AUTHOR--folk.
            PLACE--Portugal.
            DATE--possibly created 16th-18th century?
            ENGLISH TITLE--OH ENTER DEAR SHEPHERDS (translated by
                         Olga Paul).
            DIFFERING FIRST LINES--ENTRAC, ENTRAC PASTORINHOS;
                                 OH, ENTER, ENTER, DEAR
                                 SHEPHERDS.
Music: COMPOSER--folk.
            PLACE--Portugal.
            DATE--possibly created 16th-18th century?
Found: RTW

61. ARE MY EARS ON STRAIGHT?

Lyrics: AUTHOR--Melville Abner Leven (1914-   ).
            PLACE--United States.
            DATE--published 1953.
            DIFFERING FIRST LINE--I'M A LITTLE DOLL WHO WAS
                                DROPPED AND BROKEN.
Music: COMPOSER--Melville Abner Leven (1914-   ).
            PLACE--United States.
            DATE--published 1953.
Found: SEV

62. ARISE AND WAKE

Lyrics: AUTHOR--folk.
            PLACE--England.
            DATE--created 15th century.
            VARIANT VERNACULAR TITLES--NOWELL, NOWELL; NOWELL,
                                     NOWELL: OUT OF YOUR SLEEP;
                                     NOWEL. OUT OF YOUR SLEEP
                                     ARISE.
            DIFFERING FIRST LINES--NOWEL, NOWEL, NOWEL; NOWELL,
                                 NOWELL, NOWELL; NOEL, NOEL,
                                 NOEL!; OUT OF YOUR SLEEP ARISE
                                 AND WAKE.
Music: COMPOSER--folk.
            PLACE--England.
            DATE--created 15th century.
            VARIANT TUNES--two other 15th century English folk
                         tunes.
Found: MEC, MED, THF, EAR
Notes: The lyrics are very similar to those for OUT OF YOUR
            SLEEP.

63. AS I LAY UPON A NIGHT

      Lyrics: AUTHOR--folk.
                 PLACE--England.
                 DATE--created 15th century.
                 DIFFERING FIRST LINE--HER LOOKING WAS SO LOVELY.
      Music: COMPOSER--folk.
                 PLACE--England.
                 DATE--created 15th century.
                 VARIANT TUNE--another 15th century English folk tune.
      Found: MED, THF, MEC
      Notes: Although the first line of the first verse of this
                 song is the same as that for the carol ALMA
                 REDEMPTORIS MATER, the two songs have no relation.

64. AS I SAT ON A SUNNY BANK

      Lyrics: AUTHOR--folk.
                 PLACE--England.
                 DATE--probably created 15th or 16th century.
                 VARIANT VERNACULAR TITLES--SUNNY BANK; THE SUNNY
                                            BANKS.
                 DIFFERING FIRST LINE--AS I SAT ON THE SUNNY BANKS.
      Music: COMPOSER--folk.
                 PLACE--England.
                 DATE--probably created 15th or 16th century.
                 VARIANT TUNE--another English folk tune.
      Found: OXF, PEN, CCM, OCC, SHA
      Notes: The carol was possibly first published in 1666.

65. AS JOSEPH WAS A-WALKING

      Lyrics: AUTHOR--folk.
                 PLACE--England.
                 DATE--possibly created 15th or 16th century.
                 VARIANT VERNACULAR TITLES--THE CHERRY TREE CAROL;
                                            JOSEPH AND THE ANGEL.
      Music: COMPOSER--folk.
                 PLACE--England.
                 DATE--possibly created 15th or 16th century.
                 VARIANT TUNES--folk tune from the Appalachian region;
                                another folk tune from England; tune by
                                Richard Runciman Terry (1865-1938).
      Found: OXF, THF, SIM, TRA, UNI
      Notes: Although this carol is sometimes identified as THE
                 CHERRY TREE CAROL, it is actually only part 2 of that
                 song; part 1 is the carol JOSEPH WAS AN OLD MAN;
                 part 3 is an Easter song; there are Appalachian lyrics
                 which are used with the Appalachian tune and which are
                 a fair amount different from the lyrics from England;
                 the 15th-16th century tune is also used with a widely
                 variant set of lyrics with the same title, written by
                 Henry John Gauntlett (1805-1876); the variant

Appalachian tune is also used for the carol JOSEPH AND
MARY (Kentucky 1); look under THE CHERRY TREE CAROL
in the index for all related carols.

66. AS ON THE NIGHT

Lyrics: AUTHOR--George Wither (1588-1667).
PLACE--England.
DATE--published 1623.
DIFFERING FIRST LINES--AS ON THE NIGHT BEFORE THE
BLESSED MORN; AS ON THE NIGHT
BEFORE THIS HAPPY MORN.
Music: COMPOSER--Orland Gibbons (1583-1625).
PLACE--England.
DATE--written early 17th century.
Found: FYF, CHO

67. AS WITH GLADNESS MEN OF OLD

Lyrics: AUTHOR--William Chatterton Dix (1837-1898).
PLACE--England.
DATE--published 1859.
Music: COMPOSER--probably Conrad Kocher (1786-1872).
PLACE--Germany.
DATE--published 1838.
VARIANT TUNES--tunes by Henry Walford Davies (1869-
1941) and Robert Frederick Smith (ca.
1830-1905).
Found: MANY
Notes: William Henry Monk (1823-1889) adapted Kocher's tune
(which originally was written for the chorale TREUER
HEILAND in a collection edited by Kocher) to Dix's
lyrics; the whole carol was published in 1861; the
tune is also used for the hymn FOR THE BEAUTY OF THE
EARTH.

68. THE ASHWELL CAROL

Lyrics: AUTHOR--John Catterick or Catrik (d. 1419).
PLACE--Ashwell, England.
DATE--written late 14th or early 15th century.
DIFFERING FIRST LINES--GLORIA IN EXCELSIS DEO!; ANGELS
IN THE SKIES ARE SINGING.
Music: COMPOSER--folk.
PLACE--Russia.
DATE--possibly created medieval period.
Found: PEN

69. AU SAINT NAU

Lyrics: AUTHOR--folk.
PLACE--Poitou, France.

DATE--probably created 15th century.
ENGLISH TITLE--TO NOEL (translated by Edward Bliss
                Reed [1872-1940]).
DIFFERING FIRST LINE--AU SAINCT NAU.
Music: COMPOSER--folk.
PLACE--probably Poitou, France.
DATE--probably created 15th or 16th century.
Found: CTH, TIE, SMI

70. AULD LANG SYNE

Lyrics: AUTHOR--some verses, Robert Burns (1759-1796); verse 1
                and other verses, folk.
PLACE--Scotland.
DATE--Burns' verses, written 1788; other verses,
                possibly created 16th-18th century.
DIFFERING FIRST LINE--SHOULD AULD ACQUAINTANCE BE
                                FORGOT.
Music: COMPOSER--folk.
PLACE--Scotland.
DATE--possibly created 16th-18th century?
Found: MANY

71. AUR TXIKI

Lyrics: AUTHOR--folk.
PLACE--Basque region, Spain and France.
DATE--possibly created 16th-18th century?
ENGLISH TITLE--LOVELY BABY, MARY BORE HIM (translated
                by John Gray [1866-1934]).
Music: COMPOSER--folk.
PLACE--Basque region, Spain and France.
DATE--possibly created 16th-18th century?
Found: THF, UNI

72. AVE DOMINA CELI REGINA

Lyrics: AUTHOR--anonymous.
PLACE--England.
DATE--created 15th century.
VARIANT VERNACULAR TITLE--AVE DOMINA.
DIFFERING FIRST LINES--WORSHIP BE THE BIRTH OF THEE;
                                WORSHIPT BE THE BIRTH OF THEE.
Music: COMPOSER--anonymous.
PLACE--England.
DATE--created 15th century.
Found: MEC, MED, THF

73. AVE DUTEK KALUM HELA HELA

Lyrics: AUTHOR--D.J. Stembo.
PLACE--Ceylon.

DATE--probably written 20th century.
ENGLISH TITLE--SINHALESE CAROL (translated by William
Leonard Reed).
DIFFERING FIRST LINE--WHILE EASTERN SHEPHERDS WATCHED
THEIR FLOCKS BY NIGHT.

Music: COMPOSER--D.J. Stembo.
PLACE--Ceylon.
DATE--probably written 20th century.

Found: REF

74. AVE MARIA

Lyrics: AUTHOR--Franz Schubert (1797-1828).
PLACE--Austria.
DATE--written April 1825.
DIFFERING FIRST LINE--AVE MARIA! JUNGFRAU MILD.

Music: COMPOSER--Franz Schubert (1797-1828).
PLACE--Austria.
DATE--written April 1825.

Found: BAE

Notes: The lyrics were based on THE LADY OF THE LAKE by
Walter Scott (1771-1832).

75. AWAKE, AWAKE, YE DROWSY SOULS

Lyrics: AUTHOR--folk.
PLACE--England (possibly Shropshire).
DATE--possibly created 16th-18th century?
VARIANT VERNACULAR TITLES--THE LAMB OF GOD; NEW YEAR'S
CAROL.

Music: COMPOSER--folk.
PLACE--England (possibly Shropshire).
DATE--possibly created 16th-18th century?

Found: UNI, OXF, SHA

76. AWAY IN A MANGER

Lyrics: AUTHOR--anonymous, possibly from German Lutheran
community of Pennsylvania.
PLACE--United States.
DATE--published 1885.
DIFFERING FIRST LINE--AWAY IN A MANGER, NO CRIB FOR A
BED.

Music: COMPOSER--James Ramsey Murray (1841-1905).
PLACE--United States.
DATE--published 1887.
VARIANT TUNES--FLOW GENTLY, SWEET AFTON by Jonathan E.
Spilman (1812-1896); tune by William
James Kirkpatrick (1838-1921); other
tunes.

Found: MANY

Notes: The entire carol has been incorrectly attributed to
Martin Luther (1483-1546) because it was misrepresented

by the notation "Luther's Cradle Hymn" in an 1887 song
collection by Murray; the tune has been erroneously
attributed to a "Carl Mueller".

77. THE BABE IN BETHLEHEM'S MANGER LAID

Lyrics: AUTHOR--folk.
PLACE--England (possibly Kent).
DATE--probably created late 18th century.
VARIANT VERNACULAR TITLES--THE SAVIOUR'S WORK; THE
BABE IN BETHLEM'S MANGER;
THE BABE OF BETHLEHEM.
DIFFERING FIRST LINE--THE BABE IN BETHLEM'S MANGER
LAID.
Music: COMPOSER--folk.
PLACE--England (possibly Kent).
DATE--probably created late 18th century.
Found: OXF, OBE, SIM, THF, UNI

78. THE BABE OF BETHLEHEM

Lyrics: AUTHOR--folk.
PLACE--Southern States.
DATE--probably created 18th or early 19th century.
DIFFERING FIRST LINES--YE NATIONS ALL, ON YOU I CALL;
YE NATIONS ALL, ON YE I CALL.
Music: COMPOSER--folk.
PLACE--Southern States.
DATE--probably created 18th or early 19th century.
Found: SEA, SEE, LAN
Notes: The song was probably first published in 1835.

79. BABY'S FIRST CHRISTMAS

Lyrics: AUTHOR--Stephan Charles and Van Roberts.
PLACE--United States.
DATE--published 1956.
DIFFERING FIRST LINE--HANG UP THE BABY'S STOCKING,
DEAR.
Music: COMPOSER--Stephan Charles and Van Roberts.
PLACE--United States.
DATE--published 1956.
Found: NOR, SEV

80. BALLADE DE JÉSUS-CHRIST

Lyrics: AUTHOR--folk.
PLACE--France.
DATE--probably created 17th century.
ENGLISH TITLE--BALLAD OF JESUS CHRIST (translated by
George K. Evans).

DIFFERING FIRST LINES--JÉSUS CHRIST S'HABILLE EN
                       PAUVE; JESUS CHRIST CAME IN
                       GARMENT LOWLY.

Music: COMPOSER--folk.
           PLACE--France.
           DATE--probably created 17th century.
Found: INT

81. BALOO, LAMMY

Lyrics: AUTHOR--folk.
           PLACE--Scotland.
           DATE--possibly created 16th or 17th century.
           DIFFERING FIRST LINE--THIS DAY TO YOU IS BORN A CHILD.
Music: COMPOSER--folk.
           PLACE--Scotland.
           DATE--created around 1600.
Found: INT, OBE, SIM, HEL

82. BALULALOW

Lyrics: AUTHOR--James Wedderburn (1495?-1553), John Wedderburn
           (1500?-1556), and/or Robert Wedderburn (ca.
           1510-1557).
           PLACE--England.
           DATE--published 1567.
           VARIANT VERNACULAR TITLE--O MY DEIR HEART.
           DIFFERING FIRST LINES--O MY DEARE HERT, YOUNG JESU
                       SWEIT; O MY DEAR HEART, YOUNG
                       JESUS SWEET; O MY DEIR HERT,
                       YOUNG JESUS SWEIT.
Music: COMPOSER--Peter Warlock (1894-1930).
           PLACE--England.
           DATE--possibly written 1925.
           VARIANT TUNE--tune by Benjamin Britten (1913-1976).
Found: OXF, REE, BRI, APP, CAT
Notes: The lyrics are part of a poem, ANE SANG OF THE BIRTH
           OF CHRIST, which is a translation of the carol VOM
           HIMMEL HOCH, DA KOMM ICH HER.

83. BARN JESUS

Lyrics: AUTHOR--Hans Christian Andersen (1805-1875).
           PLACE--Denmark.
           DATE--published 1849.
           VARIANT VERNACULAR TITLE--BARN JESUS I EN KRYBBE LAD.
           ENGLISH TITLES--CHILD JESUS (translated by George K.
                       Evans); CHILD JESUS CAME TO EARTH THIS
                       DAY.
           DIFFERING FIRST LINES--BARN JESUS I EN KRYBBE LAA;
                       CHILD JESUS IN A MANGER LAY.

Music: COMPOSER--Niels Vilhelm Gade (1817-1890).
           PLACE--Denmark.
           DATE--published 1859.
Found: INT, HUT, OBE, PRE

84. BE MERRY, BE MERRY

     Lyrics: AUTHOR--folk.
                PLACE--England.
                DATE--created 15th century.
                DIFFERING FIRST LINES--A PRINCIPAL POINT OF CHARITY;
                                       A PRINC'PAL POINT OF CHARITY.
     Music: COMPOSER--folk.
                PLACE--England.
                DATE--created 15th century.
                VARIANT TUNE--another 15th century English folk tune.
     Found: MEC, MED, THF, EAR

85. BEATLES FOR CHRISTMAS

     Lyrics: AUTHOR--Mary James and Tony Clark.
                PLACE--United States.
                DATE--published 1964.
                VARIANT VERNACULAR TITLE--I WANT THE BEATLES FOR
                                          CHRISTMAS.
                DIFFERING FIRST LINE--IF ANYBODY ASKS WHAT I WANT FOR
                                      CHRISTMAS.
     Music: COMPOSER--Mary James and Tony Clark.
                PLACE--United States.
                DATE--published 1964.
     Found: SEV

86. BEHOLD A SILLY TENDER BABE

     Lyrics: AUTHOR--Robert Southwell (ca. 1561-1595).
                PLACE--England.
                DATE--written late 16th century.
                VARIANT VERNACULAR TITLES--NEW PRINCE, NEW POMP; NEW
                                           PRINCE, NEW POMPE; BEHOULDE
                                           A SELY TENDER BABE; IN
                                           FREEZING WINTER NIGHT.
                DIFFERING FIRST LINE--BEHOLD A SIMPLE TENDER BABE.
     Music: COMPOSER--John Ireland (1879-1962).
                PLACE--England.
                DATE--probably written early 20th century.
                VARIANT TUNES--tune by Benjamin Britten (1913-1976);
                               anonymous tune from Germany, possibly
                               by David Gregorius Corner (1585-1648),
                               published in Corner's 1625 collection
                               GEISTLICHE GESANGBUCH; folk tune from
                               England.
     Found: OXF, BRI, OWE, UNI, CCB

87. BEHOLD THAT STAR!

    Lyrics: AUTHOR--Thomas Washington Talley.
                PLACE--probably Nashville, Tennessee.
                DATE--probably written first half of 20th century.
    Music: COMPOSER--Thomas Washington Talley.
                PLACE--probably Nashville, Tennessee.
                DATE--probably written first half of 20th century.
    Found: INT, WIL, LAN, ONS, ONT

88. BEHOLD THE GREAT CREATOR MAKES

    Lyrics: AUTHOR--Thomas Pestel (ca. 1595-ca. 1659).
                PLACE--England.
                DATE--published 1659.
    Music: COMPOSER--folk.
                PLACE--England.
                DATE--created 15th or 16th century.
    Found: HAR, ENG
    Notes: The tune is also used for the carol THIS ENDRIS NIGHT.

89. BELEN'EN SORTU ZAIGU

    Lyrics: AUTHOR--folk.
                PLACE--Basque region, Spain and France.
                DATE--possibly created 16th-18th century?
                ENGLISH TITLE--IN MIDDLE WINTER THEY SET OUT (trans-
                          lated by John O'Connor [1870-1952]).
                DIFFERING FIRST LINES--BELEN'EN SORTU ZAIGU JINKOA;
                                       IN MIDDLE WINTER THEY SET OUT
                                       FROM HOME.
    Music: COMPOSER--folk.
                PLACE--Basque region, Spain and France.
                DATE--possibly created 16th-18th century?
    Found: THF, MON

90. THE BELLS OF CHRISTMAS

    Lyrics: AUTHOR--Mary Stuart Krolik.
                PLACE--United States.
                DATE--published 1967.
                DIFFERING FIRST LINE--HEAR THE BELLS ON CHRISTMAS MORN.
    Music: COMPOSER--Mary Stuart Krolik.
                PLACE--United States.
                DATE--published 1967.
    Found: ONS, HAP

91. BERGER, SECOUE TON SOMMEIL PROFOND!

    Lyrics: AUTHOR--folk.
                PLACE--France.

DATE--probably created 17th century; possibly first
       published 1842.
VARIANT VERNACULAR TITLE--CHANTONS, BERGERS NOEL,
       NOEL.
ENGLISH TITLES--SHEPHERDS, SHAKE OFF YOUR DROWSY
       SLEEP; SHEPHERD, SHAKE OFF YOUR DROWSY
       SLEEP; SHEPHERDS! SHAKE OFF.
Music: COMPOSER--folk.
PLACE--Besancon region, France.
DATE--probably created 17th century.
Found: INT, OXF, OBE, UNI, RSC
Notes: The tune is the melody CHANTONS, BARGIÉS, NOUÉ, NOUÉ;
the tune is also used for the carol CAROL OF THE
ADVENT.

92. BETHLEHEM'S STALL

Lyrics: AUTHOR--K.W. Simpson.
PLACE--England.
DATE--probably written early 20th century.
DIFFERING FIRST LINE--BETHLEHEM'S DARKENED CITY.
Music: COMPOSER--folk.
PLACE--Basque region, Spain and France.
DATE--possibly created 16th-18th century?
Found: THF, UNI
Notes: The tune is the melody ABETS ZAGUN GUZIEK.

93. BETLEHEMS STJÄRNA

Lyrics: AUTHOR--Viktor Rydberg (1828-1895).
PLACE--Sweden.
DATE--probably written second half of 19th century.
VARIANT VERNACULAR TITLE--GLÄNS ÖVER SJÖ OCH STRAND.
ENGLISH TITLE--SHINE OVER LAKE AND STRAND (translated
       by Noel Wirén).
Music: COMPOSER--Alice Charlotte Sandström Tegnér (1864-
       1943).
PLACE--Sweden.
DATE--written late 19th or early 20th century.
Found: SWE, GLA, JUL

94. THE BIRTHDAY OF A KING

Lyrics: AUTHOR--William Harold Neidlinger (1863-1924).
PLACE--United States.
DATE--written around 1890.
DIFFERING FIRST LINE--IN THE LITTLE VILLAGE OF
       BETHLEHEM.
Music: COMPOSER--William Harold Neidlinger (1863-1924).
PLACE--United States.
DATE--written around 1890.
Found: SIM, ONS, ONT

95. BLACK CHRISTMAS

    Lyrics: AUTHOR--Richard William Wolf (1928-).
               PLACE--United States.
               DATE--published 1970.
               DIFFERING FIRST LINE--BITTER DAYS, DECEMBER NIGHTS.
    Music: COMPOSER--Richard William Wolf (1928-).
               PLACE--United States.
               DATE--published 1970.
    Found: ONT

96. BLAKE'S CRADLE SONG

    Lyrics: AUTHOR--William Blake (1757-1827).
               PLACE--England.
               DATE--published 1789.
               DIFFERING FIRST LINE--SWEET DREAMS, FORM A SHADE.
    Music: COMPOSER--Ralph Vaughan Williams (1872-1958).
               PLACE--England.
               DATE--published 1928.
    Found: OXF

97. BLESSED BE THAT MAID MARIE

    Lyrics: AUTHOR--folk.
               PLACE--England.
               DATE--possibly created 15th or 16th century.
    Music: COMPOSER--probably folk, possibly William Ballet.
               PLACE--England.
               DATE--probably created 16th century; oldest known
                    text in Ballet's LUTE BOOK (ca. 1600).
    Found: INT, SHE, UNI, CCO, COF

98. THE BLESSED BIRTH

    Lyrics: AUTHOR--George Wither (1588-1667).
               PLACE--England.
               DATE--published 1623.
               VARIANT VERNACULAR TITLE--THAT SO THY BLESSED BIRTH,
                          O CHRIST.
    Music: COMPOSER--Orlando Gibbons (1583-1625).
               PLACE--England.
               DATE--written early 17th century.
               VARIANT TUNE--tune by Henry Walford Davies (1869-1941).
    Found: HUT, CHO

99. BLUE CHRISTMAS

    Lyrics: AUTHOR--Billy Hayes (1906-) and Jay W. Johnson
                   (1903-).
               PLACE--United States.

                DATE--published 1948.
                DIFFERING FIRST LINE--I'LL HAVE A BLUE CHRISTMAS
                                      WITHOUT YOU.
   Music: COMPOSER--Billy Hayes (1906-   ) and Jay W. Johnson
                          (1903-   ).
                PLACE--United States.
                DATE--published 1948.
   Found: HAP

100. THE BOAR'S HEAD

   Lyrics: AUTHOR--probably Richard Smert.
                PLACE--probably Devonshire, England.
                DATE--probably written second half of 15th century.
                VARIANT VERNACULAR TITLE--NOWELL, NOWELL: THE BOARËS
                                          HEAD.
                DIFFERING FIRST LINES--NOWELL, NOWELL, NOWELL, NOWELL;
                                       NOEL, NOEL, NOEL, NOEL; THE
                                       BOAR'S HEAD THAT WE BRING HERE;
                                       THE BOARËS HEAD THAT WE BRING
                                       HERE.
   Music: COMPOSER--probably Richard Smert.
                PLACE--probably Devonshire, England.
                DATE--probably written second half of 15th century.
   Found: EAR, MEC
   Notes: This song, which has religious lyrics, is not to be
                confused with the much better-known and predominantly
                secular THE BOAR'S HEAD CAROL.

101. THE BOAR'S HEAD CAROL

   Lyrics: AUTHOR--anonymous.
                PLACE--probably Oxford, England.
                DATE--probably created 15th century.
                VARIANT VERNACULAR TITLES--CAROL ON BRINGING IN THE
                                           BOAR'S HEAD; THE BORE'S
                                           HEED; CAPUT APRI DEFERO.
                DIFFERING FIRST LINES--THE BOAR'S HEAD IN HAND BEAR I;
                                       THE BORE'S HEED IN HAND BRING I.
   Music: COMPOSER--anonymous.
                PLACE--probably Oxford, England.
                DATE--probably created 15th century.
   Found: MANY
   Notes: The song has been used in Christmas celebrations at
                Queen's College, Oxford for over 500 years; by legend,
                a student at the college who was walking in nearby
                woods on Christmas day killed a wild boar by thrusting
                a book by Aristotle down the beast's throat and that
                evening the animal was served to the student body with
                great ceremony thus beginning the annual festivities;
                the carol was first published in Wynken de Worde's
                1521 collection CHRISTMASSE CAROLLES; it is one of the
                earliest printed carols.

102. BONDJOÛ, WÈSÈNE, DWÈRMEZ-VE ÈCO?

   Lyrics: AUTHOR--folk.
             PLACE--Walloon region, Belgium and France.
             DATE--possibly created 15th-17th century?
             ENGLISH TITLE--ARE YOU A-SLEEPING? (translated by
                      Edward Bliss Reed [1872-1940]).
             DIFFERING FIRST LINE--ARE YOU A-SLEEPING, ONE AND ALL?
   Music: COMPOSER--folk.
             PLACE--Walloon region, Belgium and France.
             DATE--possibly created 15th-17th century?
   Found: CNI, DOU

103. BREAK FORTH, O LIVING LIGHT OF GOD

   Lyrics: AUTHOR--Frank von Christierson (1900-   ).
             PLACE--probably California.
             DATE--written around 1952.
   Music: COMPOSER--William Jones (1726-1800).
             PLACE--England.
             DATE--published 1789.
   Found: MET
   Notes: The tune is also used for the carol THE KING SHALL
             COME.

104. BRICH AN, DU SCHÖNES MORGENLICHT

   Lyrics: AUTHOR--Johann Rist (1607-1667).
             PLACE--Germany.
             DATE--published 1641.
             ENGLISH TITLE--BREAK FORTH, O BEAUTEOUS HEAVENLY LIGHT
                      (translated by John Troutbeck [1833-
                      1889]).
   Music: COMPOSER--Johann Schop (ca. 1590-ca. 1664).
             PLACE--Germany.
             DATE--published 1641.
   Found: INT, SIM, REE, CCO, MET
   Notes: Johann Sebastian Bach (1685-1750) adapted Schop's tune
             extensively for use in his CHRISTMAS ORATORIO (1734),
             and Bach's version is the one normally used for the
             carol today.

105. BRIGHT AND JOYFUL IS THE MORN

   Lyrics: AUTHOR--James Montgomery (1771-1854).
             PLACE--probably Sheffield, England.
             DATE--published 1819.
   Music: COMPOSER--J.D. Jones (1827-1870).
             PLACE--Wales.
             DATE--written mid-19th century.
   Found: TRE, PIL
   Notes: Jones may well have arranged an old Welsh tune instead
             of composing a completely new melody.

106. BRIGHTEST AND BEST

    Lyrics: AUTHOR--Reginald Heber (1783-1826).
             PLACE--England.
             DATE--published 1811.
             VARIANT VERNACULAR TITLES--BRIGHTEST AND BEST OF THE
                                SONS OF THE MORNING; STAR
                                OF THE EAST.
    Music: COMPOSER--James Procktor Harding (1850-1911).
             PLACE--probably London, England.
             DATE--written June 1892.
             VARIANT TUNES--tune by J.F. Thrupp (1827-1867); United
                                States folk tune; 17th century German
                                tune.
    Found: INT, REE, UNI, YAL, MET
    Notes: The lyrics are similar to those for the United States
             carol STAR IN THE EAST; almost surely, this mainstream
             song preceded the United States folk song; one of the
             folk tunes used with the United States carol is also
             used with this carol.

107. BUON NATALE

    Lyrics: AUTHOR--Bob Saffer (1910-   ) and Frank Linale.
             PLACE--United States.
             DATE--published 1959.
             DIFFERING FIRST LINE--BUON NATALE MEANS MERRY
                                CHRISTMAS TO YOU.
    Music: COMPOSER--Bob Saffer (1910-   ) and Frank Linale.
             PLACE--United States.
             DATE--published 1959.
    Found: ONS, ONT

108. BURGUNDIAN CAROL

    Lyrics: AUTHOR--Oscar Brand (1920-   ).
             PLACE--United States.
              DATE--published 1951.
              DIFFERING FIRST LINE--THE WINTER SEASON OF THE YEAR.
    Music: COMPOSER--Oscar Brand (1920-   ).
             PLACE--United States.
              DATE--published 1951.
    Found: ULT

109. C-H-R-I-S-T-M-A-S

    Lyrics: AUTHOR--Jenny Lou Carson.
             PLACE--United States.
              DATE--published 1949.
              DIFFERING FIRST LINE--WHEN I WAS BUT A YOUNGSTER.
    Music: COMPOSER--Eddie Arnold (1918-   ).
             PLACE--United States.

Found: DATE--published 1949.
ULT, ONS, ONT

110. CALM ON THE LISTENING EAR OF NIGHT

Lyrics: AUTHOR--Edmund Hamilton Sears (1810-1876).
PLACE--Massachusetts.
DATE--published 1834.
Music: COMPOSER--John Bacchus Dykes (1823-1876).
PLACE--England.
DATE--published 1866.
VARIANT TUNES--tune by Edward John Hopkins (1818-
1901); folk tune from Devonshire,
England; tune by Richard Storrs Willis
(1819-1900).
Found: SIM, HUT, BAP, TRE, CHW
Notes: The tune by Dykes was originally composed for the hymn
JESUS, THE VERY THOUGHT OF THEE; the tune by Willis is
also used for the carols IT CAME UPON THE MIDNIGHT
CLEAR and WHILE SHEPHERDS WATCHED THEIR FLOCKS.

111. CAMPANA SOBRE CAMPANA

Lyrics: AUTHOR--folk.
PLACE--Andalusia, Spain.
DATE--possibly created 17th-19th century?
VARIANT VERNACULAR TITLE--CAMPANAS DE BELÉN.
ENGLISH TITLE--BELLS OVER BETHLEHEM (translated by
George K. Evans).
DIFFERING FIRST LINE--BELLS OVER BETHLEHEM PEALING.
Music: COMPOSER--folk.
PLACE--Andalusia, Spain.
DATE--possibly created 17th-19th century?
VARIANT TUNE--tune by Joaquín Nin y Castellanos (1879-
1949), composer from Cuba.
Found: INT, MON, MOO, CAN, NIN

112. CAN I WAIT UP FOR SANTA CLAUS?

Lyrics: AUTHOR--Steve Allen (1921-   ).
PLACE--United States.
DATE--published 1953.
Music: COMPOSER--Steve Allen (1921-   ).
PLACE--United States.
DATE--published 1953.
Found: HAP

113. CANÇÃO DE NATAL

Lyrics: AUTHOR--folk.
PLACE--Portugal.
DATE--possibly created 17th-19th century?

                VARIANT VERNACULAR TITLE--BEIJAI O MENINO.
                ENGLISH TITLE--A KISS FOR THE BABY (translated by
                        Elizabeth Poston [1905-   ]).
Music: COMPOSER--folk.
                PLACE--Portugal.
                DATE--possibly created 17th-19th century?
Found: PEN

114. CANDLEMAS EVE

     Lyrics: AUTHOR--Robert Herrick (1591-1674).
                 PLACE--England.
                 DATE--published 1648.
                 VARIANT VERNACULAR TITLE--TWELFTH NIGHT SONG.
                 DIFFERING FIRST LINE--DOWN WITH THE ROSEMARY AND BAYS.
     Music: COMPOSER--Elizabeth Maconchy (1907-   ).
                 PLACE--England.
                 DATE--published 1967.
                 VARIANT TUNE--English folk tune.
     Found: OXF, APP, ECS

115. CANDY KID

     Lyrics: AUTHOR--Tony Romeo.
                 PLACE--United States.
                 DATE--published 1968.
                 DIFFERING FIRST LINE--FEELIN' SO DEPRESSED.
     Music: COMPOSER--Tony Romeo.
                 PLACE--United States.
                 DATE--published 1968.
     Found: ONS, ONT

116. CANTEMOS

     Lyrics: AUTHOR--folk.
                 PLACE--Venezuela.
                 DATE--possibly created 18th or 19th century?
                 ENGLISH TITLE--WE ARE SINGING (translated by George K.
                         Evans).
                 DIFFERING FIRST LINES--CANTEMOS, CANTEMOS; SINGING, WE
                         ARE SINGING!
     Music: COMPOSER--folk.
                 PLACE--Venezuela.
                 DATE--possibly created 18th or 19th century?
     Found: INT

117. CANTIAM TUTTI

     Lyrics: AUTHOR--folk.
                 PLACE--Italy.
                 DATE--probably created 16th or 17th century.

ENGLISH TITLE--O SHEPHERDS SING TOGETHER (translated
                  by K.W. Simpson).
Music: COMPOSER--folk.
            PLACE--Italy.
            DATE--probably created 16th or 17th century.
Found: THF, ICC
Notes: The words and melody were possibly first published in
            1674.

118. CANTIQUE DE NOËL

Lyrics: AUTHOR--Placide Cappeau (1808-1877).
            PLACE--France.
            DATE--written 1847.
            VARIANT VERNACULAR TITLES--MINUIT, CHRÉTIENS; NOËL;
                                CANTIQUE POUR NOËL.
            ENGLISH TITLES--O HOLY NIGHT and CHRISTMAS SONG (two
                  titles for the same translation by
                  John Sullivan Dwight [1818-1893]);
                  O CHRISTMAS NIGHT.
Music: COMPOSER--Adolphe Adam (1803-1856).
            PLACE--Paris, France.
            DATE--written 1847.
Found: MANY
Notes: This is the best-known French carol; the song was
            probably first published around 1855, in London.

119. CANZONE D'I ZAMPOGNARI

Lyrics: AUTHOR--folk.
            PLACE--Sicily, Italy.
            DATE--possibly created 17th century.
            VARIANT VERNACULAR TITLE--IL ZAMPOGNARI.
            ENGLISH TITLES--CAROL OF THE BAGPIPERS (four different
                  translations, one by Theodore Baker
                  [1851-1934], another by Gordon Hitch-
                  cock, another by Ruth Heller [1920-
                     ], another by Henry William Simon
                  [1901-   ]); ON THAT MOST BLESSED
                  NIGHT and BAGPIPER'S CAROL (two titles
                  for the same translation by Marx E.
                  Oberndorfer [1876-   ]).
            DIFFERING FIRST LINES--QUANNO NASCETTE NINNO A BETTE-
                        LEMME; WHEN CHRIST OUR LORD WAS
                        BORN AT BETHLEHEM AFAR; AND
                        WHEN THE CHILD WAS BORN AT
                        BETHLEHEM; A STAR SHONE UP IN
                        HEAVEN.
Music: COMPOSER--folk.
            PLACE--Sicily, Italy.
            DATE--possibly created 17th century.
Found: INT, SIM, TRA, OBE, UNI

Notes: It is possible that George Frederick Handel (1685-
          1759) discovered the melody during his 1708 Italian
          travels and used it for the opening of HE SHALL FEED
          HIS FLOCK in his 1742 oratorio THE MESSIAH; this is
          perhaps the best-known Italian carol.

120. THE CARNAL AND THE CRANE

Lyrics: AUTHOR--folk.
           PLACE--England.
           DATE--probably created 15th or 16th century.
           VARIANT VERNACULAR TITLE--THE CROW AND THE`CRANE.
           DIFFERING FIRST LINE--AS I PASSED BY A RIVERSIDE.
Music: COMPOSER--folk.
           PLACE--England.
           DATE--probably created 15th or 16th century.
Found: OXF, SEA
Notes: One of the carols entitled THE MIRACULOUS HARVEST has
           this title as a variant; these lyrics are different
           from those for the other carol, but the same tune is
           used for both carols.

121. CAROL OF THE ADVENT

Lyrics: AUTHOR--Eleanor Farjeon (1881-   ).
           PLACE--England.
           DATE--written early 20th century.
           DIFFERING FIRST LINE--PEOPLE LOOK EAST. THE TIME IS
                                 NEAR.
Music: COMPOSER--folk.
           PLACE--Besancon region, France.
           DATE--probably created 17th century.
Found: OXF, YAL
Notes: The tune is the melody CHANTONS, BARGIÉS, NOUÉ, NOUÉ;
           The tune is also used for the carol BERGER, SECOUE
           TON SOMMEIL PROFOUND!

122. CAROL OF THE BELLS

Lyrics: AUTHOR--anonymous.
           PLACE--United States.
           DATE--earliest known publication 1972.
           VARIANT VERNACULAR TITLE--UKRAINIAN CAROL.
           DIFFERING FIRST LINE--HARK TO THE BELLS, HARK TO THE
                                 BELLS.
Music: COMPOSER--Mykola Dmytrovich Leontovych (1877-1921).
           PLACE--Ukraine.
           DATE--written early 20th century.
Found: SEV, ULT
Notes: This is not the original or most popular version of
           CAROL OF THE BELLS; see the other carol of this name
           for the original version; the tune is also used for
           the carols RING, CHRISTMAS BELLS and COME, DANCE AND
           SING.

123. CAROL OF THE BELLS

    Lyrics: AUTHOR--Peter J. Wilhousky (1902-1978).
              PLACE--United States.
              DATE--published 1936.
              VARIANT VERNACULAR TITLE--UKRAINIAN CAROL.
              DIFFERING FIRST LINE--HARK! HOW THE BELLS, SWEET
                          SILVER BELLS.
    Music: COMPOSER--Mykola Dmytrovich Leontovych (1877-1921).
              PLACE--Ukraine.
              DATE--written early 20th century.
    Notes: These lyrics are the original English words set to
              Leontovych's music, and the most popular version;
              the other and later carol of this name uses somewhat
              similar lyrics and the same music; the tune is also
              used for the carols RING, CHRISTMAS BELLS and
              COME, DANCE AND SING.

124. THE CAROL OF THE BIRDS

    Lyrics: AUTHOR--John Jacob Niles (1892-1980).
              PLACE--United States.
              DATE--published 1943.
              DIFFERING FIRST LINES--OH A MANY A BIRD DID WAKE AND
                          FLY; OH, MANY A BIRD DID WAKE
                          AND FLY.
    Music: COMPOSER--John Jacob Niles (1892-1980).
              PLACE--United States.
              DATE--published 1943.
    Found: NIL, LAN

125. CAROL OF THE BIRDS

    Lyrics: AUTHOR--John Wheeler.
              PLACE--Australia.
               DATE--probably written mid-20th century.
              DIFFERING FIRST LINE--OUT ON THE PLAINS THE BROLGAS
                          ARE DANCING.
    Music: COMPOSER--William Garnet James (1895-   ).
              PLACE--Australia.
               DATE--probably written mid-20th century.
    Found: UNI

126. CAROL OF THE FLOWERS

    Lyrics: AUTHOR--Willys Peck Kent (1877-   ).
              PLACE--United States.
               DATE--probably written early 20th century.
              VARIANT VERNACULAR TITLE--THE SONG OF THE THREE WISE
                        MEN.
              DIFFERING FIRST LINE--IN THE EARLY MORNING AS I WENT
                        ON MY WAY.

Music: COMPOSER--folk.
           PLACE--probably Basses-Pyrénées, France.
           DATE--probably created 18th century.
Found: SIM
Notes: The tune is also used for the spring song CAROL OF
           THE FLOWERS (NOUÈL DE LAS FLOUS) and the Christmas
           carol COME WITH US, SWEET FLOWERS.

127. CAROL OF THE MOTHER

      Lyrics: AUTHOR--Wihla Hutson.
                  PLACE--United States.
                  DATE--published 1954.
                  DIFFERING FIRST LINE--SLEEP, BABY MINE.
      Music: COMPOSER--Alfred Burt (1919 or 1920-1954).
                  PLACE--United States.
                  DATE--published 1954.
      Found: BUR

128. CAROL OF THE SHEPHERDS

      Lyrics: AUTHOR--Arnold Freed (1926-   ).
                  PLACE--United States.
                  DATE--published 1972.
                  VARIANT VERNACULAR TITLE--HOW MUCH FARTHER MUST WE GO?
                  DIFFERING FIRST LINE--WE ARE SHEPHERDS FROM AFAR.
      Music: COMPOSER--Arnold Freed (1926-   ).
                  PLACE--United States.
                  DATE--published 1972.

129. CAROL, SWEETLY CAROL

      Lyrics: AUTHOR--Frances Jane Crosby Van Alstyne (1820-1915).
                  PLACE--United States.
                  DATE--written second half of 19th century.
                  DIFFERING FIRST LINE--CAROL, SWEETLY CAROL, A
                                        SAVIOUR BORN TODAY.
      Music: COMPOSER--Theodore E. Perkins (1831-   ).
                  PLACE--United States.
                  DATE--probably written second half of 19th century.
                  VARIANT TUNES--anonymous tune; tune by Edward Bunnett
                                 (1834-   ).
      Found: ONS, CHO, HUT

130. CAROLING, CAROLING

      Lyrics: AUTHOR--Wihla Hutson
                  PLACE--United States.
                  DATE--published 1954.
                  DIFFERING FIRST LINE--CAROLING, CAROLING, NOW WE GO.
      Music: COMPOSER--Alfred Burt (1919 or 1920-1954).

PLACE--United States.
DATE--published 1954.
Found: BUR, ULT, HAP

131. CAUX CAROL

Lyrics: AUTHOR--Morris Martin (1910-   ).
PLACE--England.
DATE--possibly written 1949.
DIFFERING FIRST LINE--SHEEP NOR SHEPHERDS, NONE ARE
HERE.
Music: COMPOSER--Paul Petrocokino (1910-   ).
PLACE--England.
DATE--probably written 1949.
Found: REE

132. THE CEDAR OF LEBANON

Lyrics: AUTHOR--Richard Frederick Littledale (1833-1890).
PLACE--England.
DATE--written second half of 19th century.
Music: COMPOSER--Erik Routley (1917-1982).
PLACE--England.
DATE--written 20th century.
VARIANT TUNE--English folk tune, possibly 15th-17th
century.
Found: UNI, CHO, HUT

133. CÉLÉBRONS LA NAISSANCE

Lyrics: AUTHOR--anonymous.
PLACE--France.
DATE--probably created 15th century; possibly first
published 1766.
ENGLISH TITLES--WE CELEBRATE THE BIRTH (translated by
Bernard Gasso [1926-   ]); WE SING
IN CELEBRATION (translated by George
K. Evans); O PUBLISH THE GLAD STORY.
Music: COMPOSER--folk.
PLACE--France.
DATE--probably created 15th century.
Found: INT, TRA, ONT, ONS
Notes: The tune is also used for the carols CHANTONS! JE
VOUS EN PRIE, NOUS VOICI DANS LA VILLE, ADAM E SA
COUMPAGNO, and A DAY, A DAY OF GLORY!

134. CEREMONIES FOR CHRISTMAS

Lyrics: AUTHOR--Robert Herrick (1591-1674).
PLACE--England.
DATE--published 1648.

                  DIFFERING FIRST LINE--COME BRING WITH A NOISE.
Music: COMPOSER--folk.
                  PLACE--England.
                  DATE--possibly created 15th-17th century?
Found: UNI

135. CESTIT SVIETU

Lyrics: AUTHOR--folk.
                  PLACE--Croatia, Yugoslavia.
                  DATE--possibly created 16th-18th century?
                  ENGLISH TITLE--HAPPINESS THE SUN IS BRINGING (trans-
                              lated by Olga Paul).
Music: COMPOSER--folk.
                  PLACE--Croatia, Yugoslavia.
                  DATE--possibly created 16th-18th century?
Found: RTW

136. CHANTICLEER

Lyrics: AUTHOR--William Austin (1587-1633).
                  PLACE--England.
                  DATE--published 1635.
                  VARIANT VERNACULAR TITLES--CHANTICLEER'S CAROL; ALL
                                        THIS NIGHT BRIGHT ANGELS
                                        SING.
                  DIFFERING FIRST LINE--ALL THIS NIGHT SHRILL
                                        CHANTICLEER.
Music: COMPOSER--folk.
                  PLACE--England.
                  DATE--possibly created 16th-18th century?
                  VARIANT TUNES--tunes by Norman Fulton (1909-   ),
                                  Arthur Seymour Sullivan (1842-1900),
                                  James T. Field, and Frank Fruttchey.
Found: OXF, APP, HUT, STA
Notes: There are two different versions of the lyrics, both
                  having the same words for verses 2 and 3, but with
                  different words for verse 1.

137. CHANTONS! JE VOUS EN PRIE

Lyrics: AUTHOR--Lucas Le Moigne.
                  PLACE--France.
                  DATE--probably written first half of 15th century.
                  VARIANT VERNACULAR TITLES--OR DITES NOUS, MARIE; OR,
                                        NOUS DITES MARIE.
                  ENGLISH TITLES--NOW TELL US, GENTLE MARY (translated
                                  by W.B. Lindsay and Ruth Heller
                                  [1920-   ]); NOW SING WE ALL FULL
                                  SWEETLY; NOW LET US SING, I PRAY
                                  THEE! (translated by K.W. Simpson).
Music: COMPOSER--folk.

PLACE--France.
DATE--probably created 15th century.
VARIANT TUNE--folk tune probably from Burgundy,
    France.
Found: HUT, THF, HEL, TIE, SMI
Notes: The main tune is also used for the carols CÉLÉBRONS
LA NAISSANCE, NOUS VOICI DANS LA VILLE, ADAM E SA
COUMPAGNO, and A DAY, A DAY OF GLORY!

138. THE CHERRY TREE

Lyrics: AUTHOR--folk.
PLACE--probably Kentucky.
DATE--probably created 18th or 19th century.
DIFFERING FIRST LINE--WHEN JOSEPH WAS AN OLDEN MAN.
Music: COMPOSER--folk.
PLACE--probably Kentucky.
DATE--probably created 18th or 19th century.
Found: TCC
Notes: This is another version of THE CHERRY TREE CAROL,
with lyrics very similar to those for other versions,
but with a different tune; look under THE CHERRY TREE
CAROL in the index for all related carols.

139. CHILD OF GOD

Lyrics: AUTHOR--folk (Black spiritual).
PLACE--probably Georgia or Louisiana.
DATE--probably created 18th or 19th century.
VARIANT VERNACULAR TITLES--THE LITTLE CRADLE ROCKS
    TONIGHT IN GLORY; THE
    LITTLE CRADLE ROCKS
    TONIGHT.
DIFFERING FIRST LINES--IF ANYBODY ASK YOU WHO I AM;
    IF ANYBODY ASK YE WHO I AM; IF
    ANYBODY ASKS YOU WHO I AM.
Music: COMPOSER--folk (Black spiritual).
PLACE--probably Georgia or Louisiana.
DATE--probably created 18th or 19th century.
Found: SEA, SEE, LAN

140. CHILDREN, GO WHERE I SEND THEE!

Lyrics: AUTHOR--folk (Black spiritual).
PLACE--probably Kentucky or Arkansas.
DATE--probably created 19th century.
VARIANT VERNACULAR TITLES--THE HOLY BABY; HOLY BABE;
    LITTLE BITTY BABY.
DIFFERING FIRST LINE--CHILDREN, GO AND I WILL SEND
    THEE.
Music: COMPOSER--folk (Black spiritual).
PLACE--probably Kentucky.

DATE--probably created 19th century.
VARIANT TUNE--another folk tune, probably from
                              Arkansas.
Found: INT, LOM, SEE, OWE, SEA

141. THE CHIPMUNK SONG

Lyrics: AUTHOR--Ross Bagdasarian (1919-1972).
          PLACE--United States.
          DATE--published 1958.
          VARIANT VERNACULAR TITLE--CHRISTMAS, DON'T BE LATE.
          DIFFERING FIRST LINE--CHRISTMAS, CHRISTMAS TIME IS
                              NEAR.
Music: COMPOSER--Ross Bagdasarian (1919-1972).
          PLACE--United States.
          DATE--published 1958.
Found: NOR, SEV

142. CHIQUIRRIQUITIN

Lyrics: AUTHOR--folk.
          PLACE--Andalusia, Spain.
          DATE--possibly created 15th-17th century?
          ENGLISH TITLE--O MY LOVELIEST ONE (translated by
                              George K. Evans).
Music: COMPOSER--folk.
          PLACE--Andalusia, Spain.
          DATE--possibly created 15th-17th century?
Found: INT

143. CHRIST IS BORN OF MAIDEN FAIR

Lyrics: AUTHOR--folk.
          PLACE--probably Surrey, England.
          DATE--possibly created 16th-18th century?
Music: COMPOSER--folk.
          PLACE--probably Surrey, England.
          DATE--possibly created 16th-18th century?
Found: HUT, UNI, OCC

144. CHRIST THE LORD MOST GLORIOUS

Lyrics: AUTHOR--John Antes (1740-1811).
          PLACE--United States.
          DATE--probably written second half of 18th century.
          DIFFERING FIRST LINE--CHRIST THE LORD, THE LORD MOST
                              GLORIOUS.
Music: COMPOSER--John Antes (1740-1811).
          PLACE--United States.
          DATE--probably written second half of 18th century.
Found: LAN
Notes: Antes was of the Moravian community.

145. CHRIST WAS BORN ON CHRISTMAS DAY

 Lyrics: AUTHOR--John Mason Neale (1818-1866).
      PLACE--England.
      DATE--written mid-19th century.
 Music: COMPOSER--George Edgar Oliver (1856-).
      PLACE--United States.
      DATE--written late 19th or early 20th century.
      VARIANT TUNES--tune by Charles Lee Williams (1853-
              1935), composer from England;
              anonymous tune.
 Found: HUT
 Notes: The lyrics were originally intended to be a trans-
      lation of the carol RESONET IN LAUDIBUS and are still
      commonly used with that carol's well-known tune; this
      carol (and its two variants) are simply adaptations
      of Neale's words to different tunes.

146. CHRISTBAUM

 Lyrics: AUTHOR--Peter Cornelius (1824-1874).
      PLACE--Germany.
      DATE--written mid-19th century.
      ENGLISH TITLE--THE CHRISTMAS TREE (two different
              translations, one anonymous, one by
              Herbert Newell Bate [1871-1941]).
      DIFFERING FIRST LINES--WIE SCHÖN GESCHMÜCKT DER
              FESTLICHE RAUM!; THE HOLLY'S
              UP, THE HOUSE IS ALL BRIGHT;
              THE CHRISTMAS TREE IS
              SPARKLING WITH LIGHT.
 Music: COMPOSER--Peter Cornelius (1824-1874).
      PLACE--Germany.
      DATE--written mid-19th century.
 Found: OXF, HUT

147. CHRISTIANS, AWAKE, SALUTE THE HAPPY MORN

 Lyrics: AUTHOR--John Byrom (1692-1763).
      PLACE--England.
      DATE--probably written December 1749.
      VARIANT VERNACULAR TITLE--CHRISTIANS, AWAKE.
 Music: COMPOSER--John Wainwright (1723-1768).
      PLACE--England.
      DATE--probably written December 1750.
 Found: SIM, HAW, REE, YAL, HAR

148. THE CHRISTMAS CANDY CALENDAR

 Lyrics: AUTHOR--Robert Maxwell (1921-).
      PLACE--United States.
      DATE--published 1974.

          DIFFERING FIRST LINE--IT'S SIX PINK PEPPERMINTS TO
                              CHRISTMAS.
    Music: COMPOSER--Robert Maxwell (1921-   ).
          PLACE--United States.
          DATE--published 1974.
    Found: HAP, ONT

149. CHRISTMAS DAY

    Lyrics: AUTHOR--Hal David (1921-   ).
           PLACE--United States.
           DATE--published 1968.
           DIFFERING FIRST LINE--CHRISTMAS DAY IS HERE AND SO
                                ARE WE.
    Music: COMPOSER--Burt Bacharach (1928-   ).
           PLACE--United States.
           DATE--published 1968.
    Found: SEV
    Notes: This is from the Broadway musical PROMISES, PROMISES.

150. CHRISTMAS DAY

    Lyrics: AUTHOR--Andrew Young (1885-1971).
           PLACE--England.
           DATE--published 1960.
           DIFFERING FIRST LINE--LAST NIGHT IN THE OPEN SHIPPEN.
    Music: COMPOSER--Elizabeth Poston (1905-   ).
           PLACE--England.
           DATE--published 1967.
    Found: APP

151. CHRISTMAS DREAM

    Lyrics: AUTHOR--Lloyd Weber and Tim Rice.
           PLACE--United States.
           DATE--published 1974.
           DIFFERING FIRST LINE--WATCH ME, HERE I GO.
    Music: COMPOSER--Lloyd Weber and Tim Rice.
           PLACE--United States.
           DATE--published 1974.

152. CHRISTMAS DREAMING

    Lyrics: AUTHOR--Lester Lee (1905-1956).
           PLACE--United States.
           DATE--written around 1947.
           VARIANT VERNACULAR TITLE--A LITTLE LATE THIS YEAR.
    Music: COMPOSER--Irving Gordon (1915-   ).
           PLACE--United States.
           DATE--written around 1947.

153. CHRISTMAS EVE BY THE FIRESIDE

> *Lyrics:* AUTHOR--H. Jean Diestelhorst.
> PLACE--United States.
> DATE--published 1960.
> *Music:* COMPOSER--H. Jean Diestelhorst.
> PLACE--United States.
> DATE--published 1960.
> *Found:* SEV

154. CHRISTMAS FOR COWBOYS

> *Lyrics:* AUTHOR--Steve Weisberg.
> PLACE--United States.
> DATE--published 1975.
> DIFFERING FIRST LINE--TALL IN THE SADDLE WE SPEND
> CHRISTMAS DAY.
> *Music:* COMPOSER--Steve Weisberg.
> PLACE--United States.
> DATE--published 1975.

155. CHRISTMAS HATH MADE AN END

> *Lyrics:* AUTHOR--folk.
> PLACE--England.
> DATE--possibly created 16th or 17th century; possibly
> first published 1661.
> *Music:* COMPOSER--folk.
> PLACE--England.
> DATE--possibly created 16th or 17th century.
> *Found:* CEL
> *Notes:* The second line of the lyrics is "Welladay", and the
> tune has acquired that name; the tune is also used for
> the carol OLD YORKSHIRE GOODING CAROL.

156. CHRISTMAS IN KILARNEY

> *Lyrics:* AUTHOR--John Redmond (1906-   ), James Cavanaugh
> (d. 1967), and Frank Weldon (d. 1970).
> PLACE--United States.
> DATE--written 1950.
> *Music:* COMPOSER--James Cavanaugh (d. 1967) and Frank Weldon
> (d. 1970).
> PLACE--United States.
> DATE--written 1950.

157. CHRISTMAS IN THE AIR

> *Lyrics:* AUTHOR--S. Allman.
> PLACE--United States.
> DATE--probably written 1940's or 1950's.

Music: COMPOSER--Walter Schumann (1913-1958).
           PLACE--United States.
           DATE--probably written 1940's or 1950's.

158. CHRISTMAS IN THE CITY OF ANGELS

      Lyrics: AUTHOR--Suzy Elman.
                  PLACE--United States.
                  DATE--published 1979.
                  DIFFERING FIRST LINE--THE CITY THIS TIME OF YEAR.
      Music: COMPOSER--Suzy Elman, Jack Gold, and Arnold Goland
                           (1928-   ).
                  PLACE--United States.
                  DATE--published 1979.

159. CHRISTMAS IS A TIME

      Lyrics: AUTHOR--Carolyn Gilbert.
                  PLACE--United States.
                  DATE--published 1950.
                  VARIANT VERNACULAR TITLE--CHRISTMAS IS A TIME THAT
                                            WILL NEVER CHANGE.
                  DIFFERING FIRST LINE--CHRISTMAS IS A TIME TO BE LOVING.
      Music: COMPOSER--Carolyn Gilbert.
                  PLACE--United States.
                  DATE--published 1950.
      Found: SEV

160. CHRISTMAS IS COMING

      Lyrics: AUTHOR--folk.
                  PLACE--England.
                  DATE--possibly created 17th-19th century?
                  VARIANT VERNACULAR TITLES--A ROUND ABOUT CHRISTMAS;
                                             PLEASE PUT A PENNY IN THE
                                             OLD MAN'S HAT.
      Music: COMPOSER--Edith Nesbit Bland (1858-1924).
                  PLACE--England.
                  DATE--written late 19th or early 20th century.
                  VARIANT TUNES--tunes by Henry Walford Davies (1869-
                                 1941) and Nick Reynolds (1933-   ).
      Found: SHE, SIM, SEV, REE, FCC
      Notes: This is based on a nursery rhyme.

161. CHRISTMAS IS FOR CHILDREN

      Lyrics: AUTHOR--Sammy Cahn (1913-   ).
                  PLACE--United States.
                  DATE--published 1968.
                  DIFFERING FIRST LINE--THE WORLD HAD THE LOOK OF A
                                        FAIRYTALE BOOK.
      Music: COMPOSER--Edward Chester Babcock (1913-   ).
                  PLACE--United States.
                  DATE--published 1968.
      Found: SEV

162. CHRISTMAS IS FOR CHILDREN

Lyrics: AUTHOR--Richard William Wolf (1928-   ).
           PLACE--United States.
           DATE--published 1967.
Music: COMPOSER--Richard William Wolf (1928-   ).
           PLACE--United States.
           DATE--published 1967.
Found: ONS, ONT

163. CHRISTMAS IS HERE

Lyrics: AUTHOR--Jack Kunz.
           PLACE--United States.
           DATE--published 1974.
           DIFFERING FIRST LINE--FROST-PAINTED WINDOWS LOOKING
                                 UP TO SKY'S SO CLEAR.
Music: COMPOSER--Jack Kunz.
           PLACE--United States.
           DATE--published 1974.

164. CHRISTMAS LULLABY

Lyrics: AUTHOR--John Brimhall (1928-   ).
           PLACE--United States.
           DATE--published 1961.
           DIFFERING FIRST LINE--NOW'S THE TIME TO GO TO SLEEP.
Music: COMPOSER--John Brimhall (1928-   ).
           PLACE--United States.
           DATE--published 1961.
Found: SEV

165. CHRISTMAS ON THE MOON

Lyrics: AUTHOR--Jerry Silverman.
           PLACE--United States.
           DATE--published 1968.
Music: COMPOSER--Jerry Silverman.
           PLACE--United States.
           DATE--published 1968.
Found: ONT

166. CHRISTMAS PARTY

Lyrics: AUTHOR--Pennsylvania Dutch community.
           PLACE--Pennsylvania.
           DATE--probably created 18th or 19th century.
           DIFFERING FIRST LINE--WHAT A LOVELY CHRISTMAS PARTY.
Music: COMPOSER--Pennsylvania Dutch community
           PLACE--Pennsylvania.
           DATE--probably created 18th or 19th century.

167. CHRISTMAS PRESENT

    Lyrics: AUTHOR--Sydney Robin (1912-   ).
            PLACE--United States.
            DATE--published 1964.
            DIFFERING FIRST LINE--BOXES STACKED UP TO THE CEILING.
    Music: COMPOSER--Sydney Robin (1912-   ).
            PLACE--United States.
            DATE--published 1964.
    Found: SEV

168. CHRISTMAS SNOW

    Lyrics: AUTHOR--Lawrence William Hansen (1905-   ) and
                John Brimhall (1928-   ).
            PLACE--United States.
            DATE--published 1962.
            DIFFERING FIRST LINE--SNOW, CHRISTMAS SNOW.
    Music: COMPOSER--Lawrence William Hansen (1905-   ) and
                John Brimhall (1928-   ).
            PLACE--United States.
            DATE--published 1962.
    Found: SEV

169. THE CHRISTMAS SONG

    Lyrics: AUTHOR--Mel Torme (1925-   ) and Robert Wells.
            PLACE--United States.
            DATE--published 1946.
            DIFFERING FIRST LINE--CHESTNUTS ROASTING ON AN OPEN
                             FIRE.
    Music: COMPOSER--Mel Torme (1925-   ) and Robert Wells.
            PLACE--United States.
            DATE--published 1946.
    Found: NOR, SEV

170. THE CHRISTMAS TREE

    Lyrics: AUTHOR--Ron Goodwin.
            PLACE--United States.
            DATE--published 1956.
            DIFFERING FIRST LINE--THERE ONCE WAS A TREE.
    Music: COMPOSER--Ron Goodwin.
            PLACE--United States.
            DATE--published 1956.

171. THE CHRISTMAS WALTZ

    Lyrics: AUTHOR--Sammy Cahn (1913-   ).
            PLACE--United States.
            DATE--published 1954.

                     DIFFERING FIRST LINE--FROSTED WINDOW PANES.
      Music: COMPOSER--Jule Styne (1905-   ).
                     PLACE--United States.
                     DATE--published 1954.
      Found: POP

172. CHRISTMAS WILL BE JUST ANOTHER LONELY DAY

      Lyrics: AUTHOR--Lee Jackson and Patti Seymour.
                     PLACE--United States.
                     DATE--published 1963.
                     DIFFERING FIRST LINE--IT'S CHRISTMAS EVE, AND SNOW IS
                                         ON THE GROUND.
      Music: COMPOSER--Lee Jackson and Patti Seymour.
                     PLACE--United States.
                     DATE--published 1963.
      Found: POP

173. CHRISTOPHER THE CHRISTMAS TREE

      Lyrics: AUTHOR--George T. Bowers.
                     PLACE--United States.
                     DATE--published 1969.
                     DIFFERING FIRST LINE--IN THE VALLEY OF HIDDEN HOLLOW.
      Music: COMPOSER--George T. Bowers.
                     PLACE--United States.
                     DATE--published 1969.
      Found: ONS, ONT

174. CHRISTY CHRISTMAS

      Lyrics: AUTHOR--Marty Symes (1904-1953) and Tony Starr
                             (1914-1971).
                     PLACE--United States.
                     DATE--published 1952.
                     DIFFERING FIRST LINE--CHRISTY CHRISTMAS IS LOADING
                                         SANTA'S SLEIGH.
      Music: COMPOSER--Marty Symes (1904-1953) and Tony Starr
                             (1914-1971).
                     PLACE--United States.
                     DATE--published 1952.
      Found: ONT

175. CHTIC, ABY SPAL, TAK ZPÍVALA

      Lyrics: AUTHOR--folk.
                     PLACE--Czechoslovakia.
                     DATE--possibly created 16th-18th century?
                     VARIANT VERNACULAR TITLE--CHTIC, ABY SPAL.
                     ENGLISH TITLES--SWEET MARY SINGS HER BABE TO SLEEP
                                         (translated by George K. Evans);

LULLING HER CHILD (translated by
Edward Bliss Reed [1872-1940]); MARY
WAS WATCHING (translated by Mary
Cochrane Vojácek).
DIFFERING FIRST LINE--MARY WAS WATCHING TENDERLY.
Music: COMPOSER--folk.
PLACE--Czechoslovakia.
DATE--possibly created 16th-18th century?
Found: INT, ZPE, SCC, CEI

176. CLOSE TO CHRISTMAS

Lyrics: AUTHOR--Sammy Cahn (1913-   ).
PLACE--United States.
DATE--published 1968.
VARIANT VERNACULAR TITLE--IT MUST BE GETTING CLOSE TO
CHRISTMAS.
DIFFERING FIRST LINE--IT'S NEAR THE NOEL!
Music: COMPOSER--Edward Chester Babcock (1913-   ).
PLACE--United States.
DATE--published 1968.
Found: SEV

177. CO TO ZNAMENÁ

Lyrics: AUTHOR--folk.
PLACE-- Moravia, Czechoslovakia.
DATE--possibly created 17th-19th century?
ENGLISH TITLE--WHAT IS THE MEANING? (translated by
Olga Paul).
DIFFERING FIRST LINES--CO TO ZNAMENÁ MEDLE NOVÉHO?;
WHAT IS THE MEANING OF THIS
NEW GLORY?
Music: COMPOSER--folk.
PLACE--Moravia, Czechoslovakia.
DATE--possibly created 17th-19th century?
Found: ZPE, RTW

178. COLD IS THE MORNING

Lyrics: AUTHOR--Willys Peck Kent (1877-   ).
PLACE--United States.
DATE--probably written early 20th century.
DIFFERING FIRST LINE--COLD IS THE MORNING AND BLEAK
IS THE DAY.
Music: COMPOSER--folk.
PLACE--Czechoslovakia.
DATE--probably created 17th or 18th century.
Found: SIM, TRE
Notes: The tune is also used for the carols NESEM VÁM NOVINY
and KOMMET, IHR HIRTEN.

179. COME ALL YOU WORTHY GENTLEMEN

    Lyrics: AUTHOR--folk.
             PLACE--probably Somerset, England.
             DATE--possibly created 16th-18th century?
             VARIANT VERNACULAR TITLES--SOMERSET CAROL; COMFORT
                                            AND TIDINGS OF JOY.
    Music: COMPOSER--folk.
             PLACE--probably Somerset, England.
             DATE--possibly created 16th-18th century?
    Found: OXF, REE, SEA, SHA, CFS

180. COME, DANCE AND SING

    Lyrics: AUTHOR--anonymous.
             PLACE--United States.
             DATE--published 1957.
    Music: COMPOSER--Mykola Dmytrovich Leontovych (1877-1921).
             PLACE--Ukraine.
             DATE--written early 20th century.
    Found: WIL
    Notes: The tune is also used for the carols CAROL OF THE
             BELLS (both versions) and RING, CHRISTMAS BELLS.

181. COME, DEAR CHILDREN

    Lyrics: AUTHOR--Wihla Hutson.
             PLACE--United States.
             DATE--published 1954.
             DIFFERING FIRST LINE--COME, DEAR CHILDREN, DON'T BE
                                     DALLYING.
    Music: COMPOSER--Alfred Burt (1919 or 1920-1954).
             PLACE--United States.
             DATE--published 1954.
    Found: BUR

182. COME, MAD BOYS, BE GLAD BOYS

    Lyrics: AUTHOR--folk.
             PLACE--England.
             DATE--probably created 17th century.
             DIFFERING FIRST LINE--COME, MAD BOYS, BE GLAD BOYS,
                                      FOR CHRISTMAS IS HERE.
    Music: COMPOSER--folk.
             PLACE--England.
             DATE--probably created 15th or 16th century.
    Found: SHE

183. COME, THOU LONG-EXPECTED JESUS

    Lyrics: AUTHOR--Charles Wesley (1707-1788).
             PLACE--England.

DATE--published 1744.
VARIANT VERNACULAR TITLE--HAIL, THOU LONG-EXPECTED
JESUS.
Music: COMPOSER--Rowland Hugh Prichard (1811-1887).
PLACE--Wales.
DATE--written around 1830.
VARIANT TUNES--tune probably by Christian Friedrich
Witt (1660-1716); anonymous tune; tune
by John Stainer (1840-1901); 1851 tune
by Ithamar Conkey; tune by Lowell
Mason (1792-1872).
Found: MET, PRA, HAR, LUT, ENG
Notes: The tune by Witt is also used for the carol O SOLA
MAGNARUM URBIUM.

184. COME, TUNE YOUR CHEERFUL VOICE

Lyrics: AUTHOR--folk.
PLACE--Dorsetshire, England.
DATE--probably created 17th or 18th century.
Music: COMPOSER--folk.
PLACE--Dorsetshire, England.
DATE--probably created 18th century.
Found: UNI, DOR

185. COME WITH US, SWEET FLOWERS

Lyrics: AUTHOR--anonymous.
PLACE--probably United States.
DATE--possibly written early 20th century.
VARIANT VERNACULAR TITLE--CAROL OF THE FLOWERS.
DIFFERING FIRST LINE--COME WITH US SWEET FLOW'RS, AND
WORSHIP CHRIST THE LORD.
Music: COMPOSER--folk.
PLACE--probably Basses-Pyrénées, France.
DATE--probably created 18th century.
Found: OBE, CCM
Notes: The tune is also used for the spring song CAROL OF
THE FLOWERS (NOUÈL DE LAS FLOUS) and the Christmas
song CAROL OF THE FLOWERS.

186. COME, YE LOFTY, COME, YE LOWLY

Lyrics: AUTHOR--Archer T. Gurney (1820-1887).
PLACE--England.
DATE--published 1871.
VARIANT VERNACULAR TITLE--COME! YE LOFTY.
Music: COMPOSER--Archer T. Gurney (1820-1887).
PLACE--England.
DATE--published 1871.
VARIANT TUNES--tunes by George Job Elvey (1816-1893)
and Arthur F.M. Custance.
Found: HUT, CHO, STA

187. COMO BUSCA EL TIERNO INFANTE

Lyrics: AUTHOR--folk.
PLACE--Venezuela.
DATE--possibly created 18th or 19th century?
ENGLISH TITLE--AS THE FRIGHTENED BABY JESUS (trans-
lated by George K. Evans).
Music: COMPOSER--folk.
PLACE--Venezuela.
DATE--possibly created 18th or 19th century?
Found: INT

188. CONDITOR ALME SIDERUM

Lyrics: AUTHOR--anonymous.
PLACE--Europe.
DATE--probably created 7th century.
VARIANT VERNACULAR TITLE--CREATOR ALME SIDERUM.
ENGLISH TITLES--CREATOR OF THE STARS OF NIGHT and
CREATOR OF THE STARRY NIGHT (two
titles for the same translation by
John Mason Neale [1818-1866]).
Music: COMPOSER--anonymous.
PLACE--Europe.
DATE--probably created medieval period.
VARIANT TUNE--tune by Margaret MacWilliam written
around 1925.
Found: UNI, HAR, CAT, ENG, SIG
Notes: The main tune is also used for the carol O HEILAND,
REISS DIE HIMMEL AUF.

189. CONGAUDEAT TURBA FIDELIUM

Lyrics: AUTHOR--anonymous.
PLACE--Europe.
DATE--probably created 11th century.
VARIANT VERNACULAR TITLE--CONGAUDEAT.
ENGLISH TITLES--COME YE FAITHFUL (translated by
Ronald Arbuthnott Knox [1888-1957]);
FROM CHURCH TO CHURCH (translated by
John Mason Neale [1818-1866]); O HARK
TO THE BELLS' GLAD SONG; WITH MERRY
HEART LET ALL REJOICE IN ONE (trans-
lated by Maurice Frederick Bell).
Music: COMPOSER--anonymous.
PLACE--Europe (possibly France).
DATE--possibly created 12th century.
Found: THF, OBE, COF, HUT, OXF

190. CORDE NATUS EX PARENTIS

Lyrics: AUTHOR--Aurelius Clemens Prudentius (348-ca. 413).
PLACE--Spain.

DATE--probably written early 5th century.
VARIANT VERNACULAR TITLE--CORDE NATUS.
ENGLISH TITLES--OF THE FATHER'S LOVE BEGOTTEN and
                FROM THE FATHER'S LOVE BEGOTTEN (two
                variations of the same translation by
                John Mason Neale [1818-1866] and
                Henry Williams Baker [1821-1877]);
                OF THE FATHER'S HEART BEGOTTEN (trans-
                lated by R.F. Davis).
Music: COMPOSER--anonymous.
PLACE--Europe.
DATE--probably created 13th century; possibly first
      published 1582.
VARIANT TUNE--folk tune from Belgium or France.
Found: INT, CAT, HAR, CCT, MET

191. CORRE AL PORTALICO!

Lyrics: AUTHOR--folk.
PLACE--Andalusia, Spain.
DATE--possibly created 16th-18th century?
ENGLISH TITLE--HURRY, HURRY TO THE STABLE (translated
              by John Morrison).
DIFFERING FIRST LINE--CORRE, CORRE AL PORTALICO.
Music: COMPOSER--folk.
PLACE--Andalusia, Spain.
DATE--possibly created 16th-18th century?
Found: MON, REF

192. COVENTRY CAROL

Lyrics: AUTHOR--Pageant of the Shearmen and Tailors.
PLACE--Coventry, England.
DATE--created 15th century; oldest known text (by
      Robert Croo) 1534.
VARIANT VERNACULAR TITLES--LULLY, LULLAY; LULLABY,
                    THOU LITTLE TINY CHILD;
                    LULLY, LULLA.
DIFFERING FIRST LINES--LULLY, LULLA, THOU LITTLE TINY
                    CHILD; LULLY, LULLA, YOU LITTLE
                    TINY CHILD; LULLAY, THOU LITTLE
                    TINY CHILD; LULLY, LULLA, THOW
                    LITTELL TINÉ CHILD.
Music: COMPOSER--probably Pageant of the Shearmen and Tailors.
PLACE--probably Coventry, England.
DATE--probably created 15th century; oldest known text
      1591.
VARIANT TUNES--tunes by Franz Joseph Haydn (1732-1809)
              and John La Montaine (1920-   ).
Found: MANY

193. COVERDALE'S CAROL

>*Lyrics:* AUTHOR--Miles Coverdale (1487-1568).
>PLACE--England.
>DATE--published 1546.
>VARIANT VERNACULAR TITLE--THE BLESSED SON OF GOD.
>DIFFERING FIRST LINE--NOW BLESSED BE THOU, CHRIST
>JESU.
>*Music:* COMPOSER--folk.
>PLACE--probably Herefordshire, England.
>DATE--possibly created 16th-18th century?
>VARIANT TUNE--tune by Ralph Vaughan Williams (1872-
>1958).
>*Found:* OXF, CCO, APP
>*Notes:* The lyrics are really a translation of GELOBET SEIST
>DU, JESU CHRIST, but the translation, set to two
>different tunes, has been treated as a separate carol;
>Vaughan Williams' tune was originally written for his
>cantata HODIE (1954).

194. COWBOY CAROL

>*Lyrics:* AUTHOR--Cecil Broadhurst (1908-   ).
>PLACE--England.
>DATE--probably written 1949.
>DIFFERING FIRST LINE--THERE'LL BE A NEW WORLD
>BEGINNIN' FROM T'NIGHT!
>*Music:* COMPOSER--Cecil Broadhurst (1908-   ).
>PLACE--England.
>DATE--probably written 1949.
>*Found:* REE, GOL

195. DA DROBEN VOM BERGE

>*Lyrics:* AUTHOR--folk.
>PLACE--Austria.
>DATE--possibly created 17th-19th century?
>ENGLISH TITLE--ABOVE, ON THE MOUNTAIN (translated by
>George K. Evans).
>*Music:* COMPOSER--folk.
>PLACE--Austria.
>DATE--possibly created 17th-19th century?
>*Found:* INT

196. DAME, GET UP AND BAKE YOUR PIES

>*Lyrics:* AUTHOR--folk.
>PLACE--England.
>DATE--possibly created 16th-18th century?
>VARIANT VERNACULAR TITLE--DAME GET UP.
>DIFFERING FIRST LINE--O DAME, GET UP AND BAKE YOUR
>PIES.

Music: COMPOSER--folk.
            PLACE--England.
            DATE--possibly created 16th-18th century?
Found: SHE, MAL, CCM, BMC

197. DANS CETTE ÉTABLE

Lyrics: AUTHOR--Esprit Fléchier (1632-1710).
            PLACE--France.
            DATE--probably written second half of 17th century.
            ENGLISH TITLES--IN THAT POOR STABLE and BETHLEHEM
                       (both titles for the same translation
                       by Maurice Frederick Bell); BETHLEHEM
                       (translated by John O'Connor [1870-
                       1952]); BETHLEHEM (translated by
                       Percy Dearmer [1867-1936]).
            DIFFERING FIRST LINE--JESUS IN STABLE!
Music: COMPOSER--folk.
            PLACE--France.
            DATE--possibly created 17th-19th century.
Found: OXF, ECS, THF, UNI, TIE
Notes: The tune has sometimes been called "Gounod's
            Bethlehem" because Charles Gounod (1818-1893) made an
            often-used arrangement.

198. DAVID EX PROGENIE

Lyrics: AUTHOR--anonymous.
            PLACE--England.
            DATE--created 15th century.
            ENGLISH TITLE--FROM THE ROYAL SHEPHERD'S LINE (trans-
                       lated by John O'Connor [1870-1952]).
Music: COMPOSER--anonymous.
            PLACE--England.
            DATE--created 15th century.
Found: MEC, MED, THF

199. DE BOODSCHAP VAN MARIA

Lyrics: AUTHOR--folk.
            place--Netherlands.
            DATE--possibly created 15th-17th century?
            VARIANT VERNACULAR TITLE--ER WAS EEN MAAGDETJE.
            ENGLISH TITLE--THE MESSAGE.
            DIFFERING FIRST LINE--A MESSAGE CAME TO A MAIDEN
                                       YOUNG.
Music: COMPOSER--folk.
            PLACE--Netherlands.
            DATE--possibly created 15th-17th century?
Found: OXF

200. DE DRIE KONINGEN

      Lyrics: AUTHOR--folk.
               PLACE--Belgium.
               DATE--possibly created 15th or 16th century.
               ENGLISH TITLES--THERE WERE THREE KINGS; THE THREE
                                  KINGS; THREE KINGS and THE MAGI AND
                                  KING HEROD (two titles for the same
                                  translation by Robert Graves [1895-
                                        ]).
               DIFFERING FIRST LINES--LAATST WAREN ER DRIE KONINGEN
                                       WIJS; THERE WERE THREE KINGS,
                                       ON JOURNEY DID GO; THREE KINGS
                                       ARE HERE, BOTH WEALTHY AND
                                       WISE; LATE, THREE WISE KINGS
                                       AFAR OFF DID GO.
      Music: COMPOSER--folk.
               PLACE--Belgium.
               DATE--possibly created 15th or 16th century.
               VARIANT TUNE--tune by John La Montaine (1920-   ).
      Found: SHE, OBE, OXF, HUT, WON

201. DE LARGA JORNADA

      Lyrics: AUTHOR--folk.
               PLACE--Latin America.
               DATE--possibly created 18th or 19th century?
               ENGLISH TITLE--THE LONG JOURNEY (two different trans-
                                    lations, one anonymous, one by Helen
                                    Luvaas Fjerstad).
               DIFFERING FIRST LINE--FROM A LONG JOURNEY.
      Music: COMPOSER--folk.
               PLACE--Latin America.
               DATE--possibly created 18th or 19th century?
      Found: PAZ, FJE

202. DE NEDERIGE GEBOORTE

      Lyrics: AUTHOR--folk.
               PLACE--Belgium.
                DATE--possibly created 15th-17th century?
               VARIANT VERNACULAR TITLE--ER IS EEN KINDEKEN GEBOREN
                                    OP D'AARD.
               ENGLISH TITLES--A LITTLE CHILD ON THE EARTH HAS BEEN
                                    BORN and FLEMISH CAROL (both the same
                                    translation by Robert Calverley
                                    Trevelyan [1872-1951]); THE SIMPLE
                                    BIRTH (four different translations,
                                    two anonymous, one by George K.
                                    Evans), and one by Ruth Heller
                                    [1920-   ]).

DIFFERING FIRST LINES--ER IS EEN KINDEKIN GEBOREN OP
                      D'AARD'; FROM HEAV'N THERE
                      CAME TO EARTH A BABY SO SMALL;
                      A CHILD TODAY HAS BEEN BORN ON
                      THIS EARTH; A HOLY CHILD WAS
                      BORN IN A STALL; A LITTLE
                      CHILD WAS BORN IN A STALL.

Music: COMPOSER--folk.
           PLACE--Belgium.
           DATE--possibly created 15th-17th century?
Found: INT, OBE, OXF, REE, SEA
Notes: This is perhaps the best-known carol from Belgium.

203.   DE TIERRA LEJANA VENIMOS

Lyrics: AUTHOR--probably Manuel Fernández Juncos (1846-1928).
           PLACE--Puerto Rico.
           DATE--written late 19th or early 20th century.
           VARIANT VERNACULAR TITLES--LOS REYES DE ORIENTE; LOS
                               REYES ORIENTE.
           ENGLISH TITLE--SONG OF THE WISE MEN (two different
                          translations, one by Seymour Barab
                          [1921-   ], the other by George K.
                          Evans).
           DIFFERING FIRST LINES--DE TIERRA LEJANA VENIMOS A
                               VERTE; FROM A DISTANT HOME,
                               THE SAVIOR WE COME SEEKING.
Music: COMPOSER--folk.
           PLACE--Puerto Rico.
           DATE--possibly created 18th or 19th century?
Found: INT, LUC, LOP, LAN

204.   DECK THE HALLS WITH BOUGHS OF HOLLY

Lyrics: AUTHOR--folk.
           PLACE--Wales.
           DATE--possibly created 16th century.
           VARIANT VERNACULAR TITLE--DECK THE HALL.
           DIFFERING FIRST LINE--DECK THE HALL WITH BOUGHS OF
                               HOLLY.
Music: COMPOSER--folk.
           PLACE--Wales.
           DATE--possibly created 16th century.
Found: MANY
Notes: Wolfgang Amadeus Mozart (1756-1791) used the melody
           in a duet for violin and piano; the tune is also
           used for the carol NOS GALAN.

205.   THE DECREE

Lyrics: AUTHOR--folk.
           PLACE--England.

```
                    DATE--probably created 18th century.
                    VARIANT VERNACULAR TITLE--THE BLACK DECREE.
                    DIFFERING FIRST LINE--LET CHRISTIANS ALL WITH ONE
                                         ACCORD REJOICE.
        Music:      COMPOSER--folk.
                    PLACE--England.
                    DATE--possibly created 16th-18th century?
                    VARIANT TUNES--two other folk tunes from England;
                                   tune by Arthur Henry Brown (1830-1926).
        Found:      OXF, THF, CHO, STA
```

206. DEILIG ER DEN HIMMEL BLAA

```
        Lyrics:     AUTHOR--Nicolai Frederik Severin Grundtvig (1783-
                           1872).
                    PLACE--Denmark.
                    DATE--published 1810.
                    VARIANT VERNACULAR TITLE--DEJLIG ER DEN HIMMEL BLÅ.
                    ENGLISH TITLES--BRIGHT AND GLORIOUS IS THE SKY;
                                    LOVELY IS THE DARK BLUE SKY (trans-
                                    lated by George K. Evans).
        Music:      COMPOSER--folk.
                    PLACE--Denmark.
                    DATE--possibly created 17th-19th century?
                    VARIANT TUNE--tune by Thomas Linnemann Laub (1852-
                                  1927).
        Found:      INT, FHS, LUT
```

207. DER HEILAND IST GEBOREN

```
        Lyrics:     AUTHOR--folk.
                    PLACE--Upper Austria.
                    DATE--possibly created 16th-18th century?
                    ENGLISH TITLE--THE CHRIST-CHILD IS BORN.
        Music:      COMPOSER--folk.
                    PLACE--Upper Austria.
                    DATE--possibly created 16th-18th century?
        Found:      BUD, WOR, CCM, NHW
```

208. DET KIMER NU TIL JULEFEST

```
        Lyrics:     AUTHOR--Nicolai Frederik Severin Grundtvig (1783-
                           1872).
                    PLACE--Denmark.
                    DATE--published 1817.
                    ENGLISH TITLE--THE HAPPY CHRISTMAS COMES ONCE MORE
                                   (translated by Charles Porterfield
                                    Krauth [1823-1883]).
        Music:      COMPOSER--Carl C.N. Balle (1806-1855).
                    PLACE--probably Denmark.
                    DATE--published 1850.
                    VARIANT TUNE--15th century tune.
```

Found: INT, FHS, PRE, HEL, LUT
Notes: This is perhaps the best-known Danish carol.

209. DET STÅR ETT LJUS I ÖSTERLAND

       Lyrics: AUTHOR--folk.
                PLACE--Sweden.
                DATE--possibly created 16th-18th century?
                ENGLISH TITLE--THE STAR IN THE EAST (translated by
                          Marx E. Oberndorfer [1876-   ]).
                DIFFERING FIRST LINE--THE STAR SHINES BRIGHT IN FAR-
                          OFF EAST.
       Music: COMPOSER--folk.
                PLACE--Sweden.
                DATE--possibly created 16th-18th century?
       Found: OBE, JUL, GLA

210. DIE ALRESOETSTE JESUS

       Lyrics: AUTHOR--folk.
                PLACE--Netherlands.
                DATE--created 15th century.
                ENGLISH TITLES--THERE WAS A MAID SO LOVELY and THERE
                          WAS A MAID (two titles for the same
                          translation by John O'Connor [1870-
                          1952]).
       Music: COMPOSER--folk.
                PLACE--Netherlands.
                DATE--created 15th century.
       Found: THF, UNI

211. DIE HIRTEN AUF DEM FELDE

       Lyrics: AUTHOR--folk.
                PLACE--Austria.
                DATE--possibly created 19th century.
                ENGLISH TITLE--AS LATELY WE WATCHED.
                DIFFERING FIRST LINE--AUF, AUF NUN, EHS HIARTEN.
       Music: COMPOSER--folk.
                PLACE--Austria.
                DATE--possibly created 19th century.
       Found: INT, OBE, CCM, PRE, MAR

212. DIE KÖNIGE

       Lyrics: AUTHOR--Peter Cornelius (1824-1874).
                PLACE--Germany.
                DATE--written mid-19th century.

ENGLISH TITLES--THE KINGS and THE THREE KINGS (two
different titles for the same trans-
lation by Herbert Newell Bate [1871-
1941]); THE KINGS (translated by W.G.
Rothery); THE THREE KINGS (anonymous
translation).
DIFFERING FIRST LINES--DREI KÖN'GE WANDERN AUS
MORGENLAND; THREE KINGS HAVE
WANDER'D FROM EASTERN LAND;
THREE KINGS FROM PERSIAN LANDS
AFAR; THREE KINGS HAD JOURNEY'D
FROM LANDS AFAR.
Music: COMPOSER--Peter Cornelius (1824-1874).
PLACE--Germany.
DATE--written mid-19th century.
Found: OXF, SIM, UNI, HUT, CCO
Notes: Sometimes the tune for the carol WIE SCHÖN LEUCHTET
DER MORGENSTERN is used as an accompaniment to this
carol.

213. DIES EST LETICIAE

Lyrics: AUTHOR--anonymous.
PLACE--Europe (possibly Bohemia, Czechoslovakia).
DATE--possibly created 12th-14th century.
VARIANT VERNACULAR TITLES--DIES EST LAETITIAE; DIES
EST LETICIE; DIES EST
LAETITIA.
ENGLISH TITLES--CHRISTIAN FOLK, A DAY OF JOY (trans-
lated by John O'Connor [1870-1952]);
ROYAL DAY THAT CHASETH GLOOM (trans-
lated by John Mason Neale [1818-1866]).
Music: COMPOSER--anonymous.
PLACE--Europe (possibly Bohemia, Czechoslovakia).
DATE--possibly created 12th-14th century.
Found: THF, COF, KOL
Notes: The song's oldest known text was written around 1410.

214. DIÉU VOUS GARD', NOSTE MÈSTRE

Lyrics: AUTHOR--folk.
PLACE--Provence, France.
DATE--possibly created 16th-18th century?
ENGLISH TITLE--THE GOSSOON AND THE GAFFER CAROL
(translated by John O'Connor [1870-
1952]).
DIFFERING FIRST LINE--GOD SAVE YOU KINDLY GAFFER.
Music: COMPOSER--folk.
PLACE--Provence, France.
DATE--possibly created 16th-18th century?
Found: THF, UNI

215. DING-A-LING, THE CHRISTMAS BELL

    Lyrics: AUTHOR--Jerry Foster (1935-   ) and Bill Rice.
              PLACE--United States.
              DATE--published 1970.
              DIFFERING FIRST LINE--GATHER 'ROUND AND I WILL TELL.
    Music: COMPOSER--Jerry Foster (1935-   ) and Bill Rice.
              PLACE--United States.
              DATE--published 1970.
    Found: SEV

216. DING DONG! MERRILY ON HIGH

    Lyrics: AUTHOR--George Ratcliffe Woodward (1848-1934).
              PLACE--England.
              DATE--written late 19th or early 20th century.
              VARIANT VERNACULAR TITLES--DING DONG; NOEL! MERRILY
                                 ON HIGH (modification of
                                 Woodward's lyrics by
                                 Elizabeth Poston [1905-
                                 ]).
    Music: COMPOSER--folk.
              PLACE--France.
              DATE--probably created 16th century; probably first
                  published in ORCHÉSOGRAPHIE, a 1588 treatise on
                  dancing by Thoinot Arbeau (1519-1595).
    Found: CCT, HAW, REE, PEN, SHE
    Notes: Although Woodward's lyrics (or modifications) are
              normally used, other words (anonymous), under the same
              title, are also used; the tune is the folk dance
              melody BRANLE DE L'OFFICIEL.

217. DIVES AND LAZARUS

    Lyrics: AUTHOR--folk.
              PLACE--probably Herefordshire, England.
              DATE--probably created 15th or 16th century.
              DIFFERING FIRST LINE--AS IT FELL OUT UPON ONE DAY.
    Music: COMPOSER--folk.
              PLACE--probably Herefordshire, England.
              DATE--probably created 15th or 16th century.
              VARIANT TUNES--another folk tune from Herefordshire;
                  a third folk tune from England.
    Found: OXF, THF, LEA, STA

218. DO YOU HEAR WHAT I HEAR

    Lyrics: AUTHOR--Noel Regney and Gloria Shayne.
              PLACE--United States.
              DATE--published 1962
              DIFFERING FIRST LINE--SAID THE NIGHT WIND TO THE
                  LITTLE LAMB.

Music: COMPOSER--Noel Regney and Gloria Shayne.
           PLACE--United States.
           DATE--published 1962.

219. DO YOU KNOW HOW CHRISTMAS TREES ARE GROWN?

Lyrics: AUTHOR--Hal David (1921-   )
            PLACE--United States.
            DATE--published 1969.
Music: COMPOSER--John Barry.
            PLACE--United States.
            DATE--published 1969.
Found: HAP

220. DONA NOBIS PACEM

Lyrics: AUTHOR--anonymous.
            PLACE--Europe.
            DATE--probably created medieval period.
Music: COMPOSER--anonymous.
            PLACE--Europe.
            DATE--possibly created 15th-17th century?
Found: SIM, WIL, HFW
Notes: The lyrics consist entirely of "Dona nobis pacem"
            repeated several times.

221. ¿DÓNDE ESTÁ SANTA CLAUS?

Lyrics: AUTHOR--Rod Parker, Alvin G. Greiner (1911-   ), and
                    George Scheck (1911-   ).
            PLACE--United States.
            DATE--published 1958.
            DIFFERING FIRST LINE--MAMACITA, ¿DÓNDE ESTÁ SANTA
                                  CLAUS.
Music: COMPOSER--Rod Parker, Alvin G. Greiner (1911-   ),
                    and George Scheck (1911-   ).
            PLACE--United States.
            DATE--published 1958.
Found: HAP
Notes: The song is also known as WHERE IS SANTA CLAUS?

222. DONKEY CAROL

Lyrics: AUTHOR--John Rutter.
            PLACE--England.
            DATE--published 1975.
            DIFFERING FIRST LINE--DONKEY RIDING OVER THE BUMPY
                                  ROAD.
Music: COMPOSER--John Rutter.
            PLACE--England.
            DATE--published 1975.
Found: CCF

223. DORMI, DORMI, O BEL BAMBIN

      Lyrics: AUTHOR--folk.
               PLACE--Italy.
               DATE--possibly created 16th-18th century?
               ENGLISH TITLES--SLEEP, O SLEEP, MY LOVELY CHILD
                                 (translated by George K. Evans);
                                 SLEEP, SLEEP, LOVELY BABE (translated
                                 by Ruth Heller [1920-   ]); SLEEP, O
                                 HOLY CHILD OF MINE (translated by
                                 Olga Paul); SLEEP, OH SLEEP, LITTLE
                                 BABY; SLEEP, MY DARLING (translated
                                 by Bryson Gerard).
               DIFFERING FIRST LINES--SLEEP, MY DARLING BABY SLEEP;
                                 SLEEP, MY DARLING, SLEEP, MY KING;
                                 SLEEP, OH HOLY CHILD OF MINE.
      Music: COMPOSER--folk.
               PLACE--Italy.
               DATE--possibly created 16th-18th century?
      Found: INT, SIM, SHE, RTW, HEL

224. DORS, MA COLOMBE

      Lyrics: AUTHOR--Émile Blémont (1839-1927).
               PLACE--Alsace, France.
               DATE--probably written second half of 19th century.
               ENGLISH TITLE--SLEEP, LITTLE DOVE (two different
                                   translations, one by Edward Cuthbert
                                 Nunn [1868-1914], one by Charles
                                 Fonteyn Manney [1872-1951]).
               DIFFERING FIRST LINE--SLEEP, LITTLE DOVE OF MINE.
      Music: COMPOSER--folk.
               PLACE--Alsace, France.
               DATE--probably created 17th century.
      Found: INT, NOB, TIE
      Notes: This is the French version of SCHLAF', MEIN KINDELEIN.

225. D'OÙ VIENS-TU, BERGÈRE?

      Lyrics: AUTHOR--folk.
               PLACE--France or Quebec.
               DATE--probably created 17th century.
               ENGLISH TITLES--WHENCE ART THOU, MY MAIDEN? (trans-
                                   lated by William McLennan); WHENCE, O
                                   SHEPHERD MAIDEN? (translated by John
                                   Murray Gibbon [1875-   ]); WHERE WERE
                                   YOU, OH MAIDEN? (translated by Olga
                                   Paul); THE SHEPHERDESS (translated by
                                   Ruth Heller [1920-   ]).
               DIFFERING FIRST LINE--FROM WHENCE SHEPHERDESS, DO YOU
                                   NOW COME?
      Music: COMPOSER--folk.
               PLACE--France or Quebec.

DATE--probably created 17th century.
Found: INT, TRA, SMI, JOH, RTW
Notes: If this carol is from Quebec, it is the best-known
French-Canadian carol; France, however, is the more
likely location.

226. DOWN IN YON FOREST

Lyrics: AUTHOR--folk.
PLACE--probably Derbyshire, England.
DATE--possibly created 15th century.
VARIANT VERNACULAR TITLE--CORPUS CHRISTI CAROL.
DIFFERING FIRST LINE--DOWN IN YON FOREST THERE STANDS
A HALL.
Music: COMPOSER--folk.
PLACE--probably Derbyshire, England.
DATE--possibly created 15th century.
Found: OXF, CCT, REE, UNI, BAE
Notes: A derivative of this carol was also created in the
Appalachian region; for a carol with similar lyrics
but a different tune, see ALL BELLS IN PARADISE.

227. DU GRØNNE, GLITRENDE TRE, GOD-DAG!

Lyrics: AUTHOR--Johan Jacob Krohn (1841-1925).
PLACE--Denmark.
DATE--probably written second half of 19th century.
ENGLISH TITLE--YOU GREEN AND GLITTERING TREE, GOOD
DAY! (translated by George K. Evans).
Music: COMPOSER--Christoph Ernst Friedrich Weyse (1774-
1842).
PLACE--Denmark.
DATE--probably written first half of 19th century.
Found: INT

228. DU LIEBER, HEIL'GER, FROMMER CHRIST

Lyrics: AUTHOR--Ernst Moritz Arndt (1769-1860).
PLACE--Germany.
DATE--written late 18th or early 19th century.
Music: COMPOSER--Gottlob Siegert (1789-   ).
PLACE--Germany.
DATE--published 1821.
Found: ROT, BUD, WOR

229. DUÉRMETE, NIÑO LINDO

Lyrics: AUTHOR--folk.
PLACE--probably Southwest United States.
DATE--possibly created 18th or 19th century.
VARIANT VERNACULAR TITLE--A LA RU.

ENGLISH TITLE--LULLABYE (translated by Helen Luvaas
            Fjerstad).
            DIFFERING FIRST LINE--ABOVE YOUR CRADLE, MY DEAR ONE.
Music: COMPOSER--folk.
            PLACE--probably Southwest United States.
            DATE--possibly created 18th or 19th century.
Found: SEA, FJE

230. DULCE JESUS MIO

Lyrics: AUTHOR--folk.
            PLACE--Ecuador.
            DATE--possibly created 18th or 19th century?
            ENGLISH TITLE--SWEET AND PRECIOUS JESUS (translated
                        by Olga Paul).
Music: COMPOSER--folk.
            PLACE--Ecuador.
            DATE--possibly created 18th or 19th century?
Found: RTW

231. DZIASIAJ W BETLEJEM

Lyrics: AUTHOR--folk.
            PLACE--Poland.
            DATE--possibly created 15th-17th century?
            ENGLISH TITLES--HEAR THE GLAD TIDINGS! (translated by
                        Alice Zienko and Ruth Heller [1920-
                        ]); O COME REJOICING (translated
                        by George K. Evans); HEAR! BETHLEHEM.
Music: COMPOSER--folk.
            PLACE--Poland.
            DATE--possibly created 15th-17th century?
Found: INT, REB, HEL

232. EARTHLY FRIENDS

Lyrics: AUTHOR--John Mason Neale (1818-1866).
            PLACE--England.
            DATE--written 1853.
            VARIANT VERNACULAR TITLE--EARTHLY FRIENDS WILL CHANGE
                        AND FALTER.
Music: COMPOSER--anonymous.
            PLACE--Europe (possibly Germany).
            DATE--possibly created 14th-16th century; possibly
                        first published 1582.
            VARIANT TUNE--tune by Michael Praetorius (1571-1621).
Found: OXF, COF

233. ECCE NOVUM GAUDIUM

Lyrics: AUTHOR--anonymous.
            PLACE--Europe.

                    DATE--possibly created 14th-16th century.
                    ENGLISH TITLES--HERE IS JOY FOR EVERY AGE (translated
                              by John Mason Neale [1818-1866]);
                              HERE IS JOY FOR EV'RYONE (translated
                              by Ronald Arbuthnott Knox [1888-1957]).
          Music: COMPOSER--anonymous.
                    PLACE--Europe.
                    DATE--possibly created 14th-16th century.
          Found: THF, OBE, COF
          Notes: The song was possibly first published in 1582; the
                    Latin lyrics are similar to those for the carol ECCE
                    QUOD NATURA, but the tunes are different.

234. ECCE QUOD NATURA

          Lyrics: AUTHOR--anonymous.
                    PLACE--England.
                    DATE--created 15th century.
                    ENGLISH TITLE--THOUGH THEY CANNOT PALTER (translated
                              by John O'Connor [1870-1952]).
                    DIFFERING FIRST LINES--ECCE NOVUM GAUDIUM; LO, A
                              BLITHE AND NOVEL JOY.
          Music: COMPOSER--anonymous.
                    PLACE--England.
                    DATE--created 15th century.
                    VARIANT TUNE--another 15th century English tune.
          Found: MEC, MED, THF
          Notes: The Latin lyrics are similar to those for the carol
                    ECCE NOVUM GAUDIUM, but the tunes are different.

235. ECHEN CONFITES

          Lyrics: AUTHOR--folk.
                    PLACE--Mexico.
                    DATE--possibly created 18th or 19th century?
                    ENGLISH TITLE--SCATTER THE BON BONS.
                    DIFFERING FIRST LINE--SERVE UP THE BONBONS AND
                              SUGARPLUMS.
          Music: COMPOSER--folk.
                    PLACE--Mexico.
                    DATE--possibly created 18th or 19th century?
          Found: PAZ

236. EEN KINDEKIJN IS ONS GHEBOREN

          Lyrics: AUTHOR--folk.
                    PLACE--Netherlands.
                    DATE--probably created 14th or 15th century.
                    ENGLISH TITLES--HARK! UNTO US A CHILD IS BORN (trans-
                              lated by Marguerite Vogels-Reiners);
                              A LITTLE CHILD CAME YESTER MORNING
                              (translated by John O'Connor [1870-
                              1952]).

Music: COMPOSER--folk.
            PLACE--Netherlands.
            DATE--probably created 14th or 15th century.
Found: THF, BRU, PEE

237. EEN KINT GHEBOREN IN BETHLEHEM

Lyrics: AUTHOR--folk.
            PLACE--Netherlands.
            DATE--probably created 15th century.
            ENGLISH TITLES--A CHILD IS BORN IN BETHLEHEM (trans-
                    lated by Ruth Heller [1920-   ]);
                    DUTCH CAROL (translated by Robert
                    Calverley Trevelyan [1872-1951]);
                    WHEN JUDAH'S LOYAL SOUL ALONE (trans-
                    lated by John O'Connor [1870-1952]).
Music: COMPOSER--folk.
            PLACE--Netherlands.
            DATE--probably created 15th or 16th century.
Found: OXF, THF, BRU, HEL
Notes: The lyrics were derived from the Latin carol PUER
            NATUS IN BETHLEHEM.

238. EHRE SEI GOTT

Lyrics: AUTHOR--Ludwig Ernst Gebhardi (1787-1862).
            PLACE--Germany.
            DATE--written 19th century.
            VARIANT VERNACULAR TITLE--EHRE SEI GOTT IN DER HÖHE.
            ENGLISH TITLE--GLORY TO GOD.
            DIFFERING FIRST LINE--GLORY TO GOD IN THE HIGHEST!
Music: COMPOSER--Ludwig Ernst Gebhardi (1787-1862).
            PLACE--Germany.
            DATE--written 19th century.
Found: SIM, HFW

239. EIN KIND GEBORN ZU BETHLEHEM

Lyrics: AUTHOR--folk.
            PLACE--Germany.
            DATE--probably created 16th century.
            ENGLISH TITLE--A BOY WAS BORN IN BETHLEHEM.
Music: COMPOSER--anonymous.
            PLACE--Europe (possibly Germany or Bohemia,
                    Czechoslovakia).
            DATE--probably created 14th century; supplanted by
                    its descant by 16th century.
Found: OXF, BUD
Notes: This is a German version of PUER NATUS IN BETHLEHEM;
            the tune is also used for the carol QUAE STELLA SOLE
            PULCHRIOR.

240. EIN KINDLEIN IN DER WIEGEN

Lyrics: AUTHOR--folk.
PLACE--Austria.
DATE--probably created 16th century.
ENGLISH TITLES--HE SMILES WITHIN HIS CRADLE and THE
CRADLE (both titles for the same
translation by Robert Graves [1895-
]); A BABE LIES IN THE CRADLE
(translated by Paul England); A BABY
IN THE CRADLE (translated by George K.
Evans).
Music: COMPOSER--folk.
PLACE--Austria.
DATE--probably created 16th century.
Found: OXF, INT, REE, HAW, NOB
Notes: The song was probably first published in 1590; it has
been erroneously attributed to David Gregorius Corner
(1585-1648) because it was printed in Corner's 1649
collection GEISTLICHE NACHTIGAL; the tune is also
used for the carol THE WORLD'S DESIRE.

241. EL CANT DELS OCELLS

Lyrics: AUTHOR--folk.
PLACE--Catalonia, Spain.
DATE--possibly created medieval period?
ENGLISH TITLE--CAROL OF THE BIRDS (two different
translations, one anonymous, the other
by George K. Evans).
DIFFERING FIRST LINES--EN VEURE DESPUNTAR; AL VEURE
DESPUNTAR; UPON THIS HOLY
NIGHT; WHEN ROSE THE EASTERN
STAR.
Music: COMPOSER--folk.
PLACE--Catalonia, Spain.
DATE--possibly created medieval period?
Found: INT, MON, BAE

242. EL DESEMBRE CONGELAT

Lyrics: AUTHOR--folk.
PLACE--Catalonia, Spain.
DATE--possibly created 16th-18th century?
VARIANT VERNACULAR TITLE--CANSÓ DE NADAL.
ENGLISH TITLES--THE ICY DECEMBER; CHRISTMAS SONG
(translated by Olga Paul).
DIFFERING FIRST LINES--LO DESEMBRE CONGELAT; COLD
DECEMBER'S WINDS WERE STILLED;
WINTER NOW HAS PASSED AWAY.
Music: COMPOSER--folk.
PLACE--Catalonia, Spain.
DATE--possibly created 16th-18th century?
Found: INT, MON, RTW

243. EL MINO JESUS

    Lyrics: AUTHOR--folk.
                PLACE--Puerto Rico.
                DATE--probably created late 19th or early 20th century.
                VARIANT VERNACULAR TITLES--EL SANTO NIÑO; EL NIÑO
                                    JESÚS.
                ENGLISH TITLES--THE CHILD JESUS (two different trans-
                            lations, one anonymous, one by Olga
                            Paul; THE HOLY CHILD (translated by
                            George K. Evans); THE LITTLE JESUS.
                DIFFERING FIRST LINES--MADRE, A LA PUERTA HAY UN NIÑO;
                            MOTHER, STANDING AT OUR DOOR-
                            WAY; MOTHER DEAR, A CHILD AT
                            OUR DOORSTEP; MOTHER, LOOK!
                            A CHILD AT OUR DOOR; MOTHER,
                            SEE THE CHILD SO GLORIOUS.
    Music: COMPOSER--folk.
                PLACE--Puerto Rico.
                DATE--probably created late 19th or early 20th century.
    Found: INT, SIM, SHE, OBE, LUC
    Notes: The words have been attributed to Antonio Machado
                (1875-1939), a poet from Spain; the words are somewhat
                similar to those for the carols A ESTA PUERTA LLAMA
                UN NIÑO and MADRE, EN LA PUERTA HAY UN NIÑO, but the
                tunes are different.

244. EL NOI DE LA MARE

    Lyrics: AUTHOR--folk.
                PLACE--Catalonia, Spain.
                DATE--possibly created 16th-18th century?
                ENGLISH TITLE--THE SON OF MARY (translated by George
                            K. Evans).
                DIFFERING FIRST LINES--QUÉ LI DAREM A N'EL NOI DE
                            LA MARE?; WHAT SHALL WE GIVE TO
                            THE SON OF THE VIRGIN?
    Music: COMPOSER--folk.
                PLACE--Catalonia, Spain.
                DATE--possibly created 16th-18th century?
    Found: INT, MON, MOO

245. EL REI HERODES

    Lyrics: AUTHOR--folk.
                PLACE--Catalonia, Spain.
                DATE--possibly created 16th-18th century?
                ENGLISH TITLE--KING HEROD (translated by George K.
                            Evans).
                DIFFERING FIRST LINES--ESTANT A LA CAMBRA; ONE DAY
                            JOSEPH, RESTING.
    Music: COMPOSER--folk.
                PLACE--Catalonia, Spain.

        DATE--possibly created 16th-18th century?
Found: INT

246. EL RORRO

  Lyrics: AUTHOR--folk.
         PLACE--Mexico.
         DATE--possibly created 18th or 19th century?
         ENGLISH TITLES--THE BABE (three different transla-
                 tions, one by Bernard Gasso [1926-
                 ], one by Helen Luvaas Fjerstad,
                 one by George K. Evans); ROCKING THE
                 CHILD; THE ROCKING OF THE CHILD; O,
                 RU-RU-RU, MY LITTLE JESU (translated
                 by Ruth Heller [1920-   ]).
         DIFFERING FIRST LINE--A LA RURURU.
  Music: COMPOSER--folk.
         PLACE--Mexico.
         DATE--possibly created 18th or 19th century?
  Found: INT, SHE, TRA, HEL, ONT
  Notes: This is perhaps the best-known carol from Mexico.

247. EL SAGRADO NACIMIENTO

  Lyrics: AUTHOR--folk.
         PLACE--Aragon, Spain.
         DATE--possibly created 16th-18th century?
         DIFFERING FIRST LINE--ATENCIÓN A MIS COPLICAS.
  Music: COMPOSER--folk.
         PLACE--Aragon, Spain.
         DATE--possibly created 16th-18th century?
         VARIANT TUNE--tune by Joaquín Nin y Castellanos
                 (1879-1949), composer from Cuba.
  Found: MON, MOO, CAN, NIN

248. EN BELÉN TOCAN A FUEGO

  Lyrics: AUTHOR--folk.
         PLACE--Castille, Spain.
         DATE--possibly created 17th-19th century?
         VARIANT VERNACULAR TITLE--BRINCAN Y BAILAN.
         ENGLISH TITLE--A FIRE IS STARTED IN BETHLEHEM (trans-
                 lated by George K. Evans).
         DIFFERING FIRST LINE--HERE IN BETHLEHEM THIS EVENING.
  Music: COMPOSER--folk.
         PLACE--Castille, Spain.
         DATE--possibly created 17th-19th century?
  Found: INT, MON, MOO, CAN

249. EN BĒTHLEEM SYNEDRAMOI

Lyrics: AUTHOR--anonymous.
PLACE--probably Byzantine Empire.
DATE--probably created medieval period.
VARIANT VERNACULAR TITLE--EN BĒTHLFEM SYNEDRAMON.
ENGLISH TITLES--TO BETHLEHEM THAT NIGHT and TO
BETHLEM SHEPHERD-BRETHREN RAN (two
different translations by George
Ratcliffe Woodward [1848-1934]).
Music: COMPOSER--anonymous.
PLACE--France.
DATE--probably created medieval period.
Found: CCB, COS

250. EN EL PORTAL A BELÉN

Lyrics: AUTHOR--folk.
PLACE--Puerto Rico.
DATE--possibly created 18th or 19th century?
VARIANT VERNACULAR TITLE--EN EL PORTAL DE BELÉN.
ENGLISH TITLES--AT THE CRÈCHE (translated by Seymour
Barab [1921-   ]); IN BETHLEHEM'S
CRADLE (translated by George K.
Evans).
DIFFERING FIRST LINES--HA NACIDO EN UN PORTAL; HE IS
BORN WITHIN A STABLE; IN A
STABLE LIES A BABY.
Music: COMPOSER--folk.
PLACE--Puerto Rico.
DATE--possibly created 18th or 19th century?
Found: INT, LAN
Notes: There are also several carols from Spain entitled
EN EL PORTAL DE BELÉN.

251. EN JULSÅNG

Lyrics: AUTHOR--Selim Palmgren (1878-1951).
PLACE--Finland.
DATE--probably written around 1913.
DIFFERING FIRST LINE--OCH JUNGFRUN GÖMMER TROGET
LILLA BARNET VID SIN BARM.
Music: COMPOSER--Selim Palmgren (1878-1951).
PLACE--Finland.
DATE--probably written around 1913.
Found: FIN

252. EN JUNGFRU FÖDDE ETT BARN I DAG

Lyrics: AUTHOR--folk.
PLACE--Sweden
DATE--created medieval period.

ENGLISH TITLE--TODAY THE VIRGIN HAS BORNE A CHILD
(translated by Linnea Hallenberg and
Ruth Heller [1920-   ]).
Music: COMPOSER--folk.
PLACE--Sweden.
DATE--created medieval period.
Found: JUL, GLA, HEL

253.   EN NATUS EST EMANUEL

Lyrics: AUTHOR--anonymous.
PLACE--probably Germany.
DATE--probably created medieval period; possibly
first published 1609.
ENGLISH TITLE--THIS DAY IS BORN EMMANUEL (translated
by John O'Connor [1870-1952]).
Music: COMPOSER--anonymous, possibly Michael Praetorius
(1571-1621).
PLACE--probably Germany.
DATE--published 1609.
Found: THF, UNI

254.   EN NOMBRE DEL CIELO

Lyrics: AUTHOR--folk.
PLACE--Mexico.
DATE--possibly created 18th or 19th century?
VARIANT VERNACULAR TITLE--PEDIDA DE LA POSADA.
ENGLISH TITLES--THE SEARCH FOR LODGING (translated by
Ruth Heller [1920-   ]); PRAY GIVE
US LODGING (translated by George K.
Evans).
DIFFERING FIRST LINES--PRAY GIVE US LODGING, DEAR SIR,
IN THE NAME OF HEAV'N;
LODGING, I BEG YOU, GOOD MAN,
IN THE NAME OF HEAVEN!
Music: COMPOSER--folk.
PLACE--Mexico.
DATE--possibly created 18th or 19th century?
Found: INT, HEL

255.   EN STJÄRNA GICK PÅ HIMLEN FRAM

Lyrics: AUTHOR--folk.
PLACE--Sweden.
DATE--created medieval period.
ENGLISH TITLE--THE STAR THAT LED TO BETHLEHEM (trans-
lated by Linnea Hallenberg and Ruth
Heller [1920-   ]).
DIFFERING FIRST LINE--A STAR IN HEAVEN SHONE ONE NIGHT.
Music: COMPOSER--folk.
PLACE--Sweden
DATE--created medieval period.
Found: JUL, GLA, HEL

256. ER IS EEN' JONGE MAAGD GELEGEN

Lyrics: AUTHOR--folk.
          PLACE--Belgium.
          DATE--possibly created 16th-18th century?
          VARIANT VERNACULAR TITLE--KERSTLIED.
          ENGLISH TITLES--A MAIDEN BLEST (translated by Edward
                          Bliss Reed [1872-1940]); SAINT
                          JOSEPH'S CAROL (translated by Eliza-
                          beth Poston [1905-   ]).
          DIFFERING FIRST LINES--A MAIDEN LIES HERE, BLEST BY
                          HEAVEN; O SEE A GENTLE MAIDEN
                          MOTHER.
Music: COMPOSER--folk.
          PLACE--Belgium.
          DATE--possibly created 16th-18th century?
Found: CFF, PEN

257. ES FÜHRT' DREI KÖNIGE GOTTES HAND

Lyrics: AUTHOR--folk.
          PLACE--Germany.
          DATE--probably created 15th or 16th century.
          ENGLISH TITLE--THERE CAME THREE KINGS.
          DIFFERING FIRST LINE--THERE CAME THREE KINGS FROM
                          EASTERN LAND.
Music: COMPOSER--folk.
          PLACE--Germany.
          DATE--probably created 15th or 16th century.
Found: COF, HUT
Notes: The song was probably first published in 1623.

258. ES IST EIN' ROS' ENTSPRUNGEN

Lyrics: AUTHOR--folk.
          PLACE--Germany.
          DATE--created 15th century.
          VARIANT VERNACULAR TITLE--ES IST EIN' ROS'.
          ENGLISH TITLES--LO, HOW A ROSE E'ER BLOOMING (trans-
                          lated by Theodore Baker [1851-1934]);
                          THERE IS A FLOWER (translated by
                          Ursula Vaughan Williams [1911-   ]);
                          A NOBLE FLOWER OF JUDA (translated by
                          Anthony G. Petti); THE WORLD'S FAIR
                          ROSE (translated by Elizabeth Poston
                          [1905-   ]); LO! A FAIR ROSE IS
                          BLOOMING; THE ROSE (translated by
                          Percy W. Young [1912-   ]); THE NOBLE
                          STEM OF JESSE; LO, HOW A ROSE; BEHOLD,
                          A LOVELY FLOWER; I KNOW A FLOWER
                          (translated by George Ratcliffe Woodward
                          [1848-1934]); I KNOW A ROSE TREE SPRING-
                          ING; BEHOLD A BRANCH IS GROWING.

DIFFERING FIRST LINES--THERE IS A FLOWER SPRINGING;
LO, HOW A ROSE UPSPRINGING;
HAIL, ROSE OF WONDROUS VIRTUE;
THE WORLD'S FAIR ROSE HAS
BLOSSOMED; LO, A FAIR ROSE
ABLOOMING.

Music: COMPOSER--folk.
PLACE--Germany.
DATE--created 15th century.

Found: OXF, INT, SIM, PEN, SHE

Notes: The words and melody were probably first published in
1600; the melody was harmonized by Michael Praetorius
(1571-1621) in 1609, and Praetorius' arrangement is
the one commonly used today; Johannes Brahms (1833-
1897) wrote an 1896 chorale prelude based on the
melody; another name for the carol is FLOS DE RADICE
JESSE.

259. ES KOMT EIN SCHIFF GELADEN

Lyrics: AUTHOR--probably Johannes Tauler (1290-1361).
PLACE--Germany.
DATE--probably written around 1340.
VARIANT VERNACULAR TITLE--ES KOMT EIN SCHIFF.
ENGLISH TITLES--THERE COMES A GALLEY, LADEN (trans-
lated by George Ratcliffe Woodward
[1848-1934]); SONG OF THE SHIP or
THERE COMES A GALLEY LADEN (translated
by Anne Shaw Faulker Oberndorfer [1877-
]); SONG OF THE SHIP (anonymous
translation); THERE COMES A VESSEL
LADEN (translated by Henry W. Davis).
DIFFERING FIRST LINE--THERE COMES A SHIP A-SAILING.

Music: COMPOSER--anonymous.
PLACE--Germany.
DATE--probably written 16th or early 17th century;
probably first published 1608.

Found: OXF, OBE, COF, WOR, PRE

260. ES STOT EIN LIND IM HIMMELRICH

Lyrics: AUTHOR--folk.
PLACE--Germany.
DATE--probably created 14th or 15th century.
ENGLISH TITLES--THERE STOOD IN HEAVEN A LINDEN TREE
and THE LINDEN TREE CAROL (two titles
for the same translation by George
Ratcliffe Woodward [1848-1934]).

Music: COMPOSER--folk.
PLACE--Germany.
DATE--probably created 14th or 15th century.

Found: UNI, CCO, CCB, CCF

Notes: The oldest known text was produced around 1430.

261. ES WIRD SCHO GLEI DUMPA

    Lyrics: AUTHOR--folk.
             PLACE--Austria.
             DATE--possibly created 17th-19th century?
             VARIANT VERNACULAR TITLE--ES WIRD SCHON GLEICH
                       DUNKEL.
             ENGLISH TITLES--THE TWILIGHT IS FALLING (translated
                       by George K. Evans); THE DARKNESS IS
                       FALLING; THE SHADOWS ARE FALLING
                       (paraphrase by Thomas Armstrong
                       [1898-   ]).
    Music: COMPOSER--folk.
             PLACE--Austria.
             DATE--possibly created 17th-19th century?
    Found: INT, TRA, WOR, UNI

262. ET BARN ER FØDT I BETLEHEM

    Lyrics: AUTHOR--Nicolai Frederik Severin Grundtvig (1783-
                       1872).
             PLACE--Denmark.
             DATE--published 1820.
             ENGLISH TITLE--A CHILD IS BORN IN BETHLEHEM (trans-
                       lated by George K. Evans).
    Music: COMPOSER--folk.
             PLACE--Denmark.
             DATE--probably created around 1600.
    Found: INT, FHS
    Notes: The lyrics were derived from the Latin carol PUER
             NATUS IN BETHLEHEM.

263. ETT BARN ÄR FÖTT PÅ DENNA DAG

    Lyrics: AUTHOR--folk.
             PLACE--Sweden.
             DATE--possibly created 15th-17th century?
             ENGLISH TITLE--A TENDER CHILD WAS BORN THIS DAY
                       (translated by Olga Paul).
    Music: COMPOSER--folk.
              PLACE--Sweden.
              DATE--probably created 15th century.
    Found: RTW, GLA, JUL

264. ETZEN BADA MARIA?

    Lyrics: AUTHOR--folk.
             PLACE--Basque region, Spain and France.
             DATE--possibly created 16th-18th century?
             ENGLISH TITLES--WHO WERE THE SHEPHERDS and WHO WERE
                       THE SHEPHERDS, MARY? (both titles for
                       the same translation by John Gray
                       [1866-1934]).

Music: COMPOSER--folk.
             PLACE--Basque region, Spain and France.
             DATE--possibly created 16th-18th century?
Found: THF, UNI

265. EVERETT THE EVERGREEN

Lyrics: AUTHOR--Bobby Fischer.
             PLACE--United States.
             DATE--published 1973.
             DIFFERING FIRST LINE--EV'RETT THE EVERGREEN.
Music: COMPOSER--Bobby Fischer.
             PLACE--United States.
             DATE--published 1973.
Found: ONS, ONT

266. EVERYWHERE, EVERYWHERE, CHRISTMAS TONIGHT

Lyrics: AUTHOR--Phillips Brooks (1835-1893).
             PLACE--probably Philadelphia, Pennsylvania.
             DATE--written between 1862 and 1868.
             DIFFERING FIRST LINE--CHRISTMAS IN LANDS OF THE FIR
                                  TREE AND PINE.
Music: COMPOSER--Lewis Henry Redner (1831-1908).
             PLACE--probably Philadelphia, Pennsylvania.
             DATE--written between 1862 and 1868.
Found: INT, OBE, HUT, PRE

267. EXULTATION

Lyrics: AUTHOR--anonymous, possibly folk.
             PLACE--probably Southern States.
             DATE--probably created 18th or 19th century.
             DIFFERING FIRST LINE--COME AWAY TO THE SKIES.
Music: COMPOSER--anonymous, possibly folk.
             PLACE--probably Southern States.
             DATE--probably created 18th or 19th century.
Found: LAN, SEE

268. FALADE BEN BAIXO

Lyrics: AUTHOR--folk.
             PLACE--Galicia, Spain.
             DATE--possibly created 16th-18th century?
             ENGLISH TITLE--WE'LL SPEAK VERY SOFTLY (translated by
                                  George K. Evans).
Music: COMPOSER--folk.
             PLACE--Galicia, Spain.
             DATE--possibly created 16th-18th century?
Found: INT, MOO

269. FALAN-TIDING

    Lyrics: AUTHOR--folk.
            PLACE--England.
            DATE--probably created 16th or 17th century.
            VARIANT VERNACULAR TITLE--OUT OF THE ORIENT.
            DIFFERING FIRST LINE--OUT OF THE ORIENT CRYSTAL SKIES.
    Music: COMPOSER--folk.
            PLACE--Tyrol, Austria.
            DATE--possibly created 16th-18th century?
    Found: OXF, ENG
    Notes: The tune is also used for the carol IHR HIRTEN
            STEHET ALLE AUF VON EUREM TIEFEN SCHLAF.

270. FANFARE

    Lyrics: AUTHOR--Martin Shaw (1875-1958).
            PLACE--England.
            DATE--probably written first half of 20th century.
            DIFFERING FIRST LINE--GLORIA IN EXCELSIS DEO.
    Music: COMPOSER--Martin Shaw (1875-1958).
            PLACE--ENGLAND.
            DATE--probably written first half of 20th century.
    Found: UNI

271. FANNE, CORAIGE, LE DIALE À MORT

    Lyrics: AUTHOR--Bernard de la Monnoye (1641-1728).
            PLACE--Burgundy, France.
            DATE--probably written around 1700.
            VARIANT VERNACULAR TITLE--FANNE, CORAIGE.
            ENGLISH TITLES--CHEER UP OLD WOMAN (translated by
                        John O'Connor [1870-1952]); SHEPHERD
                        AND WIFE (translated by Alfred
                        Raymond Bellinger [1893-   ]).
            DIFFERING FIRST LINES--CHEER UP OLD WOMAN, SATAN IS
                        DEAD; CHEERILY WIFE! THE DEVIL
                        IS DEAD!
    Music: COMPOSER--probably folk, possibly Bernard de la
                        Monnoye (1641-1728).
            PLACE--Burgundy, France.
            DATE--probably created 17th or 18th century.
    Found: THF, CNT

272. FARMER'S CAROL

    Lyrics: AUTHOR--Edward Devlin.
            PLACE--possibly Canada.
            DATE--probably written first half of 20th century.
            DIFFERING FIRST LINE--COME, WIFE AND CHILDREN, LET US
                        SEE THE LIGHT.

Music: COMPOSER--Paul Petrocokino (1910-   ).
            PLACE--England.
            DATE--possibly written 1949.
Found: REE

273. FELIZ NAVIDAD

Lyrics: AUTHOR--Jose Feliciano (1945-   ).
            PLACE--United States.
            DATE--published 1970.
Music: COMPOSER--Jose Feliciano (1945-   ).
            PLACE--United States.
            DATE--published 1970.

274. FESANS RAIJOUISSANCE

Lyrics: AUTHOR--Christin Prost (d. 1676).
            PLACE--probably Besancon region, France.
            DATE--written 17th century; possibly first published
                1842.
            ENGLISH TITLE--SO, BROTHER (paraphrase by Alan
                Alexander Milne [1882-1956]).
            DIFFERING FIRST LINE--NOW, BROTHERS, LIFT YOUR VOICES.
Music: COMPOSER--folk.
            PLACE--Besancon region, France.
            DATE--possibly created 15th-17th century?
Found: OXF
Notes: The tune is the air JE SUIS DANS LA TRISTESSE or
            DE TURLU TURLUTU.

275. THE FIRST NOEL

Lyrics: AUTHOR--folk.
            PLACE--possibly Cornwall, England.
            DATE--possibly created 16th century.
            DIFFERING FIRST LINE--THE FIRST NOEL, THE ANGELS SAY.
Music: COMPOSER--Henry John Gauntlett (1805-1876).
            PLACE--England.
            DATE--probably written mid-19th century.
Found: HUT
Notes: This song should not be confused with the famous
            carol, THE FIRST NOWELL, whose lyrics are similar
            but whose tune is different; for yet another carol
            with somewhat similar lyrics and a different tune,
            see FYFE'S NOEL.

276. THE FIRST NOWELL

Lyrics: AUTHOR--folk.
            PLACE--probably Cornwall, England.
            DATE--probably created 16th century; probably first
                published 1823.

VARIANT VERNACULAR TITLE--THE FIRST NOWEL.
DIFFERING FIRST LINES--THE FIRST NOWELL THE ANGEL DID
                      SAY; THE FIRST NOWEL THAT THE
                      ANGEL DID SAY; THE FIRST NOEL
                      THAT THE ANGEL DID SAY.
Music: COMPOSER--folk.
            PLACE--probably Cornwall, England.
            DATE--probably created 16th century; probably first
                published 1833.
Found: MANY
Notes: There is some opinion that the carol is from France,
            but without basis; the chorus of the first-published
            tune is much different from the present version, which
            appeared by the 1870's (see notes for FYFE'S NOEL);
            in addition to FYFE'S NOEL, another carol with
            similar lyrics but a different tune is THE FIRST NOEL;
            this is perhaps the best-known carol of completely
            English origin.

277. FRANCIS KINDLEMARSH'S CAROL

Lyrics: AUTHOR--Francis Kindlemarsh (fl. ca. 1570).
            PLACE--England.
            DATE--published 1589.
            DIFFERING FIRST LINE--FROM VIRGIN'S WOMB THIS CHRIST-
                                  MAS DAY DID SPRING.
Music: COMPOSER--Orlando Gibbons (1583-1625).
            PLACE--England.
            DATE--probably written early 17th century.
Found: APP

278. THE FRIENDLY BEASTS

Lyrics: AUTHOR--probably Robert Davis.
            PLACE--probably United States.
            DATE--first known text 1934, but probably older.
            DIFFERING FIRST LINE--JESUS OUR BROTHER, KIND AND
                                  GOOD.
Music: COMPOSER--anonymous.
            PLACE--probably France; possibly England.
            DATE--created 12th century.
Found: INT, SHE, CCM, TOM, ULT
Notes: The tune is also used for the Latin hymn ORIENTIS
            PARTIBUS.

279. FRÖHLICH SOLL MEIN HERZE SPRINGEN

Lyrics: AUTHOR--Paul Gerhardt (1607-1676).
            PLACE--Germany.
            DATE--published 1653.

ENGLISH TITLES--ALL MY HEART THIS NIGHT REJOICES
                     (translated by Catherine Winkworth
                     [1827-1878]); ALL THE SKIES TONIGHT
                     SING O'ER US! (translated by John
                     O'Connor [1870-1952]); others.
Music: COMPOSER--Johann Georg Ebeling (1637-1676).
           PLACE--Germany.
           DATE--published 1666.
           VARIANT TUNES--1894 tune by Horatio Parker (1863-
                     1919); another 1666 tune by Ebeling;
                     other tunes.
Found: INT, UNI, CCT, MET, OWE
Notes: Both the original German words and Winkworth's
           translation are used with Ebeling's tune; Parker's
           tune (United States) is used with Winkworth's
           translation.

280. FROM EVERY SPIRE ON CHRISTMAS EVE

Lyrics: AUTHOR--Eleanor Augusta Hunter (1855-   ).
           PLACE--United States.
           DATE--written late 19th or early 20th century.
           DIFFERING FIRST LINE--FROM EV'RY SPIRE ON CHRISTMAS
                     EVE.
Music: COMPOSER--George Coles (1792-1858).
           PLACE--United States.
           DATE--written early or mid-19th century.
Found: PRE, CCC, ONS

281. FROM THE EASTERN MOUNTAINS

Lyrics: AUTHOR--Godfrey Thring (1823-1903).
           PLACE--England.
           DATE--written 1873; published 1874.
Music: COMPOSER--Arthur Henry Mann (1850-1929).
           PLACE--England.
           DATE--published 1889.
           VARIANT TUNES--tunes by George B. Lissant, Ralph
                     Vaughan Williams (1872-1958), William
                     Savage Pitts (1830-1918), and Henry G.
                     Trembath.
Found: SIM, PRS, ONT, ENG, TRE

282. FROSTY THE SNOW MAN

Lyrics: AUTHOR--Walter E. Rollins (1906-1973).
           PLACE--United States.
           DATE--written 1950.
           VARIANT VERNACULAR TITLE--FROSTY THE SNOWMAN.
Music: COMPOSER--Steve Edward Nelson (1907-   ).
           PLACE--United States.
           DATE--written 1950.
Found: ULT, ONS, ONT

283. FUM, FUM, FUM!

    Lyrics: AUTHOR--folk.
                 PLACE--Catalonia, Spain.
                 DATE--possibly created 16th-18th century?
                 ENGLISH TITLES--FOOM, FOOM, FOOM! (two different
                              translations, one by George K. Evans,
                              one by Henry William Simon [1901-
                              ]); FUM, FUM, FUM (several
                              different translations by Ruth Heller
                              [1920-   ] and others.
                 DIFFERING FIRST LINES--VEINTICINCO DE DICIEMBRE;
                                    VEINTECINCO DE DICIEMBRE;
                                    A VINT-I-CINC DE DESEMBRE;
                                    ON DECEMBER TWENTY FIVE;
                                    ON DECEMBER FIVE AND TWENTY;
                                    ON DECEMBER TWENTYFIFTH;
                                    ON THIS JOYFUL CHRISTMAS DAY
                                    SING FUM, FUM, FUM.
    Music: COMPOSER--folk.
                 PLACE--Catalonia, Spain.
                 DATE--possibly created 16th-18th century?
    Found: INT, SIM, SHE, TRA, MOO
    Notes: This is perhaps the best-known carol from Spain.

284. FYFE'S NOEL

    Lyrics: AUTHOR--folk.
                 PLACE--possibly Cornwall, England.
                 DATE--possibly created 16th century.
                 VARIANT VERNACULAR TITLE--THE FIRST NOEL.
                 DIFFERING FIRST LINE--THE FIRST NOEL AN ANGEL SUNG.
    Music: COMPOSER--folk.
                 PLACE--England.
                 DATE--possibly created 16th century.
    Found: GAS, FYF
    Notes: This song should not be confused with the famous
                 carol, THE FIRST NOWELL, whose lyrics are similar but
                 whose tune is different; this was probably first
                 published in CHRISTMAS, ITS CUSTOMS AND CAROLS, an
                 1860 collection by William Wallace Fyfe; the notes
                 for the words "Born is the King" in this carol may
                 have been substituted for the equivalent notes of the
                 first-published (1833) version of the famous carol,
                 thus creating the present (1870's) version of the
                 famous carol; for yet another carol with somewhat
                 similar words and a different tune, see THE FIRST
                 NOEL.

285. GABRIEL'S MESSAGE

    Lyrics: AUTHOR--Sabine Baring-Gould (1834-1924).
                 PLACE--England.

DATE--probably written second half of 19th century.
VARIANT VERNACULAR TITLE--THE ANGEL GABRIEL FROM
                 HEAVEN CAME.

Music: COMPOSER--folk.
PLACE--Basque region, Spain and France.
DATE--possibly created 16th-18th century?

Found: CCT, UNI, CCF, REF, CAT

286. GATHER AROUND THE CHRISTMAS TREE

Lyrics: AUTHOR--John Henry Hopkins (1820-1891).
PLACE--United States.
DATE--probably written mid-19th century.

Music: COMPOSER--John Henry Hopkins (1820-1891).
PLACE--United States.
DATE--probably written mid-19th century.

Found: INT, HUT, OWE, CCM, PRE

287. GDY SIE CHRYSTUS RODZI

Lyrics: AUTHOR--folk.
PLACE--Poland.
DATE--possibly created 15th-17th century?
ENGLISH TITLES--ON THE NIGHT WHEN JESUS CAME (trans-
    lated by Alice Zienko and Ruth Heller
    [1920-   ]); CHRIST IS BORN THIS
    EVENING (translated by George K.
    Evans); JESUS CHRIST IS BORN; WHEN
    CHRIST WAS BORN; CHRIST IS BORN.
DIFFERING FIRST LINES--GOD THE CHRIST IS BORN ON THIS
                HOLY NIGHT; CHRIST THE LORD IS
                BORN THIS NIGHT.

Music: COMPOSER--folk.
PLACE--Poland.
DATE--possibly created 15th-17th century?

Found: INT, TRA, OBE, REB, HEL

288. GEBOR'N IST UNS EIN KINDELEIN

Lyrics: AUTHOR--folk.
PLACE--Germany.
DATE--probably created 16th century; possibly first
    published 1634.
ENGLISH TITLE--TO US IS BORN A LITTLE CHILD.

Music: COMPOSER--folk.
PLACE--Germany.
DATE--created 15th century; possibly first published
    1544.
VARIANT TUNE--16th century tune from Germany.

Found: COF, HUT, OXF, OBE, PRE

289. GELOBET SEIST DU, JESU CHRIST

  Lyrics: AUTHOR--verse 1, folk; verses 2-7, Martin Luther
                  (1483-1546).
              PLACE--Germany.
              DATE--verse 1, probably created 14th century; verses
                  2-7, published 1524.
              VARIANT VERNACULAR TITLES--GELOBET SEIS TU JESU
                                    CHRIST; GELOBET SEYST DU,
                                    JESU CHRIST.
              ENGLISH TITLES--ALL PRAISE TO THEE, ETERNAL LORD; WE
                  PRAISE, O CHRIST YOUR HOLY NAME
                  (translated by F. Samuel Janzow);
                  HAIL! JESU CHRIST, BLESSED FOR AYE.
  Music: COMPOSER--folk.
              PLACE--Germany.
              DATE--probably created 14th or 15th century.
              VARIANT TUNE--tune by Thomas Tallis (ca. 1505-1585).
  Found: COF, BUD, HUT, LUT, SIG
  Notes: The tune has been attributed to Bartholomaeus Gesius
              (d. 1613), who probably made an arrangement around
              1600; for an English derivative, see COVERDALE'S
              CAROL.

290. GENTLE MARY LAID HER CHILD

  Lyrics: AUTHOR--Joseph Simpson Cook (1859-1933).
              PLACE--Canada.
              DATE--written 1919.
  Music: COMPOSER--anonymous.
              PLACE--Europe.
              DATE--created 13th century; probably first published
                  in the 1582 collection PIAE CANTIONES.
  Found: MET, SIG
  Notes: The tune originally was a spring song, TEMPUS ADEST
              FLORIDUM; the tune is also used for the carol GOOD
              KING WENCESLAS.

291. GESÙ BAMBIN L'E NATO

  Lyrics: AUTHOR--folk.
              PLACE--Italy.
              DATE--possibly created 16th-18th century?
              ENGLISH TITLES--JESUS, THE NEW-BORN BABY (translated
                          by George K. Evans); JESUS WAS BORN TO
                          MARY (translated by Olga Paul).
  Music: COMPOSER--folk.
              PLACE--Italy.
              DATE--possibly created 16th-18th century?
  Found: INT, RTW

292. GESÙ BAMBINO

    Lyrics: AUTHOR--Pietro Alessandro Yon (1886-1943).
              PLACE--United States.
              DATE--published 1917.
              ENGLISH TITLE--THE INFANT JESUS.
              DIFFERING FIRST LINES--NEL L'UMILE CAPANNA; WHEN
                                          BLOSSOMS FLOWERED 'MID THE
                                          SNOWS.
    Music: COMPOSER--Pietro Alessandro Yon (1886-1943).
              PLACE--United States.
              DATE--published 1917.
    Found: ULT
    Notes: The original lyrics were in both Italian and English,
              with the English words by Frederick Herman Martens
              (1874-1932).

293. THE GINGERBREAD HOUSE

    Lyrics: AUTHOR--Roger LaVoie.
              PLACE--United States.
              DATE--published 1971.
              DIFFERING FIRST LINE--COME WITH ME TO THE GINGERBREAD
                                            HOUSE.
    Music: COMPOSER--Roger LaVoie.
              PLACE--United States.
              DATE--published 1971.
    Found: ONS

294. GLORY TO GOD IN HEIGHTS OF HEAVEN

    Lyrics: COMPOSER--Walter Hayward Shewring (1906-   ).
              PLACE--England.
              DATE--probably written late 1920's or early 1930's.
    Music: COMPOSER--folk.
               PLACE--probably Wiltshire, England.
              DATE--possibly created 16th-18th century?
    Found: THF, UNI

295. GLORY TO THAT NEWBORN KING

    Lyrics: AUTHOR--folk (Black spiritual).
              PLACE--United States.
               DATE--probably created 18th or 19th century.
               DIFFERING FIRST LINE--O MARY WHAT YOU GOIN' TO NAME
                                          THAT PRETTY LITTLE BABY?
    Music: COMPOSER--folk (Black spiritual).
              PLACE--United States.
               DATE--probably created 18th or 19th century.
    Found: ANS
    Notes: For carols with somewhat similar lyrics but different
              tunes, see MARY, WHAT ARE YOU GOING TO NAME THAT PRETTY
              LITTLE BABY? and WHAT YOU GONNA CALL YO' PRETTY LITTLE
              BABY?

296. GLOUCESTERSHIRE WASSAIL

    Lyrics: AUTHOR--folk.
              PLACE--probably Gloucestershire, England.
              DATE--probably created 18th century.
              VARIANT VERNACULAR TITLES--WASSAIL, WASSAIL;
                                        GLOUCESTERSHIRE WASSAILERS'
                                        SONG; WASSAIL SONG.
              DIFFERING FIRST LINE--WASSAIL, WASSAIL ALL OVER THE
                                        TOWN!
    Music: COMPOSER--folk.
              PLACE--probably Gloucestershire, England.
              DATE--probably created 18th century.
              VARIANT TUNE--another English folk tune.
    Found: MANY
    Notes: The lyrics are somewhat similar to SOMERSET WASSAIL,
              but the melody is different.

297. GO TELL IT ON THE MOUNTAIN

    Lyrics: AUTHOR--folk (Black spiritual).
              PLACE--United States.
              DATE--probably created late 19th or early 20th century.
    Music: COMPOSER--folk (Black spiritual).
              PLACE--United States.
              DATE--probably created late 19th or early 20th century.
    Found: INT, SIM, LEI, SEE, MET
    Notes: The song (words and music) has been attributed to
              Frederick J. Work; the lyrics were adapted and the
              music was arranged by John W. Work (1901-1967).

298. GOD BLESS THE MASTER OF THIS HOUSE

    Lyrics: AUTHOR--folk.
              PLACE--England.
               DATE--probably created 17th century.
    Music: COMPOSER--folk.
               PLACE--probably Cornwall, England.
               DATE--possibly created 17th century.
              VARIANT TUNES--tune from Tyrol, Austria; folk tune
                                        probably from Surrey, England.
    Found: SHE, REE, UNI, OCC
    Notes: The lyrics appear to be a paraphrase of GOOD-BYE; the
              Cornwall tune is also used for the FURRY DAY CAROL
              (May); the Surrey tune possibly may be from the
              Gypsy community.

299. GOD GIVE YE MERRY CHRISTMASTIDE

    Lyrics: AUTHOR--folk.
              PLACE--England.
               DATE--possibly created 16th or 17th century.

                      VARIANT VERNACULAR TITLE--GOD GIVE YE MERRY
                                      CHRISTMAS TIDE.

Music: COMPOSER--folk.
            PLACE--England.
            DATE--possibly created 16th or 17th century.
Found: BMC, HUT

300. GOD REST YOU MERRY, GENTLEMEN

Lyrics: AUTHOR--folk (first version, possibly the Waits of
                 London, a city-supported band).
          PLACE--probably London, England.
          DATE--probably created 16th century; major variations,
                 18th century.
          VARIANT VERNACULAR TITLE--GOD REST YOU MERRY.
Music: COMPOSER--folk (possibly the Waits of London, a city-
                 supported band).
          PLACE--probably London, England.
          DATE--probably created 16th century.
          VARIANT TUNES--18th century folk tune from Cornwall,
                      England; tune by Lewis Henry Redner
                      (1831-1908).
Found: MANY
Notes: This is the carol sung to Scrooge in Charles Dickens'
          A CHRISTMAS CAROL; it has had significant cultural
          influence in Great Britain; the comma is sometimes
          misplaced after "You" in the first line, thereby
          giving the impression that this basically religious
          song is predominantly a secular one; the carol was
          probably first published in the 18th century; it is
          perhaps the best known carol of completely English
          origin.

301. GOD'S DEAR SON WITHOUT BEGINNING

Lyrics: AUTHOR--folk.
          PLACE--England.
          DATE--possibly created 15th or 16th century.
          VARIANT VERNACULAR TITLE--GOD'S DEAR SON.
Music: COMPOSER--folk.
          PLACE--England.
          DATE--possibly created 15th or 16th century.
Found: OXF, THF, GAS, GIF, ECF
Notes: The song was probably first published in 1822.

302. THE GOLDEN CAROL

Lyrics: AUTHOR--folk.
          PLACE--England.
          DATE--probably created 15th century.
          DIFFERING FIRST LINE--NOW IS CHRISTEMAS YCOME.
Music: COMPOSER--Ralph Vaughan Williams (1872-1958).

PLACE--England.
DATE--published 1928.

Found: OXF
Notes: There is another song entitled THE GOLDEN CAROL with
           different lyrics and melody.

303.   THE GOLDEN CAROL

Lyrics: AUTHOR--probably folk, possibly R.E. Lonsdale (19th
                century).
            PLACE--England.
            DATE--possibly created 17th-19th century?
            VARIANT VERNACULAR TITLES--WE SAW A LIGHT SHINE OUT
                                AFAR; STAR OF CHRISTMAS
                                MORNING.
Music: COMPOSER--folk.
            PLACE--England.
            DATE--possibly created 16th-18th century?
            VARIANT TUNE--another English tune, possibly by Henry
                John Gauntlett (1805-1876).
Found: SHE, OBE, UNI, THF, ONS
Notes: A completely new set of words (anonymous, 20th
            century, probably from the United States), which
            begins "The star we've waited for so long", is also
            used; there is another song entitled THE GOLDEN CAROL
            with different lyrics and melody.

304.   GOLDEN MORNINGS

Lyrics: AUTHOR--Percy Dearmer (1867-1936).
            PLACE--England.
            DATE--written late 19th or early 20th century.
            DIFFERING FIRST LINE--THEY SAW THE LIGHT SHINE OUT
                                AFAR.
Music: COMPOSER--folk.
            PLACE--England.
            DATE--possibly created 16th-18th century?
Found: OXF, NOB

305.   GOOD-BYE

Lyrics: AUTHOR--folk.
            PLACE--England (possibly Yorkshire).
            DATE--probably created 17th century; possibly first
                published in 1829.
            DIFFERING FIRST LINE--GOD BLESS THE MASTER OF THIS
                                HOUSE.
Music: COMPOSER--folk.
            PLACE--probably Yorkshire, England.
            DATE--probably created 17th century.
            VARIANT TUNE--folk tune probably from Leeds, England,
                        probably created in 17th or 18th century.

Found: OXF, PEN, YAL
Notes: This song is sometimes treated as a separate carol,
and sometimes as final or near final verses of
WASSAIL SONG; despite the compatibility of the
lyrics of WASSAIL SONG and GOODBYE, they appear to be
from different sources; the same music is used for
both.

306. GOOD CHRISTIAN MEN, REJOICE

Lyrics: AUTHOR--John Mason Neale (1818-1866).
PLACE--England.
DATE--published 1853.
Music: COMPOSER--probably anonymous; possibly Heinrich Suso
(d. 1366).
PLACE--Germany.
DATE--created 14th century.
Found: MANY
Notes: Neale's lyrics were freely paraphrased from the
medieval Latin-German carol IN DULCI JUBILO (probably
first published 1533); by legend, the tune and
original words were written by the Dominican mystic
Suso after he danced with angels and sang the song
with them.

307. GOOD DAY, SIR CHRISTMAS

Lyrics: AUTHOR--folk.
PLACE--England.
DATE--created 15th century.
VARIANT VERNACULAR TITLE--GODAY, MY LORD.
DIFFERING FIRST LINES--GOOD DAY GOOD DAY; GODAY,
GODAY; GOOD DAY, SIR CHRISTMAS,
OUR KING; GOOD DAY SIR
CRISTEMAS OUR KING; GODAY, SIRE
CHRISTËMAS, OUR KING.
Music: COMPOSER--folk.
PLACE--England.
DATE--created 15th century.
Found: MEC, MED, EAR

308. GOOD KING WENCESLAS

Lyrics: AUTHOR--John Mason Neale (1818-1866).
PLACE--England.
DATE--published 1853.
Music: COMPOSER--anonymous.
PLACE--Europe.
DATE--created 13th century; probably first published
in the 1582 collection PIAE CANTIONES.
Found: MANY

Notes: Neale's lyrics, which are often and severely criti-
            cized, were a substitute for a spring song, TEMPUS
            ADEST FLORIDUM, which appeared with the tune in PIAE
            CANTIONES; the tune is also used for the carol
            GENTLE MARY LAID HER CHILD.

309. GRAN DEI, RIBON, RIBÉNE

     Lyrics: AUTHOR--Bernard de la Monnoye (1641-1728).
                 PLACE--Burgundy, France.
                 DATE--probably written around 1700.
                 ENGLISH TITLE--THE TRUMPET CAROL (translated by John
                              O'Connor [1870-1952]).
                 DIFFERING FIRST LINE--TANTARA! MIGHTY GOD!
     Music: COMPOSER--probably folk, possibly Bernard de la
                              Monnoye (1641-1728).
                 PLACE--Burgundy, France.
                 DATE--probably created 17th or 18th century.
     Found: THF, UNI

310. GREAT BIG STARS

     Lyrics: AUTHOR--folk (Black spiritual).
                 PLACE--United States.
                 DATE--probably created 18th or 19th century.
     Music: COMPOSER--folk (Black spiritual).
                 PLACE--United States.
                 DATE--probably created 18th or 19th century.
     Found: SEE

311. GREEN GROW'TH THE HOLLY

     Lyrics: AUTHOR--folk.
                 PLACE--England.
                 DATE--possibly created 16th century.
     Music: COMPOSER--anonymous, possibly Henry VIII (1491-1547).
                 PLACE--England.
                 DATE--probably written early 16th century; first
                              known text around 1515.
     Found: OXF
     Notes: The first verse of the words was a refrain of a love
                 song; the other verses were added by the editors of
                 THE OXFORD BOOK OF CAROLS.

312. HAIL! BLESSED VIRGIN MARY!

     Lyrics: AUTHOR--George Ratcliffe Woodward (1848-1934).
                 PLACE--England.
                 DATE--possibly first published 1920.
     Music: COMPOSER--anonymous.
                 PLACE--Italy.

              DATE--published 1689.
        Found: CCT, UNI, CCF

313.   HAIL, MARY, FULL OF GRACE

        Lyrics: AUTHOR--folk.
                PLACE--England.
                DATE--created 15th century.
                DIFFERING FIRST LINE--THE HOLY GHOST IS TO THEE SENT.
        Music: COMPOSER--folk.
                PLACE--England.
                DATE--created 15th century.
                VARIANT TUNES--two other 15th century English folk
                            tunes.
        Found: MEC, MED, THF, EAR, UNI

314.   HAIL TO THE LORD'S ANOINTED

        Lyrics: AUTHOR--James Montgomery (1771-1854).
                PLACE--England.
                DATE--probably written December 1821; published 1822.
        Music: COMPOSER--anonymous.
                PLACE--Germany.
                DATE--published 1784.
                VARIANT TUNES--1605 German tune, probably by Bartholo-
                            maeus Gesius (d. 1613); tune by Johann
                            Crüger (1598-1662), adapted from a work
                            of Crüger's by William Henry Monk (1823-
                            1889); tune by George James Webb
                            (1803-1887).
        Found: MET, HAR, ENG, MEN, PIL

315.   HAJEJ, NYNJEJ

        Lyrics: AUTHOR--folk.
                PLACE--Czechoslovakia.
                DATE--possibly created 14th-16th century?
                VARIANT VERNACULAR TITLES--HAJEJ, NYNEJ, JEZISKU;
                                        HAJEJ, NYNEJ.
                ENGLISH TITLES--ROCKING, ROCKING SONG, LULLABY, and
                            LITTLE JESUS, SWEETLY SLEEP (all four
                            the same translation by Percy Dearmer
                            [1867-1936]); ROCKING CAROL (trans-
                            lated by George K. Evans); SHEPHERD'S
                            ROCKING CAROL (translated by Elizabeth
                            Poston [1905-   ]).
                DIFFERING FIRST LINES--JESUS, JESUS, BABY DEAR; HUSH
                                     YOU, JESUS, BABY KING.
        Music: COMPOSER--folk.
                PLACE--Czechoslovakia.
                DATE--possibly created 14th-16th century?
                VARIANT TUNE--tune by John La Montaine (1920-   ).

Found: OXF, INT, SIM, SHE, SON
Notes: This is perhaps the best-known Czech carol.

316.   THE HAMPSHIRE MUMMERS' CHRISTMAS CAROL

    Lyrics: AUTHOR--folk.
              PLACE--probably Hampshire, England.
              DATE--possibly created 17th-19th century?
              DIFFERING FIRST LINE--THERE IS SIX GOOD DAYS ALL IN
                                      THE WEEK.
    Music: COMPOSER--folk.
              PLACE--probably Hampshire, England.
              DATE--possibly created 17th-19th century?
    Found: BRO

317.   HAPPY BIRTHDAY, JESUS

    Lyrics: AUTHOR--Estelle Levitt (1941-   ).
              PLACE--United States.
              DATE--published 1977.
    Music: COMPOSER--Lee J. Pockriss (1927-   ).
              PLACE--United States.
              DATE--published 1977.

318.   HAPPY HOLIDAY

    Lyrics: AUTHOR--Irving Berlin (1888-   ).
              PLACE--United States.
              DATE--written 1941.
    Music: COMPOSER--Irving Berlin (1888-   ).
              PLACE--United States.
               DATE--written 1941.
    Notes: The song was first presented in the 1942 movie
              HOLIDAY INN.

319.   HAPPY NEW YEAR, DARLING

    Lyrics: AUTHOR--Carmen Lombardo (1903-1971) and John D. Marks
                      (1909-   ).
              PLACE--United States.
              DATE--written 1950's.
    Music: COMPOSER--Carmen Lombardo (1903-1971) and John D. Marks
                      (1909-   ).
              PLACE--United States.
               DATE--written 1950's.

320.   HARDROCK, COCO AND JOE

    Lyrics: AUTHOR--Stuart Hamblen (1908-   ).
              PLACE--United States.
               DATE--published 1950.

VARIANT VERNACULAR TITLE--THE THREE LITTLE DWARFS.
DIFFERING FIRST LINE--O LEE O LAY DEE.
Music: COMPOSER--Stuart Hamblen (1908-   ).
PLACE--United States.
DATE--published 1950.
Found: ONS, ONT

321. HARK! HARK! WHAT NEWS THE ANGELS BRING

Lyrics: AUTHOR--folk.
PLACE--England.
DATE--probably created 17th or 18th century.
VARIANT VERNACULAR TITLE--THE OLD HARK.
Music: COMPOSER--folk.
PLACE--probably West Country, England.
DATE--probably created 18th century.
VARIANT TUNE--18th century folk tune from Leicester-
shire, England.
Found: GAS, GIF, GIS, CHO, UNI

322. HARK THE GLAD SOUND!

Lyrics: AUTHOR--Philip Doddridge (1702-1751).
PLACE--England.
DATE--published 1735.
VARIANT VERNACULAR TITLE--HARK THE GLAD SOUND! THE
SAVIOUR COMES.
Music: COMPOSER--Thomas Haweis (1734-1820).
PLACE--England.
DATE--published 1792.
VARIANT TUNES--anonymous 1621 English tune; English
folk tune.
Found: PRE, PRA, ENG, MEN

323. HARK! THE HERALD ANGELS SING

Lyrics: AUTHOR--Charles Wesley (1707-1788).
PLACE--probably London, England.
DATE--published 1739.
Music: COMPOSER--Felix Mendelssohn (1809-1847).
PLACE--probably Leipzig, Germany.
DATE--written 1840.
Found: MANY
Notes: Wesley's poem was originally entitled HARK HOW ALL
THE WELKIN RINGS; lines 1 and 2 of the poem were
revised by George Whitefield (1714-1770); lines 7
and 8 of the poem were revised by Martin Madan (1726-
1790); Mendelssohn's music was originally the second
chorus (GOTT IST LICHT) of the 1840 choral work
FESTGESANG, written to celebrate the 400th anniversary
of Gutenberg's invention of printing from moveable
type; the union of words and music was made by

Englishman William Hayman Cummings (1831-1915) in
1855; the whole carol was first published in 1856.

324. HARK! WHAT MEAN THOSE HOLY VOICES

Lyrics: AUTHOR--John Cawood (1775-1852).
           PLACE--England.
           DATE--published 1819.
Music: COMPOSER--Charles William Pearce (1856-1928).
           PLACE--England.
           DATE--probably written 1880's or early 1890's.
           VARIANT TUNES--1877 tune by George Benjamin Arnold
                     (1832-1902); anonymous tune, probably
                     from England; 1866 tune by Henry
                     Thomas Smart (1813-1879); tune by
                     Lowell Mason (1792-1872).
Found: HUT, CHO, PRS, BAP

325. HAUT, HAUT, PEYROT

Lyrics: AUTHOR--folk.
           PLACE--Béarn region, France.
           DATE--probably created 17th or 18th century.
           ENGLISH TITLES--NOËL; UP, UP PIERRE (translated by
                     K.W. Simpson).
           DIFFERING FIRST LINES--WAKE UP, PIERRE, AWAKEN; UP,
                     UP PIERRE, AWAKEN!
Music: COMPOSER--folk.
           PLACE--Béarn region, France.
           DATE--probably created 17th or 18th century.
Found: SHE, HUT, THF
Notes: The words have been attributed to Henri d'Andichon
           (1712-1777).

326. HAVE YOURSELF A MERRY LITTLE CHRISTMAS

Lyrics: AUTHOR--Ralph Blane (1914-   ).
           PLACE--United States.
           DATE--written 1944.
Music: COMPOSER--Hugh Martin (1914-   ).
           PLACE--United States.
           DATE--written 1944.
Found: ONS, ONT, HAP

327. THE HAWAIIAN CHRISTMAS SONG

Lyrics: AUTHOR--Al Stillman (1906-1979).
           PLACE--United States.
           DATE--published 1961.
           DIFFERING FIRST LINE--NO SNOW IS FALLING.
Music: COMPOSER--Robert Maxwell (1921-   ).

                    PLACE--United States.
                    DATE--published 1961.
          Found: ONS, ONT, HAP

328. HEARD FROM HEAVEN TODAY

      Lyrics: AUTHOR--folk (Black spiritual).
                 PLACE--probably South Carolina.
                 DATE--probably created 18th or 19th century.
                 DIFFERING FIRST LINE--HURRY ON, MY WEARY SOUL.
      Music: COMPOSER--folk (Black spiritual).
                 PLACE--probably South Carolina.
                 DATE--probably created 18th or 19th century.
      Found: SEE

329. HEAVEN BELL RING

      Lyrics: AUTHOR--folk (Black spiritual).
                 PLACE--probably South Carolina.
                 DATE--probably created 18th or 19th century.
                 DIFFERING FIRST LINE--OH, CHRISTMAS COME BUT ONCE A
                                       YEAR.
      Music: COMPOSER--folk (Black spiritual).
                 PLACE--probably South Carolina.
                 DATE--probably created 18th or 19th century.
      Found: SEE

330. HEJ, TOMTEGUBBAR

      Lyrics: AUTHOR--folk.
                 PLACE--Sweden.
                 DATE--possibly created 16th-18th century?
                 ENGLISH TITLE--HO! JOLLY GNOMES (translated by Noel
                                Wiren).
      Music: COMPOSER--folk.
                 PLACE--Sweden.
                 DATE--possibly created 16th-18th century?
      Found: SWE, GLA, JUL

331. HER KOMMER DINE ARME SMAA

      Lyrics: AUTHOR--Hans Adolf Brorson (1694-1764).
                 PLACE--Denmark.
                 DATE--published 1732.
                 ENGLISH TITLE--THY LITTLE ONES, DEAR LORD, ARE WE
                                (translated by Harriet Reynolds Spaeth
                                [1845-1925]).
      Music: COMPOSER--Johann Abraham Peter Schulz (1747-1800).
                 PLACE--Denmark or Germany.
                 DATE--probably written late 18th century.
      Found: INT, LUT

332. HERDERS HIJ IS GEBOOREN

    Lyrics: AUTHOR--folk.
              PLACE--Netherlands or Belgium.
              DATE--created 15th century.
              VARIANT VERNACULAR TITLES--HERDERS HIJ IS GHEBOREN;
                                  HERDERS, HIJ IS GEBOREN.
              ENGLISH TITLES--SHEPHERDS HE IS BORN (translated by
                    Marguerite Vogels-Reiners); SHEPHERDS
                    ARE SINGING; SHEPHERDS, WHAT JOYFUL
                    TIDINGS (translated by John O'Connor
                    [1870-1952]).
              DIFFERING FIRST LINES--SHEPHERDS, I HEAR YOU CALLING!;
                                  SHEPHERDS NOW HE IS BORN.
    Music: COMPOSER--folk.
              PLACE--Netherlands or Belgium.
              DATE--created 15th century.
    Found: SHE, THF, PEE, BOL

333. HERE COMES SANTA CLAUS

    Lyrics: AUTHOR--Gene Autry (1907-   ) and Oakley Haldeman
                    (1909-   ).
              PLACE--United States.
              DATE--written 1946.
              VARIANT VERNACULAR TITLE--HERE COMES SANTA CLAUS RIGHT
                              DOWN SANTA CLAUS LANE.
    Music: COMPOSER--Gene Autry (1907-   ) and Oakley Haldeman
                    (1909-   ).
              PLACE--United States.
              DATE--written 1946.
    Found: SEV, ONS, HAP

334. HEREFORD CAROL

    Lyrics: AUTHOR--folk.
              PLACE--probably Herefordshire, England.
              DATE--possibly created 16th-18th century?
              VARIANT VERNACULAR TITLE--THE ANGEL GABRIEL.
              DIFFERING FIRST LINE--COME ALL YOU FAITHFUL CHRISTIANS.
    Music: COMPOSER--folk.
              PLACE--probably Herefordshire, England.
              DATE--possibly created 16th-18th century?
    Found: OXF, LEA

335. HERR CHRIST, DER EINIG GOTTS SOHN

    Lyrics: AUTHOR--Elizabeth Cruciger (ca. 1500-1535).
              PLACE--Germany.
               DATE--published 1524.
              ENGLISH TITLE--THE ONLY SON FROM HEAVEN (translated by
                    Arthur Tozer Russell [1806-1874]).

> *Music:*   COMPOSER--anonymous.
>   PLACE--Germany.
>   DATE--probably created 15th century; probably first
>   published 1524.
> *Found:*   SIG, BUD

336. HERRICK'S ODE

> *Lyrics:* AUTHOR--Robert Herrick (1591-1674).
>   PLACE--England.
>   DATE--published 1647.
>   DIFFERING FIRST LINE--IN NUMBERS, AND BUT THESE FEW.
> *Music:*   COMPOSER--Cecil Armstrong Gibbs (1889-1960).
>   PLACE--England.
>   DATE--probably written 1928.
> *Found:*   OXF

337. HET VIEL EENS HEMELS DOUWE

> *Lyrics:* AUTHOR--folk.
>   PLACE--Netherlands.
>   DATE--created 15th century.
>   ENGLISH TITLES--ALL HEAVEN ON A MAIDEN (translated by
>   John O'Connor [1870-1952]); THERE FELL
>   A HEAVENLY DEW (translated by
>   Marguerite Vogels-Reiners).
> *Music:*   COMPOSER--folk.
>   PLACE--Netherlands.
>   DATE--created 15th century.
> *Found:*   THF, BRU, PEE

338. HOLIDAY GREETINGS

> *Lyrics:* AUTHOR--Sam H. Stept (1897-1964).
>   PLACE--United States.
>   DATE--published 1945.
>   DIFFERING FIRST LINE--THE BELLS ARE RINGING IN THE
>   CHURCH ACROSS THE WAY.
> *Music:*   COMPOSER--Sam H. Stept (1897-1964).
>   PLACE--United States.
>   DATE--published 1945.
> *Found:*   HAP

339. THE HOLIDAY POLKA

> *Lyrics:* AUTHOR--Mary K. Sarlow.
>   PLACE--probably United States.
>   DATE--published 1956.
>   DIFFERING FIRST LINE--THE HALL IS GAY WITH LANTERN
>   LIGHT.
> *Music:*   COMPOSER--Donald E. Large (1909-   ).

                    PLACE--probably United States, possibly Canada.
                    DATE--published 1956.

340.   THE HOLLY AND THE IVY

       Lyrics: AUTHOR--folk.
                   PLACE--England (possibly Gloucestershire).
                   DATE--possibly created around 1700.
       Music: COMPOSER--folk.
                   PLACE--England (possibly Gloucestershire).
                   DATE--possibly created around 1700.
       Found: MANY
       Notes: Some authorities believe the song originated in
                   France; for an Australian derivative, see THE HOLLY
                   BEARS A BERRY.

341.   THE HOLLY BEARS A BERRY

       Lyrics: AUTHOR--folk.
                   PLACE--Australia.
                   DATE--probably created 19th or early 20th century.
                   DIFFERING FIRST LINE--OH, THE HOLLY BEARS A BERRY.
       Music: COMPOSER--folk.
                   PLACE--Australia.
                   DATE--probably created 19th or early 20th century.
       Found: SEA
       Notes: The lyrics were derived from the carol THE HOLLY AND
                   THE IVY, but the tunes are different.

342.   THE HOLLY BOY

       Lyrics: AUTHOR--Frank Latino.
                   PLACE--United States.
                   DATE--published 1955.
                   VARIANT VERNACULAR TITLE--THE HOLLY BOY WITH THE
                                            CHRISTMAS BALL NOSE.
                   DIFFERING FIRST LINE--WOULD YOU LIKE TO MEET THE
                                         HOLLY BOY?
       Music: COMPOSER--Frank Latino.
                   PLACE--United States.
                   DATE--published 1955.
       Found: SEV

343.   THE HOLLY TREE CAROL

       Lyrics: AUTHOR--Jean Ritchie (1922-   ).
                   PLACE--United States.
                   DATE--published 1971.
                   DIFFERING FIRST LINE--IN THE SPRING OF THE YEAR
                                         STANDS A LITTLE HOLLY TREE.
       Music: COMPOSER--Jean Ritchie (1922-   ).

                    PLACE--United States.
                    DATE--published 1971.
          Found: ONS, HAP

344. THE HOLY BOY

      Lyrics: AUTHOR--Herbert S. Brown (1901-   ).
                 PLACE--probably Kent, England.
                 DATE--written around 1937.
                 DIFFERING FIRST LINE--LOWLY, LAID IN A MANGER.
      Music: COMPOSER--John Ireland (1879-1962).
                 PLACE--England.
                 DATE--published 1917.
      Found: SIM, REF
      Notes: The tune originally was a prelude for piano.

345. THE HOLY SON OF GOD

      Lyrics: AUTHOR--Henry More (1614-1687).
                 PLACE--England.
                 DATE--published 1668.
                 DIFFERING FIRST LINE--THE HOLY SON OF GOD MOST HIGH.
      Music: COMPOSER--anonymous.
                 PLACE--Germany.
                 DATE--probably written 16th century; possibly first
                       published 1541.
                 VARIANT TUNES--German tune published 1609; tune
                                probably by Martin Luther (1483-1546).
      Found: UNI, APP, LUT
      Notes: The first tune is from the hymn SO TREIBEN WIR DEN
                 WINTER WAS; the first variant tune is the melody DAS
                 NEUGEBORNE KINDLEIN; the second variant tune is also
                 used for the carol VOM HIMMEL HOCH, DA KOMM ICH HER.

346. THE HOLY WELL

      Lyrics: AUTHOR--folk.
                 PLACE--England (possibly Herefordshire).
                 DATE--possibly created 15th-17th century?
                 DIFFERING FIRST LINE--AS IT FELL OUT ONE MAY MORNING.
      Music: COMPOSER--folk.
                 PLACE--England.
                 DATE--possibly created 15th-17th century?
                 VARIANT TUNE--another English folk tune.
      Found: SHE, OBE, OXF, UNI, HUS
      Notes: The 15th-17th century tune is also used for the carol
                 A CHILD MY CHOICE.

347. HOME FOR THE HOLIDAYS

    Lyrics: AUTHOR--Al Stillman (1906-1979).
                 PLACE--United States.
                 DATE--published 1954.
                 VARIANT VERNACULAR TITLE--THERE'S NO PLACE LIKE HOME
                                          FOR THE HOLIDAYS.
                 DIFFERING FIRST LINE--OH, THERE'S NO PLACE LIKE HOME
                                            FOR THE HOLIDAYS.
    Music: COMPOSER--Robert Allen (1927-   ).
                 PLACE--United States.
                 DATE--published 1954.
    Found: SEV, POP, ULT, ONS, ONT

348. HOW FAR IS IT TO BETHLEHEM?

    Lyrics: AUTHOR--Frances Chesterton (1875-1938).
                 PLACE--England.
                 DATE--probably written early 20th century.
                 VARIANT VERNACULAR TITLE--CHILDREN'S SONG OF THE
                                            NATIVITY.
    Music: COMPOSER--folk.
                 PLACE--probably West country, England.
                 DATE--possibly created 16th-18th century?
                 VARIANT TUNE--tune by John Ritchie, composer from New
                                          Zealand.
    Found: OXF, CCT, YAL, NOB, UNI
    Notes: The main tune is the melody STOWEY.

349. HUSH, MY DEAR, LIE STILL AND SLUMBER

    Lyrics: AUTHOR--Isaac Watts (1674-1748).
                 PLACE--England.
                 DATE--published 1715.
                 VARIANT VERNACULAR TITLES--HUSH, MY BABE; HUSH, MY
                                            BABE, LIE STILL AND
                                          SLUMBER; CRADLE HYMN;
                                          CRADLE SONG; WATT'S CRADLE
                                          SONG.
    Music: COMPOSER--Johann Sebastian Bach (1685-1750).
                 PLACE--Germany.
                   DATE--written first half of 18th century.
                 VARIANT TUNES--folk tunes from Appalachian region and
                                          Northumberland, England; tune by
                                          Stanley Taylor (1902-1972).
    Found: INT, SIM, OXF, NOB, APP
    Notes: Bach's music reportedly was taken from a now lost
                 cantata.

350. I BELIEVE IN SANTA CLAUS

    Lyrics: AUTHOR--Raymond B. Egan (1890-   ).
            PLACE--United States.
            DATE--published 1945.
    Music: COMPOSER--John Frederick Coots (1897-   ).
            PLACE--United States.
            DATE--published 1945.
    Found: NOR, SEV

351. I DENNE SØDE JULETID

    Lyrics: AUTHOR--folk.
            PLACE--Norway.
            DATE--possibly created 16th-18th century?
            ENGLISH TITLE--AT CHRISTMAS TIME WHEN ALL IS GAY
                        (translated by Olga Paul).
    Music: COMPOSER--folk.
            PLACE--Norway.
            DATE--possibly created 16th-18th century?
    Found: RTW

352. I HEARD THE BELLS ON CHRISTMAS DAY

    Lyrics: AUTHOR--Henry Wadsworth Longfellow (1807-1882).
            PLACE--probably Cambridge, Massachusetts.
            DATE--probably written December 25, 1863 (sometimes
                dated December 25, 1864); first published 1867.
    Music: COMPOSER--John Baptiste Calkin (1827-1905).
            PLACE--England.
            DATE--published 1872.
            VARIANT TUNES--tunes by John D. Marks (1909-   ),
                        John Bishop (ca. 1665-1737), and Alfred
                        Herbert Brewer (1865-1928).
    Found: MANY
    Notes: Longfellow's poem, whose theme is partly Christmas and
            partly antiwar, was originally called CHRISTMAS BELLS;
            Calkin's music was originally written for the 1848
            hymn FLING OUT THE BANNER! LET IT FLOAT, by George
            Washington Doane (1799-1859); Calkin's tune is also
            used for the carol MACHT HOCH DIE TÜR DIE TOR' MACH
            WEIT.

353. I SAW MOMMY KISSING SANTA CLAUS

    Lyrics: AUTHOR--Tommie Connor.
            PLACE--United States.
            DATE--written 1952.
            DIFFERING FIRST LINE--CHRISTMAS TOYS ALL OVER THE
                        PLACE.
    Music: COMPOSER--Tommie Connor.
            PLACE--United States.
            DATE--written 1952.

354. I SAW THREE SHIPS

    Lyrics: AUTHOR--folk.
              PLACE--England.
              DATE--possibly created 15th century.
              VARIANT VERNACULAR TITLE--ON CHRISTMAS DAY IN THE
                                    MORNING.
              DIFFERING FIRST LINE--I SAW THREE SHIPS COME SAILING
                                    IN.
    Music: COMPOSER--folk.
              PLACE--England.
              DATE--possibly created 15th century.
              VARIANT TUNES--tune by Reginald Jacques (1894-   );
                                other tunes.
    Found: MANY
    Notes: For an American derivative, see the other carol of
              the same name; for a carol with somewhat similar
              lyrics, see THE THREE SHIPS.

355. I SAW THREE SHIPS

    Lyrics: AUTHOR--folk.
              PLACE--probably Virginia.
              DATE--probably created 18th or 19th century.
              VARIANT VERNACULAR TITLE--CHRISTMAS DAY IN THE
                                    MORNING.
              DIFFERING FIRST LINE--AS I SAT ON A SUNNY BANK.
    Music: COMPOSER--folk.
               PLACE--probably Virginia.
               DATE--probably created 18th or 19th century.
    Found: LAN, SEE
    Notes: This should not be confused with the much more famous
              carol of the same name, of which this is a derivative;
              for a carol with somewhat similar lyrics, see THE
              THREE SHIPS.

356. I SING OF A MAIDEN

    Lyrics: AUTHOR--folk.
              PLACE--England.
              DATE--created 15th century.
              VARIANT VERNACULAR TITLES--I SING OF A MAYDEN; AS DEW
                                    IN APRILLE.
              DIFFERING FIRST LINES--I SING OF A MAIDEN THAT IS
                                MAKELESS; I SING OF A MAYDEN
                                THAT IS MAKELES.
    Music: COMPOSER--Martin Shaw (1875-1958).
              PLACE--England.
              DATE--published 1928.
              VARIANT TUNES--tunes by Benjamin Britten (1913-1976),
                            David Farquhar (1928-)(New Zealand
                            composer), Patrick Hadley (1899-   ),
                            Richard Runciman Terry (1865-1938),
                            and Lennox Berkeley (1903-   ).
    Found: OXF, CCT, UNI, REF, BRI

357. I SING THE BIRTH WAS BORN TONIGHT

    Lyrics: AUTHOR--Ben Jonson (1573-1637).
              PLACE--England.
              DATE--written 1600.
              VARIANT VERNACULAR TITLES--BEN JONSON'S CAROL; I SING
                                            THE BIRTH.
    Music: COMPOSER--Rutland Boughton (1878-1960).
              PLACE--England.
              DATE--probably written early 20th century.
              VARIANT TUNES--tunes by George Clement Martin (1844-
                            1916), Robert Frederick Smith, (ca. 1830-
                            1905), William Mathias (1934-   ), and
                            Michael Praetorius (1571-1621).
    Found: OXF, HUT, CHO, APP, REF

358. I WANT AN OLD-FASHIONED CHRISTMAS

    Lyrics: AUTHOR--Florence Tarr (1907-1951).
              PLACE--United States.
              DATE--published 1945.
    Music: COMPOSER--Fay Foster (1886-1960).
              PLACE--United States.
              DATE--published 1945.
    Found: ONS

359. I WONDER AS I WANDER

    Lyrics: AUTHOR--John Jacob Niles (1892-1980).
              PLACE--United States.
              DATE--written 1933; published 1934.
              DIFFERING FIRST LINE--I WONDER AS I WANDER OUT UNDER
                                  THE SKY.
    Music: COMPOSER--John Jacob Niles (1892-1980).
              PLACE--United States.
               DATE--written 1933; published 1934.
    Found: BAE, ULT, REF, NIL, LAN
    Notes: The first two lines of the words, and the inspiration
              for the rest of the words and the tune, came from a
              folk song heard in North Carolina.

360. ICH STEH AN DEINER KRIPPEN HIER

    Lyrics: AUTHOR--Paul Gerhardt (1607-1676).
              PLACE--Germany.
               DATE--published 1656.
               VARIANT VERNACULAR TITLE--ICH STEH' AN DEINER KRIPPE
                                    HIER.
              ENGLISH TITLES--BESIDE THY CRADLE HERE I STAND (trans-
                            lated by John Troutbeck [1833-1889]);
                            BESIDE THY CRADLE; CHRISTMAS SONG.
              DIFFERING FIRST LINE--I STAND BESIDE THY CRADLE HERE.

    Music: COMPOSER--anonymous.
              PLACE--Germany.
              DATE--possibly created 16th or 17th century.
    Found: INT, SIM, TRA, OWE, BUD
    Notes: Johann Sebastian Bach (1685-1750) used the words and melody in his CHRISTMAS ORATORIO (1734).

361.   IF IT DOESN'T SNOW ON CHRISTMAS

    Lyrics: AUTHOR--Milton H. Pascal (1908-   ).
              PLACE--United States.
              DATE--written around 1949.
    Music: COMPOSER--Gerald Marks (1900-   ).
              PLACE--United States.
              DATE--written around 1949.

362.   IHR HIRTEN STEHET ALLE AUF VON EUREM TIEFEN SCHLAF

    Lyrics: AUTHOR--folk.
              PLACE--Tyrol, Austria.
              DATE--possibly created 16th-18th century?
              VARIANT VERNACULAR TITLE--IHR HIRTEN STEKET ALLE AUF VON EUREM TIEFEN SCHLAF.
              ENGLISH TITLE--COME, SHEPHERDS, COME! SHAKE OFF YOUR SLEEP.
    Music: COMPOSER--folk.
              PLACE--Tyrol, Austria.
              DATE--possibly created 16th-18th century?
    Found: HUT, BUD
    Notes: The tune is also used for the carol FALAN-TIDING.

363.   IHR KINDERLEIN, KOMMET

    Lyrics: AUTHOR--Christoph von Schmid (1768-1854).
              PLACE--Germany.
              DATE--probably written first half of 19th century.
              ENGLISH TITLE--O COME, LITTLE CHILDREN (several different translations by George K. Evans, Ruth Heller [1920-   ], and others).
    Music: COMPOSER--Johann Abraham Peter Schulz (1747-1800).
              PLACE--probably Denmark.
              DATE--probably written between 1787 and 1795.
    Found: INT, SIM, SHE, HEL, TRA

364.   IL EST NÉ, LE DEVIN ENFANT

    Lyrics: AUTHOR--folk.
              PLACE--France.

DATE--possibly created 18th century.
ENGLISH TITLES--HE IS BORN, THE HOLY CHILD (trans-
                    lated by George K. Evans); HE IS BORN
                    (translated by Edward Bliss Reed
                    [1872-1940]); YEA, THE HEAVENLY CHILD
                    IS BORN (translated by Olga Paul);
                    BORN IS HE, LITTLE CHILD DIVINE
                    (translated by John Morrison); HE IS
                    BORN, THE HOLY ONE! (translated by
                    K.W. Simpson); BORN ON EARTH THE
                    DIVINE CHRIST CHILD (translated by
                    Jacqueline Froom); BORN IS JESUS, THE
                    INFANT KING.
DIFFERING FIRST LINES--DEPUIS PLUS DE QUATRE MILLE
                    ANS; OVER FOUR THOUSAND YEARS
                    HAVE PASSED; HE IS BORN, DIVINE
                    IS HE.
Music: COMPOSER--folk.
           PLACE--France.
           DATE--created 18th century.
Found: INT, THF, CCT, RTW, CSE
Notes: The song was possibly first published in 1867; the
           tune is the air LA TÊTE BIZARDE.

365.   I'LL BE HOME FOR CHRISTMAS

Lyrics: AUTHOR--Kim Gannon (1900-   ).
           PLACE--United States.
           DATE--written 1943.
           DIFFERING FIRST LINE--I'M DREAMING TONIGHT OF A
                    PLACE I LOVE.
Music: COMPOSER--Walter Kent (1911-   ).
           PLACE--United States.
           DATE--written 1943.
Found: NOR, POP, ULT, ONS, HAP

366.   IMMORTAL BABE

Lyrics: AUTHOR--Joseph Hall (1574-1656).
           PLACE--England.
           DATE--published 1660.
           VARIANT VERNACULAR TITLE--FOR CHRISTMAS DAY.
           DIFFERING FIRST LINE--IMMORTAL BABE, WHO THIS DEAR
                    DAY.
Music: COMPOSER--folk.
           PLACE--Germany.
           DATE--created 16th century.
           VARIANT TUNES--tunes by Heinrich Schütz (1585-1672)
                    and Robert Frederick Smith (ca. 1830-
                    1905).
Found: OXF, PRE, STA, CHO

367.   IN BETHLEHEM CITY

    Lyrics: AUTHOR--George Ratcliffe Woodward (1848-1934).
            PLACE--England.
            DATE--written late 19th or early 20th century.
            DIFFERING FIRST LINE--IN BETHLEHEM CITY, ON CHRISTMAS
                                   DAY MORN.
    Music: COMPOSER--folk.
            PLACE--Worcestershire, England.
            DATE--possibly created 16th-18th century?
    Found: THF, UNI

368.   IN DULCI JUBILO

    Lyrics: AUTHOR--probably anonymous; possibly Heinrich Suso
                  (d. 1366).
            PLACE--Germany.
            DATE--created 14th century.
    Music: COMPOSER--probably anonymous; possibly Heinrich Suso
                  (d. 1366).
            PLACE--Germany.
            DATE--created 14th century.
    Found: MANY
    Notes: By legend, the tune and the original words were
            written by the Dominican mystic Suso after he danced
            with angels and sang the song with them; the song was
            probably first published in 1533; the original words
            were in Latin and German; the Latin words are retained
            in the carol today; the best-known translation of the
            German lyrics is by Robert Lucas de Pearsall (1795-
            1856); John Mason Neale (1818-1866) made a free para-
            phrase of the lyrics, attached them to the melody, and
            thus produced the well-known carol GOOD CHRISTIAN MEN,
            REJOICE.

369.   IN HOC ANNI CIRCULO

    Lyrics: AUTHOR--anonymous.
            PLACE--Europe.
            DATE--probably created 14th century.
            ENGLISH TITLE--IN THE ENDING OF THE YEAR (translated
                        by John Mason Neale [1818-1866]).
    Music: COMPOSER--anonymous.
            PLACE--Europe.
            DATE--probably created 14th or 15th century.
            VARIANT TUNE--another tune of the same period.
    Found: KOL, COF

370.   IN NATALI DOMINI

    Lyrics: AUTHOR--anonymous.
            PLACE--probably Germany.

DATE--created 14th century.
ENGLISH TITLE--ON THE BIRTHDAY OF THE LORD (two
                        different translations, one anonymous,
                        the other by Richard Frederick Little-
                        dale [1833-1890]).
Music: COMPOSER--anonymous.
            PLACE--Germany.
            DATE--probably created 14th century; possibly first
                        published 1544.
            VARIANT TUNES--tune by John Bacchus Dykes (1823-1876),
                        composer from England; other tunes.
Found: COF, HUT, STA, KOL

371. IN THE BLEAK MID-WINTER

Lyrics: AUTHOR--Christina Rossetti (1830-1894).
            PLACE--England.
            DATE--published 1872.
            VARIANT VERNACULAR TITLE--MID-WINTER.
Music: COMPOSER--Gustav Holst (1874-1934).
            PLACE--England.
            DATE--published 1906.
            VARIANT TUNE--tune by Thomas Banks Strong (1861-   ).
Found: OXF, REE, APP, MET, HUT

372. IN THE FIELD WITH THEIR FLOCKS ABIDING

Lyrics: AUTHOR--Frederick William Farrar (1831-1903).
            PLACE--England.
            DATE--published 1875.
Music: COMPOSER--John Farmer (1836-1901).
            PLACE--England.
            DATE--probably written second half of 19th century.
            VARIANT TUNE--tune by Arthur Henry Brown (1830-1926).
Found: ONS, ONT, CHO, HUT

373. IN THOSE TWELVE DAYS

Lyrics: AUTHOR--folk.
            PLACE--England.
            DATE--possibly created 16th century; probably first
                        published 1625.
            VARIANT VERNACULAR TITLE--A NEW DIAL.
            DIFFERING FIRST LINE--IN THOSE TWELVE DAYS LET US BE
                                    GLAD.
Music: COMPOSER--folk.
            PLACE--England.
            DATE--possibly created 16th-18th century?
Found: OXF, THF, GAS, SAN, UNI

374. THE INFANT KING

> *Lyrics:* AUTHOR--Sabine Baring-Gould (1834-1924).
>   PLACE--England.
>   DATE--probably written second half of 19th century.
>   DIFFERING FIRST LINE--SING LULLABY!
> *Music:* COMPOSER--folk.
>   PLACE--Basque region, Spain and France.
>   DATE--possibly created 16th-18th century?
> *Found:* CCT, UNI, CCF, REF
> *Notes:* The tune is also used for the carol OI! BETLEEM!

375. INKOSI JESUS

> *Lyrics:* AUTHOR--Rae Tomlin.
>   PLACE--South Africa.
>   DATE--published 1967.
>   VARIANT VERNACULAR TITLE--MY SOVEREIGN JESUS.
>   DIFFERING FIRST LINE--I WARM MY SON UPON MY BREAST.
> *Music:* COMPOSER--Edith Hugo Bosman.
>   PLACE--South Africa.
>   DATE--published 1967.
> *Found:* REF

376. INSTANTIS ADVENTUM DEI

> *Lyrics:* AUTHOR--Charles Coffin (1676-1749).
>   PLACE--France.
>   DATE--published 1736.
>   ENGLISH TITLES--THE ADVENT OF OUR GOD (translated by
>   John Chandler [1806-1876]); THE COMING
>   OF OUR LORD (translated by Robert
>   Campbell [1814-1866] and Anthony G.
>   Petti).
> *Music:* COMPOSER--Samuel Wesley (1766-1837).
>   PLACE--England.
>   DATE--written late 18th or early 19th century.
>   VARIANT TUNES--tune by Johann Balthasar König (1691-
>   1758); anonymous 1770 English tune;
>   another anonymous tune.
> *Found:* LUT, CAT, ENG

377. IRISH CAROL

> *Lyrics:* AUTHOR--probably folk, possibly Luke Wadding (1588-
>   1657).
>   PLACE--Ireland.
>   DATE--probably written 17th century.
>   VARIANT VERNACULAR TITLE--CHRISTMAS DAY IS COME
>   (anonymous paraphrase of
>   the 17th century words).
> *Music:* COMPOSER--folk.

          PLACE--Ireland.
          DATE--possibly written 16th or 17th century?
Found: OXF, SIM, SHE

378. IT CAME UPON THE MIDNIGHT CLEAR

Lyrics: AUTHOR--Edmund Hamilton Sears (1810-1876).
          PLACE--Wayland, Massachusetts.
          DATE--published December 29, 1849.
Music: COMPOSER--Richard Storrs Willis (1819-1900).
          PLACE--New York City.
          DATE--published 1850.
          VARIANT TUNES--tunes by Arthur Seymour Sullivan
                       (1842-1900) and Samuel Smith.
Found: MANY
Notes: Willis' tune was originally intended for the hymn SEE
          ISRAEL'S GENTLE SHEPHERD STAND, but soon after Sears'
          poem was published the music was rearranged to fit
          Sears' words; the rearrangement, which quite possibly
          was done in 1850, was probably by Willis, but some
          sources state that Uzziah Christopher Burnap did the
          rearrangement; subsequently, Willis also adapted his
          tune to accommodate the words of WHILE SHEPHERDS
          WATCHED THEIR FLOCKS, and the tune is sometimes used
          with that carol; the tune is also used for the carol
          CALM ON THE LISTENING EAR OF NIGHT; the song was the
          first American carol of international reputation; it
          is probably the second-best-known American carol.

379. IT'S BEGINNING TO LOOK LIKE CHRISTMAS

Lyrics: AUTHOR--Meredith Willson (1902-1984).
          PLACE--United States.
          DATE--written 1951.
          DIFFERING FIRST LINE--IT'S BEGINNING TO LOOK A LOT
                       LIKE CHRISTMAS.
Music: COMPOSER--Meredith Willson (1902-1984).
          PLACE--United States.
          DATE--written 1951.

380. JACOB'S LADDER

Lyrics: AUTHOR--folk.
          PLACE--England.
          DATE--probably created 18th or early 19th century.
          VARIANT VERNACULAR TITLE--AS JACOB WITH TRAVEL.
          DIFFERING FIRST LINE--AS JACOB WITH TRAVEL WAS WEARY
                       ONE DAY.
Music: COMPOSER--folk.
          PLACE--England.
          DATE--probably created around 18th century.
Found: OXF, HUT, STA, CAT, ECF

381. JACOTTIN GRINGOTIN VN NOE FALLOT

      Lyrics: AUTHOR--Nicolas Martin.
                  PLACE--probably Savoy region, France.
                  DATE--published 1555.
                  ENGLISH TITLE--JACQUES, COME HERE (two different
                               translations, one by Robert Reynolds,
                               one by Edward Bliss Reed [1872-1940]).
      Music: COMPOSER--Nicolas Martin.
                  PLACE--probably Savoy region, France.
                  DATE--published 1555.
      Found: WIL, CEI

382. J'ANTAN PO NOTE RUË

      Lyrics: AUTHOR--Bernard de la Monnoye (1641-1728).
                  PLACE--Burgundy, France.
                  DATE--probably written around 1700.
                  ENGLISH TITLES--I HEAR UPON THE HIGHWAY (translated
                               by John O'Connor [1870-1952]); ALONG
                               THE STREET I HEAR (translated by
                               Alfred Raymond Bellinger [1893-   ]).
      Music: COMPOSER--probably folk, possibly Bernard de la
                          Monnoye (1641-1728).
                  PLACE--Burgundy, France.
                  DATE--probably created 17th or 18th century.
      Found: THF, CNT

383. JE SAIS, VIERGE MARIE

      Lyrics: AUTHOR--folk.
                  PLACE--France.
                  DATE--possibly created 16th-18th century?
                  ENGLISH TITLE--I KNOW, O BLESSED MARY (translated by
                               K.W. Simpson).
      Music: COMPOSER--folk.
                  PLACE--France.
                  DATE--possibly created 16th-18th century?
      Found: OXF, THF

384. JE SUIS L'ARCHANGE DE DIEU

      Lyrics: AUTHOR--folk.
                  PLACE--France.
                  DATE--possibly created 16th-18th century?
                  ENGLISH TITLE--I THE ANGEL AM OF GOD! (translated by
                               K.W. Simpson).
      Music: COMPOSER--folk.
                  PLACE--France.
                  DATE--possibly created 16th-18th century?
      Found: THF, UNI

385. JEG ER SAA GLAD HVER JULEKVELD

    Lyrics: AUTHOR--Marie Wexelsen (1832-1911).
              PLACE--Norway.
              DATE--probably written second half of 19th century.
              ENGLISH TITLES--WHEN LIGHTS ARE LIT ON CHRISTMAS EVE
                              (translated by Norman Johnson);
                              CHRISTMAS EVE (translated by Gordon
                              Grimes); I AM SO GLAD EACH CHRISTMAS
                              EVE and HOW GLAD I AM EACH CHRISTMAS
                              EVE! (two titles for the same trans-
                              lation by Peter Andrew Sveeggen
                              [1881-   ]); I AM SO HAPPY ON
                              CHRISTMAS EVE (translated by Ella K.
                              Nesvig and Ruth Heller [1920-   ]);
                              I AM SO GLAD ON CHRISTMAS EVE (two
                              different translations, one anonymous,
                              other by George K. Evans).
              DIFFERING FIRST LINE--OH, GLAD I AM 'TIS CHRISTMAS
                              EVE.
    Music: COMPOSER--Peder Knudsen (1819-1863).
              PLACE--Norway.
              DATE--written mid-19th century.
    Found: INT, UNI, CAW, ULT, PRA
    Notes: This is perhaps the best-known Norwegian carol.

386. JESU PARVULE

    Lyrics: AUTHOR--Bates Gilbert Burt (1878-1948).
              PLACE--United States.
              DATE--published 1954.
              VARIANT VERNACULAR TITLE--POOR LITTLE JESUS.
    Music: COMPOSER--Alfred Burt (1919 or 1920-1954).
              PLACE--United States.
              DATE--published 1954.
    Found: BUR

387. JÉSU VÉ'N, TREZELON SAI FÉTE

    Lyrics: AUTHOR--Bernard de la Monnoye (1641-1728).
              PLACE--Burgundy, France.
              DATE--probably written around 1700.
              ENGLISH TITLES--ELOQUENT BELLS IN EVERY STEEPLE
                              (translated by John O'Connor [1870-
                              1952]); JESUS HAS COME! (translated
                              by Alfred Raymond Bellinger [1893-
                              ]).
    Music: COMPOSER--probably folk, possibly Bernard de la
                      Monnoye (1641-1728).
              PLACE--Burgundy, France.
              DATE--probably created 17th or 18th century.
    Found: THF, CNT

388.   JESULEIN, SCHÖNS KINDELEIN

     Lyrics: AUTHOR--folk.
             PLACE--Upper Bavaria, Germany.
             DATE--possibly created 17th-19th century; possibly
                 first published 1880.
             ENGLISH TITLE--BAVARIAN FOLK CAROL (translated by
                 Edward Bliss Reed [1872-1940]).
             DIFFERING FIRST LINE--LITTLE JESUS, CHILD SO SWEET.
     Music: COMPOSER--folk.
             PLACE--Germany.
             DATE--possibly created 17th-19th century?
     Found: BUD, CFI

389.   JESUS AHATONHIA

     Lyrics: AUTHOR--Jean de Brébeuf (1593-1649).
             PLACE--Ontario.
             DATE--created around 1641 or 1642.
             VARIANT VERNACULAR TITLES--JESOUS AHATONNIA; JESOUS
                            AHATONHIA; IESUS AHATONNIA;
                            JESOS AHATONHIA.
             ENGLISH TITLES--'TWAS IN THE MOON OF WINTERTIME,
                        THE HURON CAROL, and THE HURON INDIAN
                        CAROL (three titles for the same
                        translation by J.E. Middleton); TO
                        JESUS, FROM THE ENDS OF EARTH (trans-
                        lated by Ruth Heller [1920-   ]).
             DIFFERING FIRST LINE--ESTENNIALON DE TSONUE IESUS
                        AHATONNIA.
     Music: COMPOSER--folk.
             PLACE--France.
             DATE--created 16th century.
     Found: INT, JOH, UNI, SEA, HEL
     Notes: While a Jesuit missionary to the Huron Indians,
             Brébeuf created the words in the Huron language and
             set them to the French folk song UNE JEUNE PUCELLE;
             after Brébeuf was killed by invading Iroquois
             Indians, the song was orally preserved by some of the
             Hurons, and about a century after its composition
             another Jesuit priest wrote it down; this is the
             first carol known to have been created in the
             Americas; this is perhaps the best-known Canadian
             carol.

390.   JESUS' BLOEMHOF

     Lyrics: AUTHOR--folk.
             PLACE--Netherlands.
             DATE--probably created 15th century.
             VARIANT VERNACULAR TITLE--HEER JESUS HEEFT EEN HOFKEN.
             ENGLISH TITLES--THE GARDEN OF JESUS; LORD JESUS HAS A
                      GARDEN (translated by Jeremy Ashton);

KING JESUS HATH A GARDEN (translated
by George Ratcliffe Woodward [1848-
1934]); OUR MASTER HATH A GARDEN (two
different translations, one by John
Mason Neale [1818-1866], the other by
Alfred Barry [1826-1910]).
DIFFERING FIRST LINES--LORD JESUS HAS A GARDEN FULL
OF FAIREST FLOWERS; LORD JESUS
HATH A GARDEN, FULL OF FLOWERS
GAY; OUR MASTER HATH A GARDEN
FAIR, WHERE GROW SWEET FLOWERS;
OUR MASTER HATH A GARDEN WHICH
FAIR FLOW'RS ADORN; KING
JESUS HATH A GARDEN, FULL OF
DIVERS FLOW'RS.

Music: COMPOSER--folk.
PLACE--Netherlands.
DATE--probably created 15th century.
Found: OXF, HAW, THF, COS, NOB
Notes: The words and music were probably first published in
1609; this is perhaps the best-known Dutch carol.

391.   JESUS BORN IN BETH'NY

Lyrics: AUTHOR--folk.
PLACE--probably Virginia.
DATE--probably created 18th or 19th century.
VARIANT VERNACULAR TITLE--JESUS BORNED IN BETHLEA.
Music: COMPOSER--folk.
PLACE--probably Virginia.
DATE--probably created 18th or 19th century.
VARIANT TUNES--a similar tune, probably from Virginia;
a third Virginia tune.
Found: APP, SEE, TCC, LAN

392.   JESUS CHRIST THE APPLE TREE

Lyrics: AUTHOR--anonymous, possibly folk.
PLACE--probably United States.
DATE--probably created 18th century.
DIFFERING FIRST LINE--THE TREE OF LIFE MY SOUL HATH
SEEN.
Music: COMPOSER--Elizabeth Poston (1905-   ).
PLACE--England.
DATE--published 1967.
Found: APP

393.   JESUS IN DEN STAL

Lyrics: AUTHOR--folk.
PLACE--Belgium.
DATE--possibly created 15th-17th century?

ENGLISH TITLE--JESUS OF THE MANGER (paraphrase by
    Patrick Reginald Chalmers [1872-1942]).
DIFFERING FIRST LINE--SING, GOOD COMPANY, FRANK AND
    FREE!

Music: COMPOSER--folk.
           PLACE--Belgium.
           DATE--possibly created 15th-17th century?
Found: OXF

394. JESUS, JESUS, REST YOUR HEAD

Lyrics: AUTHOR--John Jacob Niles (1892-1980).
           PLACE--United States.
           DATE--written 1932; published 1935.
           VARIANT VERNACULAR TITLE--THE MANGER CRADLE SONG.
Music: COMPOSER--John Jacob Niles (1892-1980).
           PLACE--United States.
           DATE--written 1932; published 1935.
Found: NIL, TCC, LAN
Notes: The carol was inspired by a folk song heard in
           Kentucky.

395. JESUS THE CHRIST IS BORN

Lyrics: AUTHOR--John Jacob Niles (1892-1980).
           PLACE--United States.
           DATE--written 1932; published 1935.
Music: COMPOSER--John Jacob Niles (1892-1980).
           PLACE--United States.
           DATE--written 1932; published 1935.
Found: NIL, TCC
Notes: The carol was inspired by a folk song heard in
           Tennessee.

396. JINGLE BELL ROCK

Lyrics: AUTHOR--Joseph Carleton Beal (1900-   ) and James
               R. Boothe (1917-   ).
           PLACE--United States.
           DATE--written 1957.
           DIFFERING FIRST LINE--JINGLE BELL, JINGLE BELL,
               JINGLE BELL ROCK.
Music: COMPOSER--Joseph Carleton Beal (1900-   ) and
               James R. Boothe (1917-   ).
           PLACE--United States.
           DATE--written 1957.
Found: ULT, ONS, ONT

397. JINGLE BELLS

    Lyrics: AUTHOR--James S. Pierpont (1822-1893).
             PLACE--probably Boston, Massachusetts.
             DATE--written 1857.
             DIFFERING FIRST LINES--DASHING THROUGH THE SNOW;
                              WE'RE DASHING THRO' THE SNOW.
    Music: COMPOSER--James S. Pierpont (1822-1893).
             PLACE--probably Boston, Massachusetts.
             DATE--written 1857.
    Found: MANY
    Notes: The song was originally entitled ONE HORSE OPEN
             SLEIGH; the song is erroneously attributed to John
             Pierpont (1785-1866); this is probably the first
             well-known secular American carol, although UP ON
             THE HOUSETOP may have preceded it slightly; this is
             also the best-known secular American Christmas song.

398. JINGLE, JINGLE, JINGLE

    Lyrics: AUTHOR--John D. Marks (1909-   ).
             PLACE--United States.
             DATE--published 1964.
    Music: COMPOSER--John D. Marks (1909-   ).
             PLACE--United States.
             DATE--published 1964.
    Found: POP, ULT, ONS, ONT

399. JOLLY OLD SAINT NICHOLAS

    Lyrics: AUTHOR--anonymous.
             PLACE--United States.
             DATE--probably written second half of 19th or early
                 20th century.
    Music: COMPOSER--anonymous.
             PLACE--United States.
             DATE--probably written second half of 19th or early
                 20th century.
    Found: INT, NOR, SEV, POP, ULT

400. JOSEPH AND MARY

    Lyrics: AUTHOR--folk.
             PLACE--England.
             DATE--possibly created 17th century.
             DIFFERING FIRST LINES--O, JOSEPH BEING AN OLD MAN
                            TRULY; OH, JOSEPH BEING A OLD
                            MAN TRULY.
    Music: COMPOSER--folk.
             PLACE--probably Herefordshire, England.
             DATE--possibly created 17th or 18th century?
    Found: OXF, PEN, LEA

Notes: This is one of three carols with the same title, two
            from Kentucky (both associated with the trio of
            English songs collectively called THE CHERRY TREE
            CAROL), one from England; this song has no relation to
            the Kentucky-created JOSEPH AND MARY songs, nor to
            THE CHERRY TREE CAROL.

401.   JOSEPH AND MARY

Lyrics: AUTHOR--folk.
            PLACE--Kentucky.
            DATE--probably created 18th or 19th century.
            DIFFERING FIRST LINES--AS JOSEPH AND MARY; WHEN
                                   JOSEPH WAS AN OLD MAN.
Music: COMPOSER--folk.
            PLACE--probably Appalachian region.
            DATE--probably created 18th or 19th century.
Found: SHE, SEA, LAN
Notes: This is one of three carols with the same title, two
            from Kentucky (both associated with the trio of
            English songs collectively called THE CHERRY TREE
            CAROL), one from England; this song will be desig-
            nated as the Kentucky 1 version to distinguish it
            from the other Kentucky song; these words (two
            versions) are very similar to those for Kentucky 2,
            but the tunes are different; this tune is also used
            as a variant for the carol AS JOSEPH WAS A-WALKING;
            look under THE CHERRY TREE CAROL in the index for
            all related carols.

402.   JOSEPH AND MARY

Lyrics: AUTHOR--folk.
            PLACE--Kentucky.
            DATE--probably created 18th or 19th century.
            DIFFERING FIRST LINE--JOSEPH WAS AN OLD MAN.
Music: COMPOSER--folk.
            PLACE--Kentucky.
            DATE--probably created 18th or 19th century.
Found: SEE
Notes: This is one of three carols with the same title, two
            from Kentucky (both associated with the trio of
            English songs collectively called THE CHERRY TREE
            CAROL), one from England; this song will be designated
            at the Kentucky 2 version to distinguish it from the
            other Kentucky song; these words are very similar to
            those for Kentucky 1, but the tunes are different;
            although this song and JOSEPH WAS AN OLD MAN have the
            same first line ane a common association with THE
            CHERRY TREE CAROL, the two sets of lyrics and two
            tunes are considerably different; look under THE
            CHERRY TREE CAROL in the index for all related carols.

403. JOSEPH, LIEBER JOSEPH MEIN

     Lyrics: AUTHOR--anonymous.
              PLACE--Germany.
              DATE--created 14th or 15th century.
              VARIANT VERNACULAR TITLES--JOSEF, LIEBER JOSEF MEIN;
                                   MARIA UND JOSEPH.
              ENGLISH TITLES--JOSEPH, DEAREST JOSEPH MINE (three
                            different translations, one by
                            George K. Evans, another by Elizabeth
                            Poston [1905-   ], and another by
                            anonymous source); SONG OF THE CRIB;
                            JOSEPH, O DEAR JOSEPH MINE, JOSEPH
                            DEAREST.
              DIFFERING FIRST LINE--JOSEPH DEAREST, JOSEPH MILD.
     Music: COMPOSER--anonymous.
              PLACE--Germany.
              DATE--probably created 14th century.
     Found: INT, OXF, SHE, REE, PEN
     Notes: The first known text of the carol was written about
              1500; Johannes Brahms (1833-1897) used the tune in
              his song GEISTLICHES WIEGENLIED; Peter Cornelius
              (1824-1874) used the tune in his Christmas song
              cycle, CHRISTKIND; the tune is also used for the carol
              RESONET IN LAUDIBUS.

404. JOSEPH WAS AN OLD MAN

     Lyrics: AUTHOR--folk.
              PLACE--England.
              DATE--possibly created 15th or 16th century.
              VARIANT VERNACULAR TITLE--THE CHERRY TREE CAROL.
              DIFFERING FIRST LINE--O, JOSEPH WAS AN OLD MAN.
     Music: COMPOSER--folk.
              PLACE--England.
              DATE--possibly created 15th or 16th century.
              VARIANT TUNES--other English folk tunes; tune from
                                   Appalachian region.
     Found: OXF, CCT, THF, OBE, LEI
     Notes: Although this carol is sometimes identified as THE
              CHERRY TREE CAROL, it is actually only part 1 of that
              song; sometimes both part 1 and part 2 (the folk
              carol AS JOSEPH WAS A-WALKING) are printed together
              under the collective title; part 3 is an Easter song;
              although this song and JOSEPH AND MARY (Kentucky 2)
              have the same first line and a common association
              with THE CHERRY TREE CAROL, the two sets of lyrics
              and two tunes are considerably different; look under
              THE CHERRY TREE CAROL in the index for all related
              carols.

405. JOY TO THE WORLD

    Lyrics: AUTHOR--anonymous.
              PLACE--England.
              DATE--written 18th or 19th century.
    Music: COMPOSER--Nicolaus Hermann (ca. 1490-1561).
              PLACE--Germany.
              DATE--published 1554.
    Found: THF, UNI
    Notes: This carol should not be confused with the much
              better-known song of the same title; the tune is also
              used for the carol LOBT GOTT, IHR CHRISTEN ALLE
              GLEICH; the words were apparently partially derived
              from the lyrics by Isaac Watts (1674-1748) which are
              used for the more famous carol of this name.

406. JOY TO THE WORLD!

    Lyrics: AUTHOR--Isaac Watts (1674-1748).
              PLACE--England.
              DATE--published 1719.
    Music: COMPOSER--probably Lowell Mason (1792-1872).
              PLACE--United States.
              DATE--published 1839.
              VARIANT TUNE--tune by Samuel Holyoke (1762-1820).
    Found: MANY
    Notes: The first line of Watts' poem originally was "Joy to
              the earth"; the tune is commonly attributed to George
              Frederick Handel (1685-1759) because Mason in 1839
              published Watts' poem accompanied by an anonymous
              tune which had the notation "from Handel", and
              because some parts of the tune resemble some parts
              of Handel's MESSIAH; part of the lyrics were appar-
              ently used for the other carol with this name.

407. THE JOYFUL SOUNDS OF SALVATION

    Lyrics: AUTHOR--folk.
              PLACE--England.
              DATE--possibly created 17th-19th century; possibly
                    first published 1855.
              VARIANT VERNACULAR TITLE--IN THE REIGN OF GREAT CAESAR.
    Music: COMPOSER--folk.
              PLACE--England.
              DATE--possibly created 16th-18th century?
    Found: THF, UNI, SEA

408. JULEN HAR BRAGT VELSIGNET BUD

    Lyrics: AUTHOR--Bernhard Severin Ingemann (1789-1862).
              PLACE--Denmark.
               DATE--published 1839.

ENGLISH TITLE--CHRISTMAS BRINGS JOY TO EVERY HEART
(translated by Cecil Cowdrey).
Music: COMPOSER--Christoph Ernst Friedrich Weyse (1774-1842).
PLACE--Denmark.
DATE--published 1841.
Found: FHS, LUT

409. JULEN HAR ENGLELYD

Lyrics: AUTHOR--Nicolai Frederik Severin Grundtvig (1783-
1872).
PLACE--Denmark.
DATE--published 1837.
ENGLISH TITLE--ANGELS AT CHRISTMAS TIDE (translated
by Olga Paul).
Music: COMPOSER--folk.
PLACE--Denmark.
DATE--possibly created 14th or 15th century.
VARIANT TUNE--tune by Anton Peter Berggreen (1801-
1880).
Found: FHS, RTW

410. KHANTA ZAGUN GUZIEK

Lyrics: AUTHOR--folk.
PLACE--Basque region, Spain and France.
DATE--possibly created 16th-18th century?
ENGLISH TITLES--WE SING OF DAVID'S DAUGHTER (trans-
lated by John O'Connor [1870-1952]);
COMPANIONS, ALL SING LOUDLY.
Music: COMPOSER--folk.
PLACE--Basque region, Spain and France.
DATE--possibly created 16th-18th century?
Found: THF, OBE, UNI, PRE, HEL

411. KHODIT MIESIATS

Lyrics: AUTHOR--folk.
PLACE--Russia.
DATE--possibly created 16th-18th century?
ENGLISH TITLE--CHRISTMAS GREETING (translated by
Jacob Robbins).
DIFFERING FIRST LINES--KHODIT MIESIATS PO NEBU SINEMU;
THE MOON WALKS IN THE FIELDS
OF THE SKY.
Music: COMPOSER--folk.
PLACE--Russia.
DATE--possibly created 16th-18th century?
Found: RUS

412. KHRISTOS ROZHDAETSIA

Lyrics: AUTHOR--folk.
          PLACE--Russia.
          DATE--possibly created 16th-18th century?
          ENGLISH TITLE--THE CHRIST IS COMING! (translated by
                              Jacob Robbins).
          DIFFERING FIRST LINES--KHRISTOS ROZHDAETSIA, SLAVITE!;
                              THE CHRIST IS COMING, SING HIS
                              PRAISE!
Music: COMPOSER--folk.
          PLACE--Russia.
          DATE--possibly created 16th-18th century?
Found: RUS

413. KING HEROD AND THE COCK

Lyrics: AUTHOR--folk.
          PLACE--England.
          DATE--probably created 15th or 16th century.
          DIFFERING FIRST LINE--THERE WAS A STAR IN DAVID'S
                              LAND.
Music: COMPOSER--folk.
          PLACE--England.
          DATE--probably created 15th or 16th century.
Found: OXF, SEA, SHA

414. THE KING SHALL COME

Lyrics: AUTHOR--John Brownlie (1857-1925).
          PLACE--Scotland.
          DATE--published 1907.
          VARIANT VERNACULAR TITLE--THE KING SHALL COME WHEN
                              MORNING DAWNS.
Music: COMPOSER--William Jones (1726-1800).
          PLACE--England.
          DATE--published 1789.
          VARIANT TUNES--tune by Richard Farrant (ca. 1530-
                              1581); United States folk song.
Found: MET, LUT, SIG
Notes: The words are a translation of anonymous Greek lyrics;
          the main tune is also used for the carol BREAK FORTH,
          O LIVING LIGHT OF GOD.

415. KINGS IN GLORY

Lyrics: AUTHOR--Selwyn Image (1849-1930).
          PLACE--England.
          DATE--probably written early 20th century.
          VARIANT VERNACULAR TITLE--THREE KINGS IN GREAT GLORY.
          DIFFERING FIRST LINE--THREE KINGS IN GREAT GLORY OF
                              HORSES AND MEN.

  Music: COMPOSER--Martin Shaw (1875-1958).
             PLACE--England.
             DATE--probably written early 20th century.
  Found: OXF, ECF

416. KLING, GLÖCKCHEN

  Lyrics: AUTHOR--probably Karl Enslin (1814-1875).
             PLACE--Germany.
             DATE--written 19th century.
             VARIANT VERNACULAR TITLE--KLING, GLÖCKCHEN, KLING.
             ENGLISH TITLE--RING, LITTLE BELLS (translated by
                            George K. Evans).
             DIFFERING FIRST LINES--KLING, GLÖCKCHEN, KLINGELING!;
                              RING, BELLS, GO TING-A-LING-A-
                              LING.
  Music: COMPOSER--folk.
             PLACE--Germany.
             DATE--possibly created 18th or 19th century?
  Found: INT, ROT, ONT, HAP

417. KOLIADA

  Lyrics: AUTHOR--folk.
             PLACE--Ukraine.
             DATE--possibly created 16th-18th century?
             ENGLISH TITLES--YULETIDE and YULETIDE WAKES (two
                            titles for the same translation by
                            Jacob Robbins).
             DIFFERING FIRST LINES--KOLIADA, KOLIADA; YULETIDE
                              WAKES, YULETIDE BREAKS.
  Music: COMPOSER--folk.
             PLACE--Ukraine.
             DATE--possibly created 16th-18th century?
  Found: RUS, WIL

418. KOMMET, IHR HIRTEN

  Lyrics: AUTHOR--Karl Riedel (1827-1888).
             PLACE--probably Bohemia, Czechoslovakia.
             DATE--written 19th century.
             DIFFERING FIRST LINE--KOMMET, IHR HIRTEN, IHR MÄNNER
                              UND FRAUN.
  Music: COMPOSER--folk.
             PLACE--Czechoslovakia.
             DATE--probably created 17th or 18th century.
  Found: INT, WOR, NHW
  Notes: For a Czech version of this carol, see NESEM VÁM
             NOVINY; the tune is also used for the carol COLD IS
             THE MORNING.

419. LA GUIGNOLÉE

  Lyrics: AUTHOR--folk.
            PLACE--probably Quebec.
            DATE--possibly created 17th or 18th century?
            ENGLISH TITLES--HAIL TO THE MASTER AND THE MISTRESS
                (translated by Elizabeth Poston
                [1905-   ]); GREETINGS, GOOD MASTER
                and CAROL OF THE MISTLETOE SINGERS
                (two titles for the same translation
                by Ruth Heller [1920-   ]).
            DIFFERING FIRST LINE--GREETINGS, GOOD MASTER, MIS-
                                    TRESS, CHILDREN.
  Music: COMPOSER--folk.
            PLACE--probably Quebec.
            DATE--possibly created 17th or 18th century?
  Found: PEN, UNI, HEL
  Notes: This is the best-known French-Canadian carol unless
            D'OÙ VIENS TU, BERGÈRE? is also from Quebec.

420. LA JOURNADA

  Lyrics: AUTHOR--folk.
            PLACE--Venezuela.
            DATE--possibly created 18th or 19th century?
            VARIANT VERNACULAR TITLE--DIN, DIN, DIN.
            ENGLISH TITLE--THE JOURNEY (two different translations,
                one by George K. Evans, one by Ruth
                Heller [1920-   ]).
  Music: COMPOSER--folk.
            PLACE--Venezuela.
            DATE--possibly created 18th or 19th century?
  Found: INT, HEL

421. LA MARCHE DES ROIS

  Lyrics: AUTHOR--folk.
            PLACE--Provence, France.
            DATE--probably created 13th century.
            VARIANT VERNACULAR TITLES--MARCHE DE TURENNE; MARCHE
                                        DES ROIS.
            ENGLISH TITLES--THE MARCH OF THE KINGS (one transla-
                by George K. Evans, another transla-
                tion by Abbie Farwell Brown, another
                translation by Henry William Simon
                [1901-   ]); THE MARCH OF THE THREE
                KINGS and MARCH OF TURENNE (two
                titles for the same translation by
                Marx E. Oberndorfer [1876-   ]);
                MARCH OF THE KINGS.

DIFFERING FIRST LINES--CE MATIN, J'AI RENCONTRÉ LE
TRAIN; DE GRAND MATIN, J'AI
RENCONTRÉ LE TRAIN; THREE
GREAT KINGS I MET AT EARLY
MORN; YESTERDAY I MET UPON THE
WAY; THIS GREAT DAY, I MET
UPON THE WAY; AT DAWN OF DAY,
I MET THEM ON THE WAY; IN THE
MORN WE MET THE PROUD ARRAY.

Music: COMPOSER--folk.
PLACE--Provence, France.
DATE--probably created 13th century.
Found: INT, SIM, OBE, CCM, OWE
Notes: Georges Bizet (1838-1875) used an arrangement of the
tune in his incidental music for L'ARLÉSIENNE.

422. LA VIRGEN VA CAMINANDO

Lyrics: AUTHOR--folk.
PLACE--Estremadura, Spain.
DATE--possibly created 17th-19th century?
ENGLISH TITLE--OUR PURE VIRGIN WAS GOING (translated
by Olga Paul).
DIFFERING FIRST LINE--DARKER THE MOUNTAIN WAS GROWING.
Music: COMPOSER--folk.
PLACE--Estremadura, Spain.
DATE--possibly created 17th-19th century?
Found: MON, CAN, RTW

423. LAS POSADAS

Lyrics: AUTHOR--folk.
PLACE--Latin America or Spain.
DATE--if Latin America, possibly created 18th or
19th century?; if Spain, possibly created
16th-18th century?
VARIANT VERNACULAR TITLE--LOS PASTORES.
ENGLISH TITLES--THOU ART WELL CONTENT (translated by
George K. Evans); THE SHEPHERDS.
DIFFERING FIRST LINES--QUIERES QUE TE QUITE MI BIEN
DE LAS PAJAS; THOU ART WELL
CONTENT IN A STABLE SO LOWLY.
Music: COMPOSER--folk.
PLACE--Latin America or Spain.
DATE--if Latin America, possibly created 18th or 19th
century?; if Spain, possibly created 16th-18th
century?
Found: INT, FJE

424. LASCIATE I VOSTRI ALBERGHI

Lyrics: AUTHOR--folk.
PLACE--Italy.

                   DATE--probably created 16th or 17th century.
                   ENGLISH TITLE--SHEPHERDS, THE DAY IS BREAKING
                                       (translated by K.W. Simpson).
Music: COMPOSER--folk.
                   PLACE--Italy.
                   DATE--probably created 16th or 17th century.
Found: THF, ICC
Notes: The words and melody were possibly first published
                   in 1674; the tune is the melody ECCO BELLA REGINA.

425.   LASST UNS DAS KINDLEIN WIEGEN

Lyrics: AUTHOR--folk.
                   ,PLACE--Germany.
                   DATE--probably created 16th century.
                   VARIANT VERNACULAR TITLE--LASS UNS DAS KINDLEIN
                                                 WIEGEN.
                   ENGLISH TITLES--COME, ROCK THE CRADLE FOR HIM (trans-
                                       lated by George Ratcliffe Woodward
                                       [1848-1934]); COME, ROCK THE CHRIST
                                       CHILD (translated by Edward Bliss
                                       Reed [1872-1940]).
Music: COMPOSER--folk.
                   PLACE--Germany.
                   DATE--probably created 16th century.
Found: BUD, WOR, COF, CTH, HFW
Notes: The words and music were possibly first published in
                   1604.

426.   THE LAST MONTH OF THE YEAR

Lyrics: AUTHOR--probably Vera Hall (1905-1964).
                   PLACE--probably Alabama.
                   DATE--published 1953, but probably written much
                       earlier.
                   VARIANT VERNACULAR TITLE--JANUARY, FEBRUARY.
                   DIFFERING FIRST LINES--WHAT MONTH WAS MY JESUS BORN
                                                 IN?; WHAT MONTH WAS MY JESUS
                                                 BORNED IN?
Music: COMPOSER--probably Vera Hall (1905-1964).
                   PLACE--probably Alabama.
                   DATE--published 1953, but probably written much
                       earlier.
Found: ULT, SEA, SEE, ONS, HAP

427.   LE NOËL DES OISEAUX

Lyrics: AUTHOR--folk.
                   PLACE--Languedoc region, France.
                   DATE--possibly created 16th-18th century?
                   ENGLISH TITLE--CAROL OF THE BIRDS.

DIFFERING FIRST LINES--VOICI L'ÉTOILE DE NOËL;
SEE HOW THE NÖEL STAR SHINES
BRIGHT!

Music: COMPOSER--folk.
PLACE--Languedoc region, France.
DATE--possibly created 16th-18th century?
Found: SHE

428. LE SOMMEIL DE L'ENFANT JÉSUS

Lyrics: AUTHOR--folk.
PLACE--France (possibly Anjou).
DATE--probably created 18th century.
VARIANT VERNACULAR TITLE--ENTRE LE BOEUF ET L'ÂNE
GRIS.
ENGLISH TITLES--THE SLEEP OF THE INFANT JESUS (two
translations, one anonymous, one by
George K. Evans); SHELTER WHERE OX
AND ASS ARE ONE (translated by John
Morrison); 'TWIXT GENTLE OX AND ASS
SO GRAY; THE SLEEP OF THE CHILD
JESUS (translated by M.L. Hohman);
SLUMBER SONG OF THE INFANT JESUS;
HERE BETWIXT ASS AND OXEN MILD
(translated by Charles Winfred
Douglas (1867-1944); OXEN AND SHEEP
(translated by Willys Peck Kent
[1877-   ]).

DIFFERING FIRST LINES--HERE 'TWIXT THE ASS AND OXEN
MILD; LYING AMID THE OXEN
MILD; CRADL'D AMID A HERD OF
KINE; 'TWEEN OX AND ASS IN
HUMBLE SHED; OXEN AND SHEEP
THY GUARDIANS MILD.
Music: COMPOSER--folk.
PLACE--France (possibly Anjou).
DATE--probably created 18th century.
Found: INT, HUT, YAL, SIM, UNI
Notes: The carol has been attributed to François Auguste
Gevaert (1828-1908), who made a well-known
harmonization.

429. LE VERMEIL DU SOLEIL

Lyrics: AUTHOR--Nicolas Denisot (1515-1559).
PLACE--France.
DATE--published 1553.
ENGLISH TITLES--GEMS OF DAY (paraphrase by Patrick
Reginald Chalmers [1872-1942]);
MORNING HUSH (translated by John Gray
[1866-1934]).
DIFFERING FIRST LINE--ALL THE GAY GEMS OF DAY.
Music: COMPOSER--probably Marc Antoine Muret (1526-1585).

          PLACE--France.
          DATE--probably written 16th century.
  Found: OXF, THF

430. LEAD ME TO THY PEACEFUL MANGER

  Lyrics: AUTHOR--Matthew Bridges (1800-1894).
           PLACE--England.
           DATE--probably written mid-19th century.
  Music: COMPOSER--folk.
           PLACE--Basque region, Spain and France.
           DATE--possibly created 16th-18th century?
  Found: THF, UNI
  Notes: The tune is the melody EZ DUKEZU.

431. LEANABH AN AIGH

  Lyrics: AUTHOR--Mary MacDonald (1817-1890).
           PLACE--Scotland.
           DATE--written 19th century.
           ENGLISH TITLE--CHILD IN THE MANGER (translated by
                           Lachlan Macbean [1853-1931]).
  Music: COMPOSER--folk.
           PLACE--Scotland.
           DATE--possibly created 16th-18th century?
  Found: UNI, RTW, REF

432. LES ANGES DANS NOS CAMPAGNES

  Lyrics: AUTHOR--anonymous, possibly folk.
           PLACE--France.
           DATE--probably created 18th century.
           ENGLISH TITLES--ANGELS WE HAVE HEARD ON HIGH
                           (anonymous translation incorrectly
                           attributed to Earl Bowman Marlatt
                           [1892-   ]); WESTMINSTER CAROL;
                           HEARKEN ALL! WHAT HOLY SINGING;
                           ANGELS O'ER THE FIELDS WERE SINGING
                           (translated by George K. Evans);
                           BRIGHT ANGELS WE HAVE HEARD ON HIGH.
  Music: COMPOSER--anonymous, possibly folk.
           PLACE--France.
           DATE--probably created 18th century.
  Found: MANY
  Notes: The refrain (words and music) has been incorrectly
           attributed to Telesphorus, 2nd century Roman cleric;
           James Montgomery (1771-1854) used the tune as the
           first melody for ANGELS FROM THE REALMS OF GLORY, and
           the tune is still used with that carol in Great
           Britain although in large part displaced by a later
           one; the tune is also used for the carol WHEN THE
           CRIMSON SUN HAD SET.

433.   LES BOURGEOIS DE CHASTRES

      Lyrics: AUTHOR--probably _____ Crestot.
               PLACE--probably Arpajon region, France.
               DATE--probably created 16th century.
               VARIANT VERNACULAR TITLES--NOËL DE COUR; TOUS LES BUR-
                                    GEOIS DE CHASTRES; TOUS LES
                                    BOURGEOIS DE CHASTRES; TOUS
                                    LES BOURGEOIS DE CHÂTRES.
               ENGLISH TITLES--THE GOOD MEN ALL OF CHASTRES; THE
                                    FOLK THAT LIVE IN CHASTRES (trans-
                                    lated by Alfred Raymond Bellinger
                                    [1893-   ]).
      Music: COMPOSER--folk.
               PLACE--probably Arpajon region, France.
               DATE--created 16th century.
      Found: HUT, OBE, CST, TIE

434.   LET ALL THAT ARE TO MIRTH INCLINED

      Lyrics: AUTHOR--folk.
               PLACE--England.
               DATE--probably created 17th century.
      Music: COMPOSER--folk.
               PLACE--England.
               DATE--possibly created 17th century.
      Found: THF, GAS, GIF, GIS, UNI
      Notes: The song was possibly first published in 1822; for
               a carol with similar lyrics but different tunes, see
               THE SINNERS' REDEMPTION.

435.   LET IT SNOW! LET IT SNOW! LET IT SNOW!

      Lyrics: AUTHOR--Sammy Cahn (1913-   ).
               PLACE--United States.
               DATE--published 1945.
               DIFFERING FIRST LINE--OH THE WEATHER OUTSIDE IS
                                    FRIGHTFUL.
      Music: COMPOSER--Jule Styne (1905-   ).
               PLACE--United States.
               DATE--published 1945.
      Found: NOR, POP, ULT, ONS, HAP

436.   LET SUCH (SO FANTASTICAL)

      Lyrics: AUTHOR--Thomas Tusser (1524?-1580).
               PLACE--England.
               DATE--published 1557.
               VARIANT VERNACULAR TITLE--LET SUCH (SO FANTASTICAL)
                                    LIKING NOT THIS.
      Music: COMPOSER--folk.
               PLACE--England.

DATE--possibly created 15th-17th century?
Found: UNI, CCB

437.   LET'S HAVE AN OLD FASHIONED CHRISTMAS

Lyrics: AUTHOR--Larry Conley (1895-1960).
           PLACE--United States.
           DATE--published 1939.
           DIFFERING FIRST LINE--ANOTHER YEAR HAS ROLLED AROUND.
Music: COMPOSER--Joseph Solomon (1897-1947).
           PLACE--United States.
           DATE--published 1939.
Found: SEV

438.   LIEB NACHTIGALL, WACH AUF!

Lyrics: AUTHOR--folk.
           PLACE--probably Franconia, Germany.
           DATE--probably created 17th century.
           VARIANT VERNACULAR TITLES--DIE WEIHNACHTSNACHTIGALL;
                                      DIE WEIHNACHTS NACHTIGALL;
                                      WACH NACHTIGALL, WACH AUF!
           ENGLISH TITLES--DEAR NIGHTINGALE, AWAKE! (translated
                      by George K. Evans); THE CHRISTMAS
                      NIGHTINGALE (two different anonymous
                      translations); WAKE, NIGHTINGALE
                      (translated by Edward Bliss Reed
                      [1872-1940]).
           DIFFERING FIRST LINES--SWEET NIGHTINGALE, AWAKE;
                                  WAKE, NIGHTINGALE, AWAKE!;
                                  O NIGHTINGALE AWAKE!
Music: COMPOSER--folk.
           PLACE--probably Franconia, Germany.
           DATE--probably created 17th century.
Found: INT, TRA, WOR, CTH, CCM

439.   LIETI PASTORI

Lyrics: AUTHOR--folk.
           PLACE--Italy.
           DATE--probably created 16th or 17th century.
           ENGLISH TITLE--O JOYFUL SHEPHERDS (translated by
                      K.W. Simpson).
Music: COMPOSER--folk.
           PLACE--Italy.
           DATE--probably created 16th or 17th century.
Found: THF, ICC
Notes: The words and melody were possibly first published
           in 1674.

440. LIKE SILVER LAMPS IN A DISTANT SHRINE

  Lyrics: AUTHOR--William Chatterton Dix (1837-1898).
  PLACE--England.
  DATE--published 1871.
  VARIANT VERNACULAR TITLES--LIKE SILVER LAMPS; THE
  MANGER THRONE.
  Music: COMPOSER--Charles Steggall (1826-1905).
  PLACE--England.
  DATE--published 1871.
  VARIANT TUNES--tunes by George B. Lissant and Joseph
  Barnby (1838-1896).
  Found: HUT, ADU, CHO, YOU, STA

441. LIPPAI

  Lyrics: AUTHOR--folk.
  PLACE--Tyrol, Austria.
  DATE--possibly created 19th century.
  VARIANT VERNACULAR TITLE--LIPPAI, SOLLST G'SCHWIND
  AUFSTEA.
  ENGLISH TITLES--LIPPAI (three different translations,
  one by George K. Evans, another by
  Henry William Simon [1901-   ]), and
  another by anonymous source; GERMAN
  FOLK CAROL (translated by Edward
  Bliss Reed [1872-1940]).
  DIFFERING FIRST LINES--LIPPAI, STEH AUF VOM SCHLAF!;
  LIPPAI, GET OUT OF BED!;
  LIPPAI, DON'T PLAY YOU'RE DEAD!;
  LIPPAI, AWAKE, DON'T SLEEP!;
  LIPPAI, AWAKE FROM SLEEP!
  Music: COMPOSER--folk.
  PLACE--Tyrol, Austria.
  DATE--possibly created 19th century.
  Found: INT, SIM, SHE, CFO

442. LISTEN, LORDLINGS, UNTO ME

  Lyrics: AUTHOR--folk.
  PLACE--England.
  DATE--probably created 15th or 16th century.
  VARIANT VERNACULAR TITLES--LISTEN, LORDLINGS; CAROL
  FOR CHRISTMAS-EVE.
  DIFFERING FIRST LINE--LISTEN, LORDLINGS, TO OUR LAY.
  Music: COMPOSER--folk.
  PLACE--Gascony, France.
  DATE--created 16th century.
  VARIANT TUNES--15th or early 16th century English
  folk tune; tune by Frederick Arthur
  Gore Ouseley (1825-1889).
  Found: OBE, COS, STA, RTW, HEL
  Notes: The first variant tune is the melody WESTRON WYNDE,
  WHEN WYLL THOU BLOW.

443. THE LITTLE CAROL

    Lyrics: AUTHOR--Morris Martin (1910-   ).
               PLACE--England.
               DATE--possibly written around 1967.
               DIFFERING FIRST LINE--IN THIS TIME OF LITTLE THINGS.
    Music: COMPOSER--George Fraser.
               PLACE--England.
               DATE--published 1967.
    Found: REF

444. THE LITTLE DRUMMER BOY

    Lyrics: AUTHOR--Katherine K. Davis (1892-1980).
               PLACE--United States.
               DATE--published 1941.
               VARIANT VERNACULAR TITLE--CAROL OF THE DRUM.
               DIFFERING FIRST LINE--COME, THEY TOLD ME, PARUM PUM
                                     PUM PUM.
    Music: COMPOSER--Katherine K. Davis (1892-1980).
               PLACE--United States.
               DATE--published 1941.
    Found: BAE, ULT
    Notes: In 1958 Davis' CAROL OF THE DRUM had its title
               changed to THE LITTLE DRUMMER BOY, and Henry V.
               Onorati (1912-   ) and Harry Simeone (1911-   )
               were subsequently given as collaborators.

445. LITTLE GRAY DONKEY

    Lyrics: AUTHOR--Charles Tazewell (1900-1972).
               PLACE--United States.
               DATE--published 1961.
               DIFFERING FIRST LINE--O CARRY HER SAFE TO BETHLEHEM.
    Music: COMPOSER--Roger Wagner (1914-   ).
               PLACE--United States.
               DATE--published 1961.
    Found: NOR, SEV

446. LITTLE ST. NICK

    Lyrics: AUTHOR--Brian Wilson.
               PLACE--United States.
               DATE--published 1963.
               DIFFERING FIRST LINE--WAY UP NORTH, WHERE THE AIR
                                       GETS COLD.
    Music: COMPOSER--Brian Wilson.
               PLACE--United States.
               DATE--published 1963.
    Found: NOR

447. LO, HE COMES WITH CLOUDS DESCENDING

Lyrics: AUTHOR--Charles Wesley (1707-1788).
PLACE--England.
DATE--published 1758.
VARIANT VERNACULAR TITLE--NOW HE COMES WITH CLOUDS
DESCENDING (adaptation by
Anthony G. Petti).
Music: COMPOSER--William Owen (1814-1893).
PLACE--Wales.
DATE--published 1886.
VARIANT TUNES--tune by Johann G.C. Störl (1675-1719);
18th century English tune; probably
17th century French tune.
Found: MET, LUT, CAT, ENG, SIG
Notes: Wesley's lyrics were based on LO! HE COMETH, COUNT-
LESS TRUMPETS, a hymn by John Cennick (1718-1755)
which was published 1752; the French tune is also
used for the carol SIGESATO PASA SARX BROTEIA.

448. LOBT GOTT, IHR CHRISTEN ALLE GLEICH

Lyrics: AUTHOR--Nicolaus Hermann (ca. 1490-1561).
PLACE--Germany.
DATE--published 1560.
VARIANT VERNACULAR TITLE--LOBT GOTT IHR CHRISTEN
ALLZUGLEICH.
ENGLISH TITLE--LET ALL TOGETHER PRAISE OUR GOD (two
different translations, one by F.
Samuel Janzow, the other by Arthur
Tozer Russell [1806-1874]).
Music: COMPOSER--Nicolaus Hermann (ca. 1490-1561).
PLACE--Germany.
DATE--published 1554.
Found: MET, BUD, MEN, SIG, HFW
Notes: The tune originally was set to Hermann's hymn KOMMT
HER, IHR LIEBEN SCHWESTERLEIN, but when the tune was
republished six years later it was set to the carol
lyrics; the tune is also used for the carol JOY TO
THE WORLD (the anonymous one, not the famous song by
Isaac Watts).

449. THE LONESOME CHRISTMAS TREE

Lyrics: AUTHOR--Betty Maier and Charles Russell Taylor
(1915-1979).
PLACE--United States.
DATE--published 1970.
DIFFERING FIRST LINE--I'M A LONESOME CHRISTMAS TREE.
Music: COMPOSER--Betty Maier and Charles Russell Taylor
(1915-1979).
PLACE--United States.
DATE--published 1970.
Found: ONT

450. THE LORD AT FIRST DID ADAM MAKE

    Lyrics: AUTHOR--folk.
             PLACE--probably West country, England.
             DATE--possibly created 15th or 16th century.
             VARIANT VERNACULAR TITLES--THE LORD AT FIRST HAD
                                      ADAM MADE; A CAROL FOR
                                      CHRISTMAS EVE; CAROL FOR
                                      CHRISTMAS EVE.
    Music: COMPOSER--folk.
             PLACE--probably West country, England.
             DATE--possibly created 15th or 16th century.
             VARIANT TUNE--another English folk tune.
    Found: OXF, CCT, THF, UNI, RTW
    Notes: The song was probably first published in 1822.

451. LORD, WHEN THE WISE MEN CAME

    Lyrics: AUTHOR--Sidney Godolphin (1610-1643).
             PLACE--England.
             DATE--written around 1630-1640.
             DIFFERING FIRST LINE--LORD, WHEN THE WISE MEN CAME
                                      FROM AFAR.
    Music: COMPOSER--anonymous.
             PLACE--France.
             DATE--probably created 17th century; possibly first
                    published 1681.
    Found: UNI, APP

452. LOS PASTORES

    Lyrics: AUTHOR--Felix Luna.
             PLACE--Argentina.
             DATE--possibly written mid-20th century.
             ENGLISH TITLE--THE SHEPHERDS (translated by John
                    Morrison).
             DIFFERING FIRST LINE--SHEPHERDS, COME FROM FIELD AND
                    PASTURE.
    Music: COMPOSER--Ariel Ramirez (1921-   ).
             PLACE--Argentina.
             DATE--probably written mid-20th century.
    Found: REF

453. LOVE CAME DOWN AT CHRISTMAS

    Lyrics: AUTHOR--Christina Rossetti (1830-1894).
             PLACE--England.
             DATE--published 1885.
    Music: COMPOSER--folk.
             PLACE--Ireland.
             DATE--possibly created 18th or 19th century; probably
                  first published 1902.

VARIANT TUNES--tunes by Sidney Hann, John Ernest
                    Borland (1866-1937), and Edgar Pettman
                    (1867-1943).
Found: REE, MET, HUT, UNI, LUT

454. LUCIA-VISA

Lyrics: AUTHOR--folk.
           PLACE--Sweden.
           DATE--possibly created 16th-18th century?
           VARIANT VERNACULAR TITLE--GOD MORGON, MITT HERRSKAP.
           ENGLISH TITLE--LUCIA'S SONG (translated by Noel
                        Wirén).
           DIFFERING FIRST LINE--GOOD MORROW, MY GENTLES.
Music: COMPOSER--Paula Müntzing.
           PLACE--Sweden.
           DATE--possibly written around 1924.
Found: SWE, GLA, JUL

455. LULAJZE JEZUNIU

Lyrics: AUTHOR--folk.
           PLACE--Poland.
           DATE--possibly created 15th-17th century?
           ENGLISH TITLES--SLEEP, LITTLE JESUS; SLEEP, MY CHILD
                        JESUS (translated by Marx E. Obern-
                        dorfer [1876-   ]); POLISH LULLABY
                        (two different translations by Henry
                        William Simon [1901-   ] and George
                        K. Evans); ROCKABYE JESUS; LULLABY,
                        JESU (translated by Alice Zienko and
                        Ruth Heller [1920-   ]); LULLABY
                        CAROL.
           DIFFERING FIRST LINES--LULLABY, JESUS; SLEEP, LITTLE
                        JESUS, ON MOTHER'S SAFE ARM.
Music: COMPOSER--folk.
           PLACE--Poland.
           DATE--possibly created 15th-17th century?
           VARIANT TUNE--another folk tune from Poland.
Found: INT, SIM, SHE, OBE, TRA
Notes: The melody was used by Frédéric Chopin (1810-1849) in
           his SCHERZO IN B MINOR (1831 or 1832); the song is
           perhaps the best-known Polish carol.

456. LULLABY FOR CHRISTMAS EVE

Lyrics: AUTHOR--Paul Francis Webster (1907-1984).
           PLACE--United States.
           DATE--published 1964.
           DIFFERING FIRST LINE--THERE'LL BE SNOW FALLING DOWN
                        FROM THE SKIES.
Music: COMPOSER--Pete King (1914-   ).

                    PLACE--United States.
                    DATE--published 1964.
          Found: ONS, ONT, HAP

457. LULLAY MY LIKING

          Lyrics: AUTHOR--folk.
                    PLACE--England.
                    DATE--created 15th century.
                    VARIANT VERNACULAR TITLES--LULLAY, MINE LIKING; MYN
                                        LYKING; I SAW A MAIDEN.
                    DIFFERING FIRST LINES--I SAW A FAIR MAYDEN SITTEN
                                        AND SING; I SAW A FAIR MAYDEN
                                        SYTTEN AND SING; I SAW A MAIDEN
                                        SITTEN AND SING.
          Music: COMPOSER--Gustav Holst (1874-1934).
                    PLACE--England.
                    DATE--published 1919.
                    VARIANT TUNES--tune by Richard Runciman Terry (1865-
                                1938); folk tune from the Basque
                                region, Spain and France; tune by
                                David Sydney Morgan; 15th century tune
                                from England.
          Found: OXF, UNI, PEN, CCT, REF

458. L'UNICO FIGLIO

          Lyrics: AUTHOR--folk.
                    PLACE--Italy.
                    DATE--probably created 16th or 17th century.
                    ENGLISH TITLE--HOW MANY A KING A-DREAMING (translated
                                by K.W. Simpson).
          Music: COMPOSER--folk.
                    PLACE--Italy.
                    DATE--probably created 16th or 17th century
          Found: THF, ICC
          Notes: The words and melody were possibly first published in
                    1674; the tune is the melody MARIA VERGIN BEATA.

459. MACHT HOCH DIE TÜR DIE TOR' MACH WEIT

          Lyrics: AUTHOR--Georg Weissel (1590-1635).
                    PLACE--Germany.
                    DATE--published 1642.
                    ENGLISH TITLES--LIFT UP YOUR HEADS, YE MIGHTY GATES
                                and LIFT UP YOUR HEADS (both titles
                                for the same translation by Catherine
                                Winkworth [1827-1878]).
          Music: COMPOSER--Johann Anastasius Freylinghausen (1670-1739).
                    PLACE--Germany.
                    DATE--published 1704.

VARIANT TUNES--anonymous tune published 1789 in
England; tune by John Baptiste Calkin
(1827-1905).
Found: MET, UNI, PRA, HAR, LUT
Notes: Calkin's tune is also used for the carol I HEARD THE
BELLS ON CHRISTMAS DAY.

460. MADRE, EN LA PUERTA HAY UN NIÑO

Lyrics: AUTHOR--folk.
PLACE--Andalusia, Spain.
DATE--possibly created 16th-18th century?
VARIANT VERNACULAR TITLE--AY!, QUE EN ESTA TIERRA.
Music: COMPOSER--folk.
PLACE--Andalusia, Spain.
DATE--possibly created 16th-18th century?
VARIANT TUNE--tune by Joaquín Nin y Castellanos
(1879-1949), composer from Cuba.
Found: MON, CAN, NIN
Notes: The lyrics are somewhat similar to those for the
carols EL MINO JESUS and A ESTA PUERTA LLAMA UN NIÑO,
but the tunes are different.

461. MAKE WE JOY

Lyrics: AUTHOR--anonymous.
PLACE--England.
DATE--created 15th century.
VARIANT VERNACULAR TITLE--MAKE WE JOY NOW IN THIS
FEST.
DIFFERING FIRST LINES--MAKE WE JOY NOW IN THIS FEAST;
A PATRE UNIGENTITUS.
Music: COMPOSER--anonymous.
PLACE--England.
DATE--created 15th century.
VARIANT TUNE--another 15th century English tune.
Found: OXF, THF, MEC, EAR, UNI

462. MAKE WE MERRY

Lyrics: AUTHOR--folk.
PLACE--England.
DATE--probably created 15th century; first known text
around 1500.
DIFFERING FIRST LINE--MAKE WE MERRY, BOTH MORE AND
LESS.
Music: COMPOSER--Martin Shaw (1875-1958).
PLACE--England.
DATE--probably written 1926.
Found: OXF

463.   MARIA AUF DEM BERGE

   Lyrics: AUTHOR--folk.
              PLACE--Silesia, Germany.
              DATE--created 17th century.
              VARIANT VERNACULAR TITLES--UF'M BERGE, DA WEHET DER
                                         WIND; UFM BERGE, DA GEHT
                                         DER WIND.
              ENGLISH TITLES--MARY ON THE MOUNTAIN (translated by
                              Olga Paul); MARIA ON THE MOUNTAIN.
              DIFFERING FIRST LINES--AUF DEM BERGE DA GEHT DER
                                     WIND; AUF DEM BERGE DA WEHT
                                     DER WIND; AUF DEM BERGE DA
                                     GEHET DER WIND; ON THE MOUNTAIN
                                     WHERE BREEZES SIGH; ON THE
                                     MOUNTAIN THE WIND BLOWETH WILD.
   Music: COMPOSER--folk.
              PLACE--Silesia, Germany.
              DATE--created 17th century.
   Found: SIM, TRA, ROT, BUD, RTW

464.   MARIA DIE ZOUDE NAER BETHLEEM GAEN

   Lyrics: AUTHOR--folk.
              PLACE--Belgium.
              DATE--probably created 15th century.
              ENGLISH TITLE--NOW MARY MUST JOURNEY (translated by
                             Edward Bliss Reed [1872-1940]).
   Music: COMPOSER--folk.
              PLACE--Belgium.
              DATE--probably created 15th century.
   Found: CTE, NPF
   Notes: This carol's lyrics and tune are very similar to
              those for the carol MARIA DIE ZOUDE NAER BETHLEHEM.

465.   MARIA DIE ZOUDE NAER BETHLEHEM

   Lyrics: AUTHOR--folk.
              PLACE--Netherlands.
              DATE--created 15th century.
              ENGLISH TITLES--OUR LADY ON CHRISTMAS DAY and OUR
                              LADY ON CHRISTMAS EVE, two titles
                              for the same translation by John
                              O'Connor (1870-1952).
              DIFFERING FIRST LINE--OUR LADY ON CHRISTMAS EVE HAD
                                    TO GO.
   Music: COMPOSER--folk.
              PLACE--Netherlands.
              DATE--created 15th century.
   Found: THF, UNI
   Notes: This carol's lyrics and tune are very similar to
              those for the carol MARIA DIE ZOUDE NAER BETHLEEM
              GAEN.

466. MARIA DURCH EIN' DORNWALD GING

    Lyrics: AUTHOR--folk.
                PLACE--Germany.
                DATE--probably created 15th century.
                ENGLISH TITLES--MARIA WANDERS THROUGH THE THORN
                        (translated by George K. Evans);
                        MARIA WANDERED THROUGH A WOOD (trans-
                        lated by Henry William Simon [1901-
                        ]); MARIA WALKS AMID THE THORN.
    Music: COMPOSER--folk.
                PLACE--Germany.
                DATE--probably created 15th century.
    Found: INT, SIM, TRA, ROT, BUD

467. MARIA WIEGENLIED

    Lyrics: AUTHOR--Martin Boelitz (1874-1921).
                PLACE--Germany.
                DATE--published 1912.
                ENGLISH TITLES--AMID THE ROSES MARY SITS and THE
                        VIRGIN'S SLUMBER SONG (both titles
                        for the same translation by Edward
                        Teschemacher [1876-   ]).
    Music: COMPOSER--Max Reger (1873-1916).
                PLACE--Germany.
                DATE--published 1912.
    Found: JUL, REF

468. MARIAS WANDERSCHAFT

    Lyrics: AUTHOR--folk.
                PLACE--Germany.
                DATE--probably created 15th or 16th century.
                ENGLISH TITLE--MARY'S WANDERING.
                DIFFERING FIRST LINES--MARIA DE WOLLT' WANDERN GEH'N;
                        ONCE MARY WOULD GO WANDERING.
    Music: COMPOSER--folk.
                PLACE--Germany.
                DATE--probably created 15th or 16th century.
    Found: OXF, BAE

469. MARY HAD A BABY

    Lyrics: AUTHOR--folk (Black spiritual).
                PLACE--United States (possibly South Carolina).
                DATE--probably created 18th or 19th century.
    Music: COMPOSER--folk (Black spiritual).
                PLACE--United States (possibly South Carolina)
                DATE--probably created 18th or 19th century.
    Found: INT, SEE, SEA, ULT, REF
    Notes: The lyrics are similar to those for SING HALLELU.

470. MARY MILD

    Lyrics: AUTHOR--Bob Shane (1934-   ), Tom Drake, and Miriam
                      Stafford.
                PLACE--United States.
                DATE--published 1960.
                DIFFERING FIRST LINE--AS IT FELL OUT ON A COLD WINTER
                      DAY.
    Music: COMPOSER--Bob Shane (1934-   ), Tom Drake, and
                      Miriam Stafford.
                PLACE--United States.
                DATE--published 1960.
    Found: SEV

471. MARY, WHAT ARE YOU GOING TO NAME THAT PRETTY LITTLE BABY?

    Lyrics: AUTHOR--folk (Black spiritual).
                PLACE--United States.
                DATE--probably created 18th or 19th century.
                VARIANT VERNACULAR TITLE--VIRGIN MARY.
                DIFFERING FIRST LINES--THE VIRGIN MARY HADA ONE SON;
                              VIRGIN MARY HAD ONE SON.
    Music: COMPOSER--folk (Black spiritual).
                PLACE--United States.
                DATE--probably created 18th or 19th century.
                VARIANT TUNE--another Black spiritual tune.
    Found: SEE, BAE, SEA
    Notes: For carols with somewhat similar lyrics but different
                tunes, see WHAT YOU GONNA CALL YO' PRETTY LITTLE
                BABY? and GLORY TO THAT NEWBORN KING.

472. MARY'S LITTLE BOY CHILD

    Lyrics: AUTHOR--Jester Hairston (1901-   ).
                PLACE--United States.
                DATE--published 1956.
                VARIANT VERNACULAR TITLE--MARY'S BOY CHILD.
                DIFFERING FIRST LINE--LONG TIME AGO IN BETHLEHEM.
    Music: COMPOSER--Jester Hairston (1901-   ).
                PLACE--United States.
                DATE--published 1956.
    Found: ULT

473. MASTERS IN THIS HALL

    Lyrics: AUTHOR--William Morris (1834-1896).
                PLACE--England.
                DATE--published 1860.
    Music: COMPOSER--folk.
                PLACE--France (possibly Chartres).
                DATE--possibly created 17th or 18th century.
    Found: OXF, INT, SIM, REE, CCT

> *Notes:* The tune was given to Edmund Sedding (1835-1868), the
> English carol compiler, by the organist at Chartres
> Cathedral, and Sedding asked his associate Morris to
> write some lyrics; the resultant carol was published
> by Sedding in an 1860 collection.

474. MEGA KAI PARADOXON THAUMA

> *Lyrics:* AUTHOR--St. Germanus (634-734).
> PLACE--Constantinople, Byzantine Empire.
> DATE--written late 7th or early 8th century.
> ENGLISH TITLE--A GREAT AND MIGHTY WONDER (translated
>   by John Mason Neale [1818-1866]).
> *Music:*   COMPOSER--anonymous.
> PLACE--Germany.
> DATE--probably created medieval period.
> VARIANT TUNE--tune by Henry John Gauntlett (1805-
>   1876).
> *Found:*   YAL, CCO, LUT

475. MELCHIOR ET BALTHAZAR

> *Lyrics:* AUTHOR--folk.
> PLACE--Languedoc region, France.
> DATE--possibly created 16th-18th century?
> ENGLISH TITLE--MELCHIOR AND BALTHAZAR.
> *Music:*   COMPOSER--folk.
> PLACE--Languedoc region, France.
> DATE--possibly created 16th-18th century?
> *Found:*   SHE

476. MELE KALIKAMAKA

> *Lyrics:* AUTHOR--Robert Alexander Anderson (1894-   ).
> PLACE--Hawaii.
> DATE--written 1949.
> *Music:*   COMPOSER--Robert Alexander Anderson (1894-   ).
> PLACE--Hawaii.
> DATE--written 1949.

477. MENYBÖL AR ANGYAL

> *Lyrics:* AUTHOR--folk.
> PLACE--Hungary.
> DATE--possibly created 17th-19th century?
> VARIANT VERNACULAR TITLE--MENYBÖL AS ANGYAL.
> ENGLISH TITLES--ANGELS FROM HEAVEN (three different
>   translations, one by Olga Paul, one
>   by Bernard Gasso [1926-   ]), one by
>   George K. Evans); HARK TO THE ANGELS
>   (translated by Ruth Heller [1920-
>   ]).

> *Music:*   COMPOSER--folk.
>   PLACE--Hungary.
>   DATE--possibly created 17th-19th century?
> *Found:*   INT, RTW, HEL, HAP, ONS
> *Notes:*   This is perhaps the best-known Hungarian carol.

478. MERRY CHRISTMAS

> *Lyrics:* AUTHOR--Sarah C. Fouser (1889-   ).
>   PLACE--probably DeKalb, Illinois.
>   DATE--probably written 1936.
>   DIFFERING FIRST LINE--MERRY CHRISTMAS, EV'RYONE!
> *Music:*   COMPOSER--Charles E. Fouser (1889-1946).
>   PLACE--probably DeKalb, Illinois.
>   DATE--probably written 1936.
> *Found:*   SIM

479. MERRY CHRISTMAS

> *Lyrics:* AUTHOR--Walter Scott (1771-1832)
>   PLACE--Scotland.
>   DATE--published 1808.
>   DIFFERING FIRST LINE--ON CHRISTMAS EVE THE BELLS WERE
>   RUNG.
> *Music:*   COMPOSER--Martin Shaw (1875-1958).
>   PLACE--England.
>   DATE--probably written 1925.
> *Found:*   OXF
> *Notes:*   The words were adapted from the author's poem MARMION.

480. MERRY CHRISTMAS

> *Lyrics:* AUTHOR--Janice Torre.
>   PLACE--United States.
>   DATE--published 1948.
> *Music:*   COMPOSER--Fred Spielman.
>   PLACE--United States.
>   DATE--published 1948.
> *Found:*   HAP

481. MERRY CHRISTMAS DARLING

> *Lyrics:* AUTHOR--Frank Pooler (1926-   ).
>   PLACE--United States.
>   DATE--possibly written 1946.
>   DIFFERING FIRST LINE--GREETING CARDS HAVE ALL BEEN
>   SENT.
> *Music:*   COMPOSER--Richard Lynn Carpenter (1946-   ).
>   PLACE--United States.
>   DATE--possibly written 1970.
> *Found:*   POP

482. MERRY CHRISTMAS FROM OUR HOUSE TO YOUR HOUSE

  Lyrics: AUTHOR--Mort Greene (1912-).
       PLACE--United States.
       DATE--published 1957.
  Music: COMPOSER--George Cates (1911-).
       PLACE--United States.
       DATE--published 1957.

483. THE MERRY CHRISTMAS POLKA

  Lyrics: AUTHOR--Paul Francis Webster (1907-1984).
       PLACE--United States.
       DATE--published 1949.
       DIFFERING FIRST LINE--THEY'RE TUNING UP THE FIDDLES
                     NOW.
  Music: COMPOSER--Joseph Francis Burke (1914-1950).
       PLACE--United States.
       DATE--published 1949.
  Found: ULT

484. THE MIRACLE OF THE COCK

  Lyrics: AUTHOR--folk.
       PLACE--probably Sussex, England.
       DATE--possibly created 16th-18th century?
       VARIANT VERNACULAR TITLES--KING PHARAOH; KING PHARIM.
       DIFFERING FIRST LINES--KING PHAROAH SAT AMUSING;
                  KING PHARAOH SAT AMUSING;
                  KING PHARIM SAT A-MUSING.
  Music: COMPOSER--folk.
       PLACE--probably Sussex, England.
       DATE--possibly created 16th-18th century?
  Found: OBE, BRO
  Notes: This appears to be a product of the Gypsy community;
       the tune is also used for the carol THE MIRACULOUS
       HARVEST (Sussex tune).

485. THE MIRACULOUS HARVEST

  Lyrics: AUTHOR--folk.
       PLACE--England.
       DATE--possibly created 16th-18th century?
       DIFFERING FIRST LINE--RISE UP, RISE UP, YOU MERRY
                  MEN ALL.
  Music: COMPOSER--folk.
       PLACE--probably Sussex, England.
       DATE--possibly created 16th-18th century?
  Found: OXF
  Notes: The lyrics and tune are different from those for the
       other carol with this name; the tune appears to be a
       product of the Gypsy community; the tune is also used
       for the carol THE MIRACLE OF THE COCK.

486.   THE MIRACULOUS HARVEST

    Lyrics: AUTHOR--folk.
                PLACE--probably Herefordshire, England.
                DATE--possibly created 15th-17th century?
                VARIANT VERNACULAR TITLE--THE CARNAL AND THE CRANE.
                DIFFERING FIRST LINE--THERE WAS A STAR ALL IN THE
                                              EAST.
    Music: COMPOSER--folk.
                PLACE--England.
                DATE--probably created 15th or 16th century.
    Found: LEA
    Notes: The lyrics are different from those for the other
                carols named THE MIRACULOUS HARVEST and THE CARNAL
                AND THE CRANE; the tune is different from the melody
                used for the other carol named THE MIRACULOUS HARVEST,
                but is the same as the melody used for the other
                carol named THE CARNAL AND THE CRANE.

487.   MISTER SANTA

    Lyrics: AUTHOR--Francis Drake Ballard (1899-1960).
                PLACE--United States.
                DATE--published 1955.
                DIFFERING FIRST LINE--MISTER SANTA, BRING ME SOME
                                              TOYS.
    Music: COMPOSER--Francis Drake Ballard (1899-1960).
                PLACE--United States.
                DATE--published 1954.
    Found: NOR, SEV
    Notes: The lyrics are a parody of the song MISTER SANDMAN
                (1954), with the same tune used for both songs.

488.   MISTLETOE AND HOLLY

    Lyrics: AUTHOR--Frank Sinatra (1915-   ), Dok Stanford, and
                            Henry W. Sanicola (1914-1974).
                PLACE--United States.
                DATE--published 1957.
                DIFFERING FIRST LINE--OH BY GOSH, BY GOLLY.
    Music: COMPOSER--Frank Sinatra (1915-   ), Dok Stanford,
                            and Henry W. Sanicola (1914-1974).
                PLACE--United States.
                DATE--published 1957.
    Found: POP

489.   MIT DESEN NIEWEN JARE

    Lyrics: AUTHOR--folk.
                PLACE--Netherlands.
                DATE--created 15th century.

ENGLISH TITLE--A YEAR BEGINS OF JOY AND GRACE (trans-
lated by John O'Connor [1870-1952]).
Music: COMPOSER--folk.
PLACE--Netherlands.
DATE--created 15th century.
Found: THF, BRU

490. MIZERNA CICHA

Lyrics: AUTHOR--folk.
PLACE--Poland.
DATE--possibly created 15th-17th century?
ENGLISH TITLE--ONLY A MANGER BED (translated by
George K. Evans).
DIFFERING FIRST LINES--MIZERNA, CICHA, STAJENKA
LICHA; ONLY A MANGER BED FOR
THE STRANGER.
Music: COMPOSER--folk.
PLACE--Poland.
DATE--possibly created 15th-17th century?
Found: INT

491. THE MOON SHINES BRIGHT

Lyrics: AUTHOR--folk.
PLACE--England.
DATE--possibly created 16th-18th century?
VARIANT VERNACULAR TITLES--THE BELLMAN'S SONG; THE
WAITS; THE WAITS' SONG;
WAITS CAROL; THE MOON
SHONE BRIGHT.
DIFFERING FIRST LINES--THE MOON SHINES BRIGHT AND THE
STARS GIVE A LIGHT; THE MOON
SHONE BRIGHT AND THE STARS GAVE
LIGHT; OH, THE MOON SHINES
BRIGHT, AND THE STARS GIVE A
LIGHT.
Music: COMPOSER--folk.
PLACE--England (possibly Lancashire).
DATE--possibly created 16th-18th century?
VARIANT TUNES--three other English folk tunes, two
possibly from Surrey, one possibly from
Hampshire.
Found: OXF, NOB, BRO, THF, REE

492. THE MOST WONDERFUL DAY OF THE YEAR

Lyrics: AUTHOR--John D. Marks (1909-   ).
PLACE--United States.
DATE--published 1964.
DIFFERING FIRST LINES--WE'RE ON THE ISLAND OF MISFIT
TOYS; A PACKFUL OF TOYS MEANS A
SACKFUL OF JOYS.

Music: COMPOSER--John D. Marks (1909-   ).
           PLACE--United States.
           DATE--published 1964.
Found: ULT, ONS, ONT

493. MUST BE SANTA

Lyrics: AUTHOR--Hal Moore and William Arthur Fredricks
                   (1924-   ).
           PLACE--United States.
           DATE--published 1960.
           DIFFERING FIRST LINE--WHO'S GOT A BEARD THAT'S LONG
                                 AND WHITE?
Music: COMPOSER--Hal Moore and William Arthur Fredricks
                   (1924-   ).
           PLACE--United States.
           DATE--published 1960.
Found: ULT

494. MY LORD, WHAT A MORNING!

Lyrics: AUTHOR--folk (Black spiritual).
           PLACE--United States.
           DATE--probably created 18th or 19th century.
Music: COMPOSER--folk (Black spiritual).
           PLACE--United States.
           DATE--probably created 18th or 19th century.
Found: LAN

495. NÄR JULDAGSMORGON GLIMMAR

Lyrics: AUTHOR--folk.
           PLACE--Sweden.
           DATE--possibly created 17th-19th century?
           ENGLISH TITLES--WHEN CHRISTMAS MORN IS DAWNING
                           (translated by George K. Evans);
                           I TURN INTO A STABLE (translated by
                           Noel Wirén).
Music: COMPOSER--folk.
           PLACE--Germany.
           DATE--probably created 18th or 19th century.
Found: INT, SWE, GLA, JUL

496. NARODIL SE KRISTUS PÁN

Lyrics: AUTHOR--folk.
           PLACE--Bohemia, Czechoslovakia.
           DATE--possibly created 14th-16th century?
           ENGLISH TITLES--LET OUR GLADNESS KNOW NO END; BE YE
                           JOYFUL, EARTH AND SKY (translated by
                           H. Brueckner); CHRIST THE LORD IS
                           BORN (translated by Mary Cochrane
                           Vojácek).

                    DIFFERING·FIRST LINE--CHRIST THE LORD IS BORN TODAY.
      Music: COMPOSER--folk.
                    PLACE--Bohemia, Czechoslovakia.
                    DATE--possibly created 14th-16th century?
      Found: ZPE, OBE, HEL, CAW, SCC

497. NATIVITY CAROL

      Lyrics: AUTHOR--John Rutter.
                    PLACE--England.
                    DATE--published 1967.
                    DIFFERING FIRST LINE--BORN IN A STABLE SO BARE.
      Music: COMPOSER--John Rutter.
                    PLACE--England.
                    DATE--published 1967.
      Found: CCT, CCF

498. NESEM VÁM NOVINY

      Lyrics: AUTHOR--folk.
                    PLACE--Czechoslovakia.
                    DATE--probably created 17th or 18th century.
                    ENGLISH TITLES--ANGELS AND SHEPHERDS (translated by
                                    Ruth Heller [1920-   ]); THE ANGELS
                                    AND THE SHEPHERDS (two different
                                    translations by Helena Adell Dickinson
                                    (1875-   ) and Lulu Ganschow); COME,
                                    HEAR THE WONDERFUL TIDINGS (translated
                                    by George K. Evans); COME ALL YE
                                    SHEPHERDS; FROM BETHL'EM'S CITY
                                    (translated by Mary Cochrane Vojácek);
                                    HEAR WHAT GREAT NEWS WE BRING (trans-
                                    lated by Olga Paul).
                    DIFFERING FIRST LINES--NESEM VAM NOVINY POSLOUCHEJTE;
                                    SHEPHERDS, O HARK YE; COME ALL
                                    YE SHEPHERDS AND HARK TO OUR
                                    SONG!; SHEPHERDS OF JUDAH
                                    THEIR FLOCKS WATCHED BY NIGHT;
                                    COME, HEAR THE WONDERFUL
                                    TIDINGS WE BRING; FROM BETHL'EM'S
                                    CITY GLAD TIDINGS WE BRING.
      Music: COMPOSER--folk.
                    PLACE--Czechoslovakia.
                    DATE--probably created 17th or 18th century.
      Found: INT, CCT, OBE, TRA, SCC
      Notes: For a German version of this carol, see KOMMET, IHR
                    HIRTEN; the tune is also used for the carol COLD IS
                    THE MORNING; this is perhaps the best-known Czech
                    carol.

499. NESTOR, THE LONG-EARED CHRISTMAS DONKEY

    Lyrics: AUTHOR--Gene Autry (1907-   ), Don Pfrimmer, and
                   Dave Burgess.
            PLACE--United States.
            DATE--published 1975.
            DIFFERING FIRST LINE--NESTOR WAS A DONKEY WHO SELDOM
                        LAUGHED OR PLAYED.
    Music: COMPOSER--Gene Autry (1907-   ), Don Pfrimmer, and
                   Dave Burgess.
            PLACE--United States.
            DATE--published 1975.
    Found: HAP

500. THE NEW-BORN BABY

    Lyrics: AUTHOR--folk (Black spiritual).
            PLACE--United States (possibly South Carolina).
            DATE--probably created 18th or 19th century.
            VARIANT VERNACULAR TITLE--DE NEW-BORN BABY.
            DIFFERING FIRST LINE--BABY BORN IN BETHLEHEM.
    Music: COMPOSER--folk (Black spiritual).
            PLACE--United States (possibly South Carolina).
            DATE--probably created 18th or 19th century.
    Found: OBE, SEE

501. NINNA NANNA

    Lyrics: AUTHOR--folk.
            PLACE--Naples region, Italy.
            DATE--possibly created 16th or 17th century.
            ENGLISH TITLE--SLEEP MY DARLING (translated by John
                      O'Connor [1870-1952]).
    Music: COMPOSER--folk.
            PLACE--Naples region, Italy.
            DATE--possibly created 16th or 17th century.
    Found: THF, ICC

502. NIT DE VETLLA

    Lyrics: AUTHOR--folk.
            PLACE--Catalonia, Spain.
             DATE--possibly created 15th-17th century?
            DIFFERING FIRST LINE--ESTA NIT ES NIT DE VETLLA.
    Music: COMPOSER--folk.
            PLACE--Catalonia, Spain.
            DATE--possibly created 15th-17th century?
            VARIANT TUNE--tune by Joaquín Nin y Castellanos
                      (1879-1949), composer from Cuba.
    Found: MON, MOO, NIN

503. NO HAY TAL ANDAR

Lyrics: AUTHOR--folk.
            PLACE--Asturias, Spain.
            DATE--possibly created 17th-19th century?
            DIFFERING FIRST LINE--NO HAY TAL ANDAR COMO ANDAR A
                                 LA UNA.
Music: COMPOSER--folk.
            PLACE--Asturias, Spain.
            DATE--possibly created 17th-19th century?
            VARIANT TUNE--tune by Joaquín Nin y Castellanos
                         (1879-1949), composer from Cuba.
Found: MON, MOO, CAN, NIN

504. NO ROOM IN THE INN

Lyrics: AUTHOR--folk.
            PLACE--England.
            DATE--possibly created 17th or 18th century.
            DIFFERING FIRST LINE--WHEN CAESAR AUGUSTUS HAD RAISED
                                 A TAXATION.
Music: COMPOSER--folk.
            PLACE--England.
            DATE--possibly created 17th or 18th century.
Found: SIM, OXF, SAN, SEA
Notes: Both words and tune were probably first printed in
            William Sandys' CHRISTMAS CAROLS (1833), but were not
            joined in that publication; Martin Shaw (1875-1958)
            was the person responsible for the union of lyrics
            and melody and the publication of the carol in 1928.

505. NOBIS EST NATUS

Lyrics: AUTHOR--anonymous.
            PLACE--probably Germany or Poland.
            DATE--created medieval period.
            VARIANT VERNACULAR TITLE--NOBIS EST NATUS HODIE.
            ENGLISH TITLE--THIS HAPPY MORN (translated by John
                          O'Connor [1870-1952]).
            DIFFERING FIRST LINE--THIS HAPPY MORN, TODAY IS BORN.
Music: COMPOSER--anonymous.
            PLACE--probably Germany or Poland.
            DATE--created medieval period.
Found: THF, KOL

506. NOËL DES AUSELS

Lyrics: AUTHOR--folk.
            PLACE--Basses-Pyrénées, France.
            DATE--probably created 16th century.
            VARIANT VERNACULAR TITLE--NOUÈL DES AUSÈLS.

ENGLISH TITLES--CAROL OF THE BIRDS; WHENCE COMES THIS
                    RUSH OF WINGS; WHENCE COMES THIS RUSH
                    OF WINGS AFAR.
DIFFERING FIRST LINE--AICI L'ESTELO DE NADAL.
Music: COMPOSER--folk.
        PLACE--Basses-Pyrénées, France.
        DATE--probably created 16th century.
        VARIANT TUNE--tune by Dorothy Freed.
Found: INT, SIM, OBE, REF, PRE

507. NOËL! NOËL!

Lyrics: AUTHOR--folk.
         PLACE--England (possibly London).
         DATE--possibly created 16th-18th century?
         DIFFERING FIRST LINE--'TIS THE DAY, THE BLESSED DAY.
Music: COMPOSER--folk.
        PLACE--England (possibly London).
        DATE--possibly created 16th-18th century?
Found: OBE, PRE, YOU, STA

508. NOËL NOUVELET

Lyrics: AUTHOR--folk.
         PLACE--probably Provence, France.
         DATE--probably created 17th or 18th century.
         ENGLISH TITLES--CHRISTMAS COMES ANEW (translated by
                    George K. Evans); NOWELL, SING NOWELL
                    (translated by John Rutter); NOEL!
                    A NEW NOEL! (translated by K.W.
                    Simpson); NOEL, NOEL, NOEL (the same
                    translation as the previous one, but
                    altered by Gordon Hitchcock); SING WE
                    NOW OF CHRISTMAS.
Music: COMPOSER--folk.
        PLACE--probably Provence, France.
        DATE--probably created 17th or 18th century.
Found: INT, CCT, THF, UNI, OXF
Notes: Marcel Dupré (1886-1971) based his organ composition,
        VARIATIONS SUR UN VIEUX NOËL, on this carol.

509. NOEL-TIME

Lyrics: AUTHOR--John Wheeler.
         PLACE--Australia.
         DATE--published 1954.
         DIFFERING FIRST LINE--NOW ONCE AGAIN IT'S NOEL-TIME.
Music: COMPOSER--William Garnet James (1895-   ).
        PLACE--Australia.
        DATE--published 1954.
Found: REF

510. NOIÉ, NOIÉ EST VENU

    Lyrics: AUTHOR--Jacques Charles Brossard de Montaney (1638-
             1702).
          PLACE--probably Bresse region, France.
          DATE--probably written late 17th century.
          ENGLISH TITLE--NOW HAS CHRISTMAS COME AGAIN (trans-
             lated by W.B. Lindsay and Ruth Heller
             [1920-   ]).
    Music: COMPOSER--folk.
          PLACE--probably Bresse region, France.
          DATE--possibly created 16th-18th century?
    Found: HEL, TIE

511. NOS GALAN

    Lyrics: AUTHOR--K.E. Roberts.
          PLACE--probably Wales.
          DATE--probably written early 20th century.
          DIFFERING FIRST LINE--NOW THE JOYFUL BELLS ARINGING.
    Music: COMPOSER--folk.
          PLACE--Wales.
          DATE--possibly created 16th century.
    Found: OXF
    Notes: The lyrics are a paraphrase of a secular Welsh New
          Year's Eve carol of the same name; the tune is also
          used for the carol DECK THE HALLS WITH BOUGHS OF
          HOLLY.

512. NOS RESPECTU GRACIE

    Lyrics: AUTHOR--anonymous.
          PLACE--probably Germany.
          DATE--probably created 12th century.
          ENGLISH TITLE--TOUCHING GRACE, WE PRINCES THREE
             (translated by George Ratcliffe
             Woodward [1848-1934]).
    Music: COMPOSER--folk.
          PLACE--Bohemia, Czechoslovakia.
          DATE--possibly created 15th or 16th century; possibly
             first published 1566.
    Found: COF, OBE, HUT

513. NOUS ALLONS, MA MIE

    Lyrics: AUTHOR--folk.
          PLACE--France.
          DATE--possibly created 16th-18th century?
          ENGLISH TITLE--COME WITH HEARTS AFIRE (translated by
             K.W. Simpson).
    Music: COMPOSER--folk.
          PLACE--France.
          DATE--possibly created 16th-18th century?
    Found: OXF, THF, UNI

514. NOUS VOICI DANS LA VILLE

   Lyrics: AUTHOR--folk.
             PLACE--France.
             DATE--possibly created 15th century; possibly first
                   published 1766.
             ENGLISH TITLES--IN THE TOWN (paraphrase by Eleanor
                              Farjeon [1881-   ]); THE INN (trans-
                              lated by Edward Bliss Reed [1872-
                              1940]).
             DIFFERING FIRST LINES--TAKE HEART, THE JOURNEY'S
                                    ENDED; AT LAST WE'VE REACHED
                                    THE CITY.
   Music: COMPOSER--folk.
             PLACE--France.
             DATE--probably created 15th century.
   Found: OXF, SIM, SMI, COE
   Notes: The tune is also used for the carols A DAY, A DAY OF
             GLORY!, CÉLÉBRONS LA NAISSANCE, ADAM E SA COUMPAGNO,
             and CHANTONS! JE VOUS EN PRIE.

515. NOW MAKE WE MERTHE

   Lyrics: AUTHOR--folk.
             PLACE--England.
             DATE--created 15th century.
             VARIANT VERNACULAR TITLES--NOW MAKE WE MIRTHË; MAKE WE
                                        MIRTH.
             DIFFERING FIRST LINES--NOW MAKE WE MERTHÈ ALL AND
                                    SOME; NOW MAKE WE MIRTHË ALL
                                    AND SOME; NOW MAKE WE MIRTH,
                                    ALL AND SOME; NOW GOD ALMIGHTY
                                    DOWN HATH SENT.
   Music: COMPOSER--folk.
             PLACE--England.
             DATE--created 15th century.
             VARIANT TUNE--another 15th century English folk tune.
   Found: MEC, MED, THF, EAR

516. NOW MAY WE SINGEN AS IT IS

   Lyrics: AUTHOR--folk.
             PLACE--England.
             DATE--created 15th century.
             VARIANT VERNACULAR TITLE--NOW MAY WE SINGEN.
             DIFFERING FIRST LINE--THE BABE TO US THAT NOW IS BORE.
   Music: COMPOSER--folk.
             PLACE--England.
             DATE--created 15th century.
             VARIANT TUNE--another 15th century English tune.
   Found: MEC, MED, THF

517. NOW WELL MAY WE MERTHIS MAKE

Lyrics: AUTHOR--folk.
PLACE--England.
DATE--created 15th century.
VARIANT VERNACULAR TITLES--NOW WELL MAY WE MIRTH
MAKE; ALLELUIA: NOW WELL
MAY WE MIRTHES MAKE;
ALLELUIA: NOW MAY WE
MIRTHËS MAKE.
DIFFERING FIRST LINES--ALLELUIA, ALLELUIA; NOW WELL
MAY WE MIRTHËS MAKE; NOW MAY
WE MIRTHËS MAKE.
Music: COMPOSER--folk.
PLACE--England.
DATE--created 15th century.
VARIANT TUNES--two other 15th century English folk
tunes.
Found: MEC, MED, THF, EAR

518. NOWELL, NOWELL: IN BETHLEM

Lyrics: AUTHOR--folk.
PLACE--England.
DATE--created 15th century.
VARIANT VERNACULAR TITLES--NOWEL. TO US IS BORN;
NOWEL. TO US IS BORN OUR
GOD EMANUEL.
DIFFERING FIRST LINES--NOWELL, NOWELL, NOWELL!;
NOWELL, NOWELL; NOWEL, NOWEL;
NOWEL, NOWEL, NOWEL.
Music: COMPOSER--folk.
PLACE--England.
DATE--created 15th century.
VARIANT TUNE--another 15th century English folk tune.
Found: MED, MED, THF
Notes: This carol has two main variations, both having very
similar lyrics and almost identical refrains, but
with differing first lines for the first verse; one
first verse begins "In Bethlem this bird of life"
(variation, "In Bedlem this berd of life"), and the
other begins "In Bethlem that child of life"
(variation, "In Bedlem that child of life").

519. NU ÄR DET JUL IGEN

Lyrics: AUTHOR--folk.
PLACE--Sweden.
DATE--possibly created 16th-18th century?
ENGLISH TITLES--CHRISTMAS IS HERE AGAIN (translated
by Noel Wirén); CHRISTMAS HAS COME
AGAIN! (translated by Linnea Hallen-
berg and Ruth Heller [1920-   ]);

YULETIDE IS HERE AGAIN (translated by
George K. Evans); NOW IT IS CHRIST-
MASTIME (translated by Henry William
Simon [1901-   ]); DANCE CAROL.

Music: COMPOSER--folk.
            PLACE--Sweden.
            DATE--possibly created 16th-18th century?
Found: INT, SIM, TRA, SWE, JUL
Notes: The Hambo, a very popular Swedish folk dance, is
            danced to the tune around the Christmas tree; this is
            perhaps the best-known Swedish carol.

520. NU SIJT WILLEKOME, JESU LIEVEN HEER

Lyrics: AUTHOR--folk.
            PLACE--Netherlands.
            DATE--probably created 15th or 16th century.
            VARIANT VERNACULAR TITLES--NU SIJT WILLEKOME; NU
                                      SIJT WILLECOME.
            ENGLISH TITLES--NOW BE VERY WELCOME (translated by
                            Marguerite Vogels-Reiners); WELCOME,
                            CHILD OF MARY (translated by
                            Elizabeth Poston [1905-   ]);
                            WELCOME, SON OF MARY (translated by
                            John O'Connor [1870-1952]).
Music: COMPOSER--folk.
            PLACE--Netherlands.
            DATE--probably created 15th or 16th century.
Found: PEN, THF, BRU, PEE

521. NU TÄNDAS TUSEN JULELJUS

Lyrics: AUTHOR--probably Emmy Köhler.
            PLACE--Sweden.
            DATE--probably written 19th or early 20th century.
            ENGLISH TITLES--NOW LIGHT ONE THOUSAND CHRISTMAS
                            LIGHTS; A THOUSAND CHRISTMAS CANDLES
                            NOW (translated by Noel Wirén); NOW
                            SHINE A THOUSAND CANDLES BRIGHT
                            (translated by J. Irving Erickson and
                            Karl A. Olsson).
Music: COMPOSER--Emmy Köhler.
            PLACE--Sweden.
            DATE--probably written 19th or early 20th century.
Found: SHE, JUL, SWE, PRA

522. NUNC ANGELORUM GLORIA

Lyrics: AUTHOR--anonymous.
            PLACE--Europe.
            DATE--probably created medieval period.

	ENGLISH TITLE--TODAY THE LIGHT OF ANGELS BRIGHT.
Music:	COMPOSER--anonymous.
	PLACE--Europe.
	DATE--probably created medieval period.
Found:	KOL, COF

523. NUTTIN' FOR CHRISTMAS

    Lyrics: AUTHOR--Sid Tepper (1918-   ) and Roy C. Bennett
                    (1918-).
                  PLACE--United States.
                  DATE--published 1955.
                  DIFFERING FIRST LINE--I BROKE MY BAT ON JOHNNY'S
                                      HEAD.
    Music: COMPOSER--Sid Tepper (1918-   ) and Roy C. Bennett
                    (1918-).
                  PLACE--United States.
                  DATE--published 1955.
    Found: ULT, ONS, ONT

524. O BIENHEUREUSE NUIT

    Lyrics: AUTHOR--folk.
                  PLACE--Normandy, France.
                  DATE--possibly created 15th-17th century?
                  ENGLISH TITLES--O NIGHT, PEACEFUL AND BLEST!; O
                                    NIGHT, RESTFUL AND DEEP (translated
                                    by K.W. Simpson).
    Music: COMPOSER--folk.
                  PLACE--Normandy, France.
                  DATE--possibly created 15th-17th century?
    Found: THF, OBE, HUT

525. O DEUED POB CRISTION

    Lyrics: AUTHOR--folk.
                  PLACE--Wales.
                  DATE--possibly created 15th-17th century?
                  ENGLISH TITLES--POVERTY and ALL POOR MEN AND HUMBLE
                                    (two titles for the same translation
                                    by K.E. Roberts); O COME, ALL YE
                                    CHRISTIANS (translated by Marx E.
                                    Oberndorfer [1876-   ]).
    Music: COMPOSER--folk.
                  PLACE--Wales.
                  DATE--possibly created 15th-17th century?
                  VARIANT TUNE--tune by John La Montaine (1920-).
    Found: OXF, OBE, WON

526. O DU FRÖHLICHE

    Lyrics: AUTHOR--Johannes Daniel Falk (1768-1826).

PLACE--Germany.
DATE--published 1816.
ENGLISH TITLES--O YE JOYFUL PEOPLE (translated by
                    Ruth Heller [1920-   ]); O HOW
                    JOYFULLY (translated by George K.
                    Evans); OH, HOW JOYFULLY; O THOU
                    JOYFUL, O THOU WONDERFUL (translated
                    by Henry Katterjohn).
DIFFERING FIRST LINE--O YE JOYFUL ONES.

Music: COMPOSER--anonymous.
            PLACE--possibly Sicily, Italy.
            DATE--probably written second half of 18th century;
                possibly first published 1794.

Found: INT, PRE, PRA, ROT, WOR
Notes: The lyrics originally were an anonymous 16th century
            Latin hymn of praise to the Virgin Mary, O
            SANCTISSIMA; the original words have undergone many
            translations and alterations, including this derived
            German carol and its English translations; four
            English language Christmas songs, O THOU JOYFUL DAY
            and O SANCTISSIMA (three United States versions) were
            derived directly from the Latin; the tune for all six
            songs is known as SICILIAN MARINERS, but no direct
            connection with Italy has been found.

527. O GWIAZDO BETLEJEMSKA

Lyrics: AUTHOR--folk.
            PLACE--Poland.
            DATE--possibly created 15th-17th century?
            ENGLISH TITLE--O STAR O'ER BETHLEHEM SHINING (trans-
                            lated by George K. Evans).
Music: COMPOSER--folk.
            PLACE--Poland.
            DATE--possibly created 15th-17th century?
Found: INT

528. O HEARKEN YE

Lyrics: AUTHOR--Wihla Hutson.
            PLACE--United States.
            DATE--published 1954.
            DIFFERING FIRST LINE--O HEARKEN YE WHO WOULD BELIEVE.
Music: COMPOSER--Alfred Burt (1919 or 1920-1954).
            PLACE--United States.
            DATE--published 1954.
Found: BUR

529. O HEILAND, REISS DIE HIMMEL AUF

Lyrics: AUTHOR--anonymous.
            PLACE--Germany.
            DATE--probably created 16th or early 17th century;
                possibly first published 1623.

ENGLISH TITLE--O SAVIOR, REND THE HEAVENS WIDE
(translated by Martin L. Seltz [1909-
1967]).
Music: COMPOSER--anonymous.
PLACE--Europe.
DATE--probably created medieval period.
VARIANT TUNE--1666 German tune.
Found: BUD, SIG
Notes: The main tune is also used for the carol CONDITOR
ALME SIDERUM.

530. O HEILIG KIND

Lyrics: AUTHOR--folk.
PLACE--Austria.
DATE--possibly created around 1800.
ENGLISH TITLE--WE GREET THEE, HEAVENLY DOVE.
DIFFERING FIRST LINE--WE GREET THEE, BLESSED
HEAVENLY DOVE.
Music: COMPOSER--folk.
PLACE--Austria.
DATE--possibly created around 1800.
Found: CCM, NHW

531. O JESULEIN SÜSS

Lyrics: AUTHOR--Samuel Scheidt (1587-1654).
PLACE--Germany.
DATE--published 1650.
ENGLISH TITLES--O LITTLE ONE and O LITTLE ONE SWEET
(two titles for the same translation
by Percy Dearmer [1867-1936]); O JESU,
SWEET CHILD (translated by Elizabeth
Poston [1905-   ]); O JESUS, SWEET
CHILD.
Music: COMPOSER--Samuel Scheidt (1587-1654).
PLACE--Germany.
DATE--published 1650.
Found: OXF, UNI, NOB, YAL, PEN

532. O JUL MED DIN GLEDE

Lyrics: AUTHOR--Gustava Kielland.
PLACE--Norway.
DATE--probably written late 19th or early 20th century.
VARIANT VERNACULAR TITLE--O JUL MED DIN GLAEDE.
ENGLISH TITLES--CHRISTMAS, O HAPPIEST DAY! (trans-
lated by Ella K. Nesvig and Ruth
Heller [1920-   ]); O CHRISTMAS, YOU
SEASON OF CHILDLIKE DELIGHT (trans-
lated by George K. Evans).

                                     DIFFERING FIRST LINES--O JUL MED DIN GLEDE OG BARN-
                                                 LIGE LYST; O CHRISTMAS, O
                                                 CHRISTMAS, O HAPPIEST DAY!
          Music: COMPOSER--folk.
                        PLACE--Norway.
                        DATE--possibly created 18th or 19th century?
          Found: INT, HEL

533.   O KIND, O WAHRER GOTTES SOHN!

          Lyrics: AUTHOR--folk.
                        PLACE--probably Switzerland.
                        DATE--probably created 16th or early 17th century;
                              possibly first published 1625.
                        VARIANT VERNACULAR TITLE--O KIND, O WAHRER GOTTESSOHN.
                        ENGLISH TITLES--CHILD UPON THE HAY (translated by
                                        Alfred Raymond Bellinger [1893-
                                               ]); HAIL! BABE, OF GOD THE VERY
                                               SON (translated by George Ratcliffe
                                               Woodward [1848-1934]).
                        DIFFERING FIRST LINE--O CHILD THAT ART GOD'S ONLY
                                               SON!
          Music: COMPOSER--folk.
                        PLACE--probably Germany.
                        DATE--probably created 16th or early 17th century;
                              possibly first published 1623.

                        VARIANT TUNE--tune by Arnold Mendelssohn (1855-1933).
          Found: BUD, CST, COF

534.   O LAUFET, IHR HIRTEN

          Lyrics: AUTHOR--folk.
                        PLACE--Silesia, Germany.
                        DATE--possibly created 17th-19th century; possibly
                              first published 1842.
                        VARIANT VERNACULAR TITLE--LAUFET, IHR HIRTEN, LAUFT
                                                ALLE ZUGLEICH!
                        ENGLISH TITLE--COME RUNNING, YOU SHEPHERDS (trans-
                                       lated by George K. Evans).
          Music: COMPOSER--folk.
                        PLACE--Silesia or Glatz region, Germany.
                        DATE--possibly created 17th-19th century?
          Found: INT, WOR, BUD, HFW

535.   O LITTLE TOWN OF BETHLEHEM

          Lyrics: AUTHOR--Phillips Brooks (1835-1893).
                        PLACE--Philadelphia, Pennsylvania.
                        DATE--written December 1868.
          Music: COMPOSER--Lewis Henry Redner (1831-1908).
                        PLACE--Philadelphia, Pennsylvania.
                        DATE--written December 27, 1868.

VARIANT TUNES--PLOUGHBOY'S DREAM (also called
                FOREST GREEN), an English folk song;
                CHRISTMAS CAROL, by Henry Walford
                Davies (1869-1941); a tune by Joseph
                Barnby (1838-1896); others.

Found: MANY
Notes: The song was originally intended for children; the
           carol was probably first published in 1874; it is
           probably the best-known American carol.

536. O LOVELY VOICES OF THE SKY

Lyrics: AUTHOR--Felicia Dorothea Hemans (1793-1835).
          PLACE--England or Wales.
          DATE--published 1827.
          VARIANT VERNACULAR TITLE--O LOVELY VOICES.
Music: COMPOSER--folk.
          PLACE--probably England.
          DATE--possibly created 16th-18th century?
          VARIANT TUNE--tune by Oliver A. King (1855-1923).
Found: CHO, HUT, ECS

537. O MEN FROM THE FIELDS!

Lyrics: AUTHOR--Padraic Colum (1881-1972).
          PLACE--Ireland.
          DATE--probably written first half of 20th century.
Music: COMPOSER--Arnold Cooke (1906-   ).
          PLACE--England.
          DATE--published 1961.
Found: CCO

538. O MORTAL MAN, REMEMBER WELL

Lyrics: AUTHOR--folk.
          PLACE--probably Sussex, England.
          DATE--possibly created 17th-19th century?
          VARIANT VERNACULAR TITLES--SUSSEX MUMMERS' CAROL;
                              THE SUSSEX MUMMERS'
                              CHRISTMAS CAROL.
          DIFFERING FIRST LINE--WHEN RIGHTEOUS JOSEPH WEDDED
                           WAS.
Music: COMPOSER--folk.
          PLACE--probably Sussex, England.
          DATE--possibly created 17th-19th century?
Found: OXF, REE, BRO, UNI
Notes: The first verse of one version of this carol's
           lyrics is similar to the first verse of the carol
           WHEN RIGHTEOUS JOSEPH WEDDED WAS, but otherwise they
           are unrelated.

539. O PO' LITTLE JESUS

> *Lyrics:* AUTHOR--folk (Black spiritual).
>   PLACE--United States.
>   DATE--probably created 18th or 19th century.
> *Music:*   COMPOSER--folk (Black spiritual).
>   PLACE--United States.
>   DATE--probably created 18th or 19th century.
> *Found:*   INT
> *Notes:*   This is very different from another spiritual of
>   similar title, POOR LITTLE JESUS.

540. O SANCTISSIMA

> *Lyrics:* AUTHOR--anonymous.
>   PLACE--Europe.
>   DATE--created 16th century.
> *Music:*   COMPOSER--anonymous.
>   PLACE--possibly Sicily, Italy.
>   DATE--probably written second half of 18th century;
>   possibly first published 1794.
> *Found:*   SIM, CCM
> *Notes:*   This is actually not a Christmas carol, but is
>   included in carol collections because five carols
>   (O DU FRÖHLICHE, O THOU JOYFUL DAY, and O SANCTISSIMA
>   [three United States versions]) were derived from it;
>   see their notes for more information.

541. O SANCTISSIMA

> *Lyrics:* AUTHOR--anonymous.
>   PLACE--United States.
>   DATE--written 20th century.
>   DIFFERING FIRST LINE--DAY OF HOLINESS, PEACE AND
>   HAPPINESS.
> *Music:*   COMPOSER--anonymous.
>   PLACE--possibly Sicily, Italy.
>   DATE--probably written second half of 18th century;
>   possibly first published 1794.
> *Found:*   ULT
> *Notes:*   The lyrics are a derivative of the Latin carol of the
>   same name; see the notes for a similar derived carol,
>   O THOU JOYFUL DAY, for more information.

542. O SANCTISSIMA

> *Lyrics:* AUTHOR--anonymous.
>   PLACE--United States.
>   DATE--probably written early 20th century.
>   DIFFERING FIRST LINE--O THOU HOLY DAY, O THOU JOYOUS
>   DAY.
> *Music:*   COMPOSER--anonymous.

PLACE--possibly Sicily, Italy.
DATE--probably written second half of 18th century;
    possibly first published 1794.
Found: OBE
Notes: The lyrics are a derivative of the Latin carol of the
same name; see the notes for a similar derived carol,
O THOU JOYFUL DAY, for more information.

543. O SANCTISSIMA

Lyrics: AUTHOR--William Glass.
PLACE--United States.
DATE--probably written early 20th century.
DIFFERING FIRST LINE--O, THOU BEAUTIFUL, O, THOU
                     WONDERFUL.
Music: COMPOSER--anonymous.
PLACE--possibly Sicily, Italy.
DATE--probably written second half of 18th century;
    possibly first published 1794.
Found: CHT
Notes: The lyrics are a derivation of the Latin carol of the
same name; see the notes for a similar derived carol,
O THOU JOYFUL DAY, for more information.

544. O SOLA MAGNARUM URBIUM

Lyrics: AUTHOR--Aurelius Clemens Prudentius (348-ca. 413).
PLACE--Spain.
DATE--probably written early 5th century; introduced
    into the Roman Catholic breviary in 1568.
ENGLISH TITLES--EARTH HAS MANY A NOBLE CITY and
                BETHLEHEM, MOST NOBLE CITY (two
                variations of the same translation by
                Edward Caswall [1814-1878]).
Music: COMPOSER--probably Christian Friedrich Witt (1660-
           1716).
PLACE--Germany.
DATE--published 1715.
Found: ENG, CAT, MET, LUT
Notes: Prudentius' lyrics were part of his poem LIBER
CATHEMERINON; Caswall's translation (1849) originally
began "Bethlehem, of noblest cities", but was altered
to "Earth has many a noble city" in an 1861
collection; Witt was one of the editors of the
collection PSALMODIA SACRA, in which the tune first
appeared, and probably composed or arranged the
melody; the tune is also used for the carol COME, THOU
LONG-EXPECTED JESUS.

545. O TANNENBAUM

Lyrics: AUTHOR--verse 1, folk; verses 2-3, Ernest Gebhard
        Anschütz (1800-1861).

PLACE--Germany (verse 1, possibly Westphalia).
DATE--verse 1, possibly created 16th or 17th century;
        verses 2-3, written 19th century.
VARIANT VERNACULAR TITLE--O TANNENBAUM, O TANNENBAUM.
ENGLISH TITLES--O CHRISTMAS TREE (translations by
                George K. Evans and others); OH
                CHRISTMAS TREE; THE CHRISTMAS TREE
                (translated by Henry William Simon
                [1901-   ]); O TANNENBAUM; O
                CHRISTMAS PINE (translated by Frank
                Foster); OH TREE OF FIR.
DIFFERING FIRST LINE--WE STAND BEFORE THE CHRISTMAS
                                TREE.

Music: COMPOSER--folk.
             PLACE--Germany (possibly Westphalia).
             DATE--possibly created 16th or 17th century.
Found: MANY
Notes: The tune is also used for the song MARYLAND, MY
             MARYLAND; this carol is perhaps the best-known carol
             from Germany.

546.   O THE MORN, THE MERRY, MERRY MORN

Lyrics: AUTHOR--George Ratcliffe Woodward (1848-1934).
             PLACE--England.
             DATE--written late 19th or early 20th century.
Music: COMPOSER--folk.
             PLACE--England.
             DATE--probably created 16th or 17th century.
Found: UNI, CCB
Notes: The tune is the melody O THE BROOM, THE BONNY BONNY
             BROOM.

547.   O THOU JOYFUL DAY

Lyrics: AUTHOR--anonymous.
             PLACE--probably United States.
             DATE--probably written 19th century.
Music: COMPOSER--anonymous.
             PLACE--possibly Sicily, Italy.
             DATE--probably written second half of 18th century;
                 possibly first published 1794.
Found: SIM, FIR, CCM, ONS, TRE
Notes: The lyrics originally were an anonymous 16th century
             Latin hymn of praise to the Virgin Mary, O SANCTISSIMA;
             the original words have undergone many translations
             and alterations, including this derivative, O
             SANCTISSIMA (three United States versions) and the
             German carol O DU FRÖHLICHE; the tune for all six
             songs is known as SICILIAN MARINERS, but no direct
             connection with Italy has been found.

548. O'ER THE HILL AND O'ER THE VALE

    Lyrics: AUTHOR--John Mason Neale (1818-1866).
                PLACE--England.
                DATE--written mid-19th century.
    Music: COMPOSER--anonymous.
                PLACE--Europe.
                DATE--probably created medieval period.
                VARIANT TUNE--tune by F.J. Dugard.
    Found: UNI, HUT, COF
    Notes: The main tune is the melody IN VERNALI TEMPORE.

549. OF A ROSE SING WE

    Lyrics: AUTHOR--folk.
                PLACE--England.
                DATE--created 15th century.
                DIFFERING FIRST LINES--OF A ROSE SINGÈ WE; THIS ROSE
                                        IS RAILED ON A RYS; THIS ROSE
                                        IS RAILED ON A RICE.
    Music: COMPOSER--folk.
                PLACE--England.
                DATE--created 15th century.
                VARIANT TUNE--another 15th century English folk tune.
    Found: MEC, MED, THF, EAR

550. OH JERUS'LEM IN THE MORNING!

    Lyrics: AUTHOR--folk (Black spiritual).
                PLACE--United States (possibly Georgia).
                DATE--probably created 18th or 19th century.
                VARIANT VERNACULAR TITLES--MOTHER MARY, WHAT IS THE
                                        MATTER?; BABY BORN TODAY.
    Music: COMPOSER--folk (Black spiritual).
                PLACE--United States (possibly Georgia).
                DATE--probably created 18th or 19th century.
    Found: LAN, SEE

551. OH, JOSEPH TOOK MARY UP ON HIS RIGHT KNEE

    Lyrics: AUTHOR--folk.
                PLACE--probably Appalachian region, possibly Nova
                    Scotia.
                DATE--probably created 18th or 19th century.
    Music: COMPOSER--folk.
                PLACE--probably Appalachian region, possibly Nova
                    Scotia.
                DATE--probably created 18th or 19th century.
    Found: JOH
    Notes: This is a variation of THE CHERRY TREE CAROL; look
                under THE CHERRY TREE CAROL in the index for all
                related carols.

552.   OH, MARY, WHERE IS YOUR BABY?

    Lyrics: AUTHOR--folk (Black spiritual).
                PLACE--probably Louisiana.
                DATE--probably created 19th century.
                VARIANT VERNACULAR TITLE--O MARY, WHERE IS YOUR BABY?
                DIFFERING FIRST LINES--READ IN THE GOSPEL OF MATTHEW;
                                  READ IN THE GOSPEL OF MATHAYEW.
    Music: COMPOSER--folk (Black spiritual).
                PLACE--probably Louisiana.
                DATE--probably created 19th century.
    Found: SEA, SEE

553.   OH, WHO WOULD BE A SHEPHERD BOY?

    Lyrics: AUTHOR--John Gray (1866-1934).
                PLACE--England.
                DATE--written late 19th or early 20th century.
    Music: COMPOSER--folk.
                PLACE--England.
                DATE--possibly created 17th or 18th century?
    Found: SHE, THF, GAS, UNI
    Notes: The tune was probably first published, without words,
                in William Sandys' 1833 collection, CHRISTMAS CAROLS,
                ANCIENT AND MODERN, under the title LORD THOMAS; the
                first-known lyrics were Gray's.

554.   OI! BETLEEM!

    Lyrics: AUTHOR--folk.
                PLACE--Basque region, Spain and France.
                DATE--possibly created 16th-18th century?
                VARIANT VERNACULAR TITLE--OI BETLEHEM.
                ENGLISH TITLES--O BETHLEHEM! (two different transla-
                                  tions, one by John O'Connor [1870-
                                  1952], one by Elizabeth Poston [1905-
                                  ]); O BETHLEHEM (translated by
                                  George K. Evans).
    Music: COMPOSER--folk.
                PLACE--Basque region, Spain and France.
                DATE--possibly created 16th-18th century?
    Found: PEN, THF, YAL, INT, MOO
    Notes: The tune is also used for the carol THE INFANT KING;
                this is perhaps the best-known Basque carol.

555.   OJ PASTIRI

    Lyrics: AUTHOR--folk.
                PLACE--Croatia, Yugoslavia.
                DATE--possibly created 16th-18th century?
                ENGLISH TITLE--HEAR, O SHEPHERDS.
    Music: COMPOSER--folk.
                PLACE--Croatia, Yugoslavia.
                DATE--possibly created 16th-18th century?
    Found: SIM

556. OLD TOY TRAINS

  Lyrics: AUTHOR--Roger Miller (1936-   ).
            PLACE--United States.
            DATE--published 1967.
            DIFFERING FIRST LINE--LITTLE TOY TRAINS, LITTLE TOY
                                    TRACKS.
  Music: COMPOSER--Roger Miller (1936-   ).
            PLACE--United States.
            DATE--published 1967.
  Found: SEV

557. THE OLD YEAR NOW AWAY IS FLED

  Lyrics: AUTHOR--folk.
            PLACE--England.
            DATE--published 1642.
            VARIANT VERNACULAR TITLES--THE OLD YEAR NOW AWAY HAS
                                    FLED; CAROL FOR NEW YEAR'S
                                    DAY; GREENSLEEVES; THE OLD
                                    YEAR.
  Music: COMPOSER--folk.
            PLACE--England.
            DATE--created 16th century.
            VARIANT TUNE--tune by Arthur Henry Brown (1830-1926).
  Found: OXF, REE, HUT, UNI, STA
  Notes: The 16th century tune is the well-known melody
            GREENSLEEVES; it is also used for the carol WHAT
            CHILD IS THIS?

558. OLD YORKSHIRE GOODING CAROL

  Lyrics: AUTHOR--folk.
            PLACE--probably Yorkshire, England.
            DATE--possibly created 16th-18th century?
            DIFFERING FIRST LINE--WELLADAY! WELLADAY!
  Music: COMPOSER--folk.
            PLACE--England.
            DATE--possibly created 16th or 17th century.
  Found: CCM
  Notes: The tune is also used for the carol CHRISTMAS HATH
            MADE AN END.

559. ON CHRISTMAS NIGHT

  Lyrics: AUTHOR--folk.
            PLACE--probably Sussex, England.
            DATE--possibly created 18th century; possibly first
                published 1842.
            VARIANT VERNACULAR TITLES--SUSSEX CAROL; ON CHRISTMAS
                                    NIGHT ALL CHRISTIANS SING.

Music: COMPOSER--folk.
              PLACE--probably Sussex, England.
              DATE--possibly created 18th century.
              VARIANT TUNES--folk tune from Ireland; tune by John
                                La Montaine (1920-   ).
Found: OXF, INT, HAW, WON, THF

560.   ONCE IN ROYAL DAVID'S CITY

Lyrics: AUTHOR--Cecil Frances Alexander (1823-1895).
              PLACE--England.
              DATE--published 1848.
Music: COMPOSER--Henry John Gauntlett (1805-1876).
              PLACE--England.
              DATE--published 1849.
Found: MANY
Notes: The song was originally intended for children.

561.   ONS IS GEBOREN EEN KINDEKIN

Lyrics: AUTHOR--folk.
              PLACE--Netherlands.
              DATE--probably created 14th or 15th century.
              VARIANT VERNACULAR TITLE--ONS IS GHEBOREN EEN
                                KINDEKIJN.
              ENGLISH TITLES--TODAY WE WELCOME A TINY CHILD
                                (translated by George K. Evans);
                                TO US A LITTLE CHILD IS BORN (trans-
                                lated by John O'Connor [1870-1952]);
                                A CHILD OF BEAUTY WAS BORN TO US
                                (translated by Olga Paul).
Music: COMPOSER--folk.
              PLACE--Netherlands.
              DATE--probably created 14th or 15th century.
              VARIANT TUNE--tune by Marius Monnikendam (1896-   ).
Found: INT, THF, BRU, RTW

562.   ONTWAAKT, LOOPT, HERDERS, DEZEN NACHT!

Lyrics: AUTHOR--folk.
              PLACE--Belgium or France.
              DATE--possibly created 16th-18th century?
              VARIANT VERNACULAR TITLE--ONTWAEKT, LOOPT HERDERS
                                DEZEN NACHT.
              ENGLISH TITLE--THE ANGEL AND THE SHEPHERDS (trans-
                                lated by Alfred Raymond Bellinger
                                [1893-   ]).
              DIFFERING FIRST LINE--COME SHEPHERDS, COME! YOUR
                                SILENT SHEEP.
Music: COMPOSER--folk
              PLACE--Belgium or France.
              DATE--possibly created 16th-18th century?
Found: BOL, CET, SMI

563. OÙ S'EN VONT CES GAIS BERGERS

>   *Lyrics:* AUTHOR--folk.
>   PLACE--France.
>   DATE--probably created 16th or 17th century;
>   possibly first published 1679.
>   ENGLISH TITLE--WHERE DO THESE GLAD SHEPHERDS GO?
>   (translated by Edward Bliss Reed
>   [1872-1940]).
>   *Music:* COMPOSER--folk.
>   PLACE--France.
>   DATE--possibly created 16th or 17th century.
>   *Found:* TIE, SMI, CTT

564. OUR BLESSED LADY'S LULLABY

>   *Lyrics:* AUTHOR--Richard Verstegen (ca. 1548-1640).
>   PLACE--probably Antwerp, Belgium.
>   DATE--published 1591.
>   VARIANT VERNACULAR TITLE--UPON MY LAP MY SOVREIGN
>   SITS.
>   *Music:* COMPOSER--anonymous, possibly William Byrd (1543-
>   1623).
>   PLACE--England.
>   DATE--probably created 16th century.
>   VARIANT TUNE--tune by Martin Peerson (ca. 1580-
>   1650/51).
>   *Found:* THF, UNI

565. OUR LADY SAT WITHIN HER BOWER

>   *Lyrics:* AUTHOR--George Ratcliffe Woodward (1848-1934).
>   PLACE--England.
>   DATE--written late 19th or early 20th century.
>   *Music:* COMPOSER--folk.
>   PLACE--Germany.
>   DATE--probably created 16th century; possibly first
>   published 1590.
>   *Found:* RSC, CCB

566. OUT OF THE EAST

>   *Lyrics:* AUTHOR--Harry Noble (1912-1966).
>   PLACE--United States.
>   DATE--published 1941.
>   DIFFERING FIRST LINE--OUT OF THE EAST THERE CAME
>   RIDING.
>   *Music:* COMPOSER--Harry Noble (1912-1966).
>   PLACE--United States.
>   DATE--published 1941.

567. OUT OF YOUR SLEEP

    Lyrics: AUTHOR--folk.
             PLACE--England.
             DATE--probably created 15th century.
             DIFFERING FIRST LINE--OUT OF YOUR SLEEP ARISE AND
                                AWAKE.
    Music: COMPOSER--Martin Shaw (1875-1958).
             PLACE--England.
             DATE--published 1928.
             VARIANT TUNE--tune by Richard Rodney Bennett.
    Found: OXF, CCT
    Notes: The lyrics are very similar to those for ARISE AND
             WAKE.

568. PAGKA-TÁO

    Lyrics: AUTHOR--folk.
             PLACE--Philippines.
             DATE--possibly created 18th-20th century?
             ENGLISH TITLE--CHRISTMAS CAROL (translated by Olga
                                Paul).
             DIFFERING FIRST LINES--TÁLANG NAPAKALIWANAG; 'TWAS A
                                      BRILLIANT STAR IN THE SKY.
    Music: COMPOSER--folk.
             PLACE--Philippines.
              DATE--possibly created 18th-20th century?
    Found: RTW

569. PANXOLIÑA DE NADAL

    Lyrics: AUTHOR--folk.
             PLACE--Galicia, Spain.
             DATE--possibly created 16th-18th century?
              VARIANT VERNACULAR TITLE--VINDE, PICARIÑAS.
             ENGLISH TITLE--SPANISH CAROL (translated by John
                                Brande Trend [1887-1958]).
             DIFFERING FIRST LINE--UP NOW, LAGGARDLY LASSES.
    Music: COMPOSER--folk.
              PLACE--Galicia, Spain.
              DATE--possibly created 16th-18th century?
    Found: OXF, MON, MOO, CAN

570. PARADE OF THE WOODEN SOLDIERS

    Lyrics: AUTHOR--Ballard MacDonald (1882-1935).
             PLACE--United States.
             DATE--probably written 1922.
             DIFFERING FIRST LINE--THE TOYSHOP DOOR IS LOCKED UP
                                TIGHT.
    Music: COMPOSER--Leon Jessel (1871-1942).
             PLACE--Germany.
              DATE--published 1911.
    Found: ULT

Notes: The music was originally written as an instrumental
piece; the words and music were joined in a 1922
Broadway musical, CHAUVE SOURIS, which was imported
from Paris.

571. PARTON DALL'ORIENTE

Lyrics: AUTHOR--folk.
PLACE--Italy.
DATE--probably created 16th or 17th century.
ENGLISH TITLE--THREE KINGS CAME RIDING (translated by
John Gray [1866-1934]).
DIFFERING FIRST LINE--THREE KINGS CAME RIDING FROM
THE EAST.
Music: COMPOSER--folk.
PLACE--Italy.
DATE--probably created 16th or 17th century.
Found: THF, ICC
Notes: The words and melody were possibly first published in
1674; the tune is the melody ALMA CHE SCORGI.

572. PARVULUS NOBIS NASCITUR

Lyrics: AUTHOR--anonymous.
PLACE--probably Germany.
DATE--probably created 15th century; possibly first
published 1579.
ENGLISH TITLES--TO US IS BORN A LITTLE CHILD (trans-
lated by W.J. Blew); TO US A LITTLE
CHILD IS BORN (translated by John
O'Connor [1870-1952]).
Music: COMPOSER--anonymous.
PLACE--Germany.
DATE--probably created 15th century.
VARIANT TUNES--ACH! BLEIB BEI UNS, HERR JESU CHRIST,
by Johann Sebastian Bach (1685-1750);
tune by Michael Praetorius (1571-
1621).
Found: COF, THF
Notes: The 15th century melody is the tune UNS IST GEBORN
EIN KINDERLEIN.

573. PÁSLI OVCE VALASI

Lyrics: AUTHOR--folk.
PLACE--Czechoslovakia.
DATE--possibly created 15th-17th century?
ENGLISH TITLES--SHEPHERDS WATCHED THEIR FLOCKS BY
NIGHT (translated by Mary Cochrane
Vojácek); TYDILOM and SHEPHERDS WE,
THE VALASHI (both the same transla-
tion by Elizabeth Poston [1905-   ]).

Music: COMPOSER--folk.
           PLACE--Czechoslovakia.
           DATE--possibly created 15th-17th century?
Found: SIM, PEN, ZPE, SCC

574.   PAST THREE A CLOCK

Lyrics: AUTHOR--George Ratcliffe Woodward (1848-1934);
                      refrain, folk.
           PLACE--England.
           DATE--written late 19th or early 20th century;
                      refrain, possibly created 16th or 17th century.
           VARIANT VERNACULAR TITLES--PAST THREE A CLOCK, AND A
                                     FROSTY MORNING; PAST
                                     THREE O'CLOCK.
           DIFFERING FIRST LINE--BORN IS A BABY, GENTLE AS MAY
                                 BE.
Music: COMPOSER--folk.
           PLACE--England.
           DATE--probably created 16th or 17th century;
                      possibly first published 1663.
Found: REE, CCO, YOU, UNI, CCB
Notes: The tune is the melody LONDON WAITS.

575.   PASTOR LEVATE

Lyrics: AUTHOR--folk.
           PLACE--Italy.
           DATE--probably created 16th or 17th century.
           ENGLISH TITLE--SHEPHERDS, WHY DO YE TARRY? (trans-
                          lated by K.W. Simpson).
Music: COMPOSER--folk.
           PLACE--Italy.
           DATE--probably created 16th or 17th century.
Found: THF, ICC
Notes: The words and melody were possibly first published
           in 1674; the tune is the melody CHIO PUÒ MIRAR.

576.   PASTORES A BELÉN

Lyrics: AUTHOR--folk.
           PLACE--Puerto Rico.
           DATE--possibly created 18th or 19th century?
           ENGLISH TITLES--GO YE TO BETHLEHEM (translated by
                           Ruth Heller [1920-   ]); SHEPHERDS
                           IN BETHLEHEM (translated by George K.
                           Evans); SHEPHERDS TO BETHLEHEM.
           DIFFERING FIRST LINES--THE LORD TO EARTH HAS COME;
                                  TO BETHLEHEM LET'S GO.
Music: COMPOSER--folk.
           PLACE--Puerto Rico.
           DATE--possibly created 18th or 19th century?
Found: INT, SHE, CCM, HEL

577. PATAPAN

    Lyrics: AUTHOR--Bernard de la Monnoye (1641-1728).
             PLACE--Burgundy, France.
             DATE--probably written around 1700.
             VARIANT VERNACULAR TITLES--PAT-A-PAN; GUILLÔ, PRAN
                              TON TAMBORIN.
             ENGLISH TITLES--WILLIE, TAKE YOUR LITTLE DRUM
                              (translated by Percy Dearmer [1867-
                              1936]); WILLIE, GET YOUR LITTLE DRUM
                              (translated by George K. Evans);
                              DAVIE GET YOUR TAMBOURINE (translated
                              by John O'Connor [1870-1952]);
                              others.
    Music: COMPOSER--probably folk, possibly Bernard de la
                            Monnoye (1641-1728).
             PLACE--Burgundy, France.
             DATE--probably created 17th or 18th century.
    Found: OXF, INT, SIM, SHE, THF
    Notes: The carol was possibly first published in 1842.

578. PEACE ON EARTH THIS CHRISTMAS

    Lyrics: AUTHOR--Harold Dixon and Elizabeth Vaughn.
             PLACE--United States.
             DATE--published 1950.
             DIFFERING FIRST LINE--MAY THERE BE PEACE ON EARTH
                              THIS CHRISTMAS.
    Music: COMPOSER--Elizabeth Vaughn.
             PLACE--United States.
             DATE--published 1950.
    Found: SEV

579. PEDIMENTO DE LAS POSADAS

    Lyrics: AUTHOR--folk.
             PLACE--probably Latin America.
             DATE--possibly created 18th or 19th century?
             ENGLISH TITLE--THE SEARCH FOR LODGING (translated by
                            Helen Luvaas Fjerstad).
             DIFFERING FIRST LINES--QUIÉN LES DA POSADA; WHO ARE
                              THESE POOR PILGRIMS.
    Music: COMPOSER--folk.
             PLACE--probably Latin America.
             DATE--possibly created 18th or 19th century?
    Found: FJE

580. THE PEOPLE THAT IN DARKNESS SAT

    Lyrics: AUTHOR--John Morison (1749-1798).
             PLACE--Scotland.
              DATE--published 1781.

VARIANT VERNACULAR TITLES--ALL NATIONS THAT IN DARK-
NESS PINED (adaptation by
Anthony G. Petti); THE
RACE THAT LONG IN DARKNESS
PINED; TO US A CHILD OF
HOPE IS BORN.

Music: COMPOSER--anonymous.
PLACE--Scotland.
DATE--published 1635.
VARIANT TUNES--anonymous 1621 English tune; anonymous
1615 Scottish tune; tune by Lowell
Mason (1792-1872).

Found: MET, HAR, CAT, ENG, MEN
Notes: The version that begins TO US A CHILD is taken from
the final verses of Morison's hymn.

581. PERSONENT HODIE

AUTHOR--anonymous.
PLACE--Germany.
DATE--probably created 14th century.
ENGLISH TITLES--SING ALOUD ON THIS DAY! (translated
by John A. Parkinson [1920-   ]);
THE BOYS' CAROL (translated by
Elizabeth Poston [1905-   ]); LIFT
YOUR VOICES AND SING (translated by
K.W. Simpson).
DIFFERING FIRST LINE--LET THE BOYS' CHEERFUL NOISE.

Music: COMPOSER--anonymous.
PLACE--probably Germany, possibly Scandinavia.
DATE--probably created 14th century.
Found: OXF, PEN, THF, CCT, CCF
Notes: The song was possibly first published in 1582.

582. POCHVÁLEN BUD' JEZÍS KRISTUS

Lyrics: AUTHOR--folk.
PLACE--Czechoslovakia.
DATE--possibly created 16th-18th century?
VARIANT VERNACULAR TITLE--POCHVÁLEN BUD'.
ENGLISH TITLE--PRAISE TO JESUS, OUR SALVATION
(translated by George K. Evans).
Music: COMPOSER--folk.
PLACE--Czechoslovakia.
DATE--possibly created 16th-18th century?
VARIANT TUNE--another folk tune from Czechoslovakia.
Found: INT, ZPE

583. POICHÉ L'UMIL CAPANNA

Lyrics: AUTHOR--folk.
PLACE--Italy.
DATE--probably created 16th or 17th century.

ENGLISH TITLE--TO WEARY SHEPHERDS SLEEPING (trans-
lated by K.W. Simpson).
Music: COMPOSER--folk.
PLACE--Italy.
DATE--probably created 16th or 17th century.
Found: THF, ICC, UNI
Notes: The words and melody were possibly first published in
1674.

584. POOR LITTLE JESUS

Lyrics: AUTHOR--folk (Black spiritual).
PLACE--United States (possibly New York state).
DATE--probably created 18th or 19th century.
DIFFERING FIRST LINE--IT WAS POOR LITTLE JESUS.
Music: COMPOSER--folk (Black spiritual).
PLACE--United States (possibly New York state).
DATE--probably created 18th or 19th century.
Found: SEA, SEE, APP, LAN
Notes: This is very different from another spiritual of
similar title, O PO' LITTLE JESUS.

585. POSLECHNETE MNE

Lyrics: AUTHOR--folk.
PLACE--Moravia, Czechoslovakia.
DATE--possibly created 16th-18th century?
VARIANT VERNACULAR TITLE--POSLECHNETE MNE MÁLO.
ENGLISH TITLE--HEARKEN, MY GOOD SIR, I PRAY (trans-
lated by Mary Cochrane Vojáček).
Music: COMPOSER--folk.
PLACE--Moravia, Czechoslovakia.
DATE--possibly created 16th-18th century?
Found: ZPE, SCC

586. PRAY FOR US THE PRINCE OF PEACE

Lyrics: AUTHOR--folk.
PLACE--England.
DATE--created 15th century.
VARIANT VERNACULAR TITLE--PRAY FOR US.
DIFFERING FIRST LINES--PRAY FOR US, THOU PRINCE OF
PEACE; TO THEE NOW, CHRISTËS
DARLING; TO THEE NOW, CHRISTËS
OWN DARLING; TO THEE NOW
CHRISTËS DERE DERLING; TO THEE
NOW, CHRISTËS DEAR DARLING.
Music: COMPOSER--folk.
PLACE--England.
DATE--created 15th century.
VARIANT TUNES--three other 15th century English folk
tunes.
Found: MEC, MED, THF

587.   PRETTY PAPER

    Lyrics: AUTHOR--Willie Nelson (1933-   ).
             PLACE--United States.
             DATE--published 1962.
             DIFFERING FIRST LINE--CROWDED STREETS, BUSY FEET,
                                   HUSTLE BY HIM.
    Music: COMPOSER--Willie Nelson (1933-   ).
             PLACE--United States.
             DATE--published 1962.
    Found: SEV, POP

588.   PROMPTEMENT LEVEZ-VOUS

    Lyrics: AUTHOR--folk.
             PLACE--probably Burgundy, France.
             DATE--probably created 15th or 16th century.
             VARIANT VERNACULAR TITLE--PROMPTEMENT LEVEZ-VOUS MA
                              VOISIN.
             ENGLISH TITLE--NEIGHBOR MINE (translated by K.W.
                              Simpson).
             DIFFERING FIRST LINES--PROMPTEMENT LEVEZ-VOUS MON
                              VOISIN; O RISE AND COME AWAY
                              (NEIGHBOR RUN!).
    Music: COMPOSER--folk.
             PLACE--probably Burgundy, France.
             DATE--probably created 15th or 16th century.
    Found: OXF, THF

589.   PRZYBIEZELI DO BETLEEM PASTERZE

    Lyrics: AUTHOR--folk.
             PLACE--Poland.
             DATE--possibly created 15th-17th century?
             VARIANT VERNACULAR TITLE--PRZYBIEZELI DO BETLEJEM.
             ENGLISH TITLES--SHEPHERDS, COME A-RUNNING; SHEPHERDS
                       CAME TO BETHLEHEM (translated by
                       George K. Evans); SHEPHERDS HURRIED
                       TO BETHLEHEM.
             DIFFERING FIRST LINES--PRZBIEZELI DO BETLEJEM PASTERZE;
                            SHEPHERDS, COME A-RUNNING TO
                            BETHLEHEM; SHEPHERDS COME A-
                            RUNNING INTO BETHLEHEM; SHEPHERDS
                            CAME TO BETHLEHEM THAT HOLY DAY.
    Music: COMPOSER--folk.
             PLACE--Poland.
             DATE--possibly created 15th-17th century?
    Found: INT, TRA, OBE, SHE

590.   PSALLIMUS CANTANTES

    Lyrics: AUTHOR--anonymous.
             PLACE--England.

DATE--probably created 15th century.
ENGLISH TITLE--CAST AWAY THE OLDEN (translated by
                                       John O'Connor [1870-1952]).
Music: COMPOSER--anonymous.
           PLACE--England.
           DATE--probably created 15th century.
Found: THF, MED

591. PSALLITE UNIGENITO

Lyrics: AUTHOR--anonymous.
            PLACE--Germany.
            DATE--possibly created 14th-16th century; possibly
                 first published 1582.
            ENGLISH TITLE--SING, O SING!
            DIFFERING FIRST LINE--SING, O SING! HAIL THE HOLY
                                               ONE!
Music: COMPOSER--probably Michael Praetorius (1571-1621).
            PLACE--Germany.
            DATE--published 1609.
Found: TRA, COS

592. PUER NATUS IN BETHLEHEM

Lyrics: AUTHOR--anonymous.
            PLACE--Europe (possibly Germany or Bohemia,
                 Czechoslovakia).
            DATE--probably created 14th century.
            VARIANT VERNACULAR TITLE--PUER NATUS.
            ENGLISH TITLES--A CHILD IS BORN IN BETHLEHEM; A BOY
                               WAS BORN IN BETHLEHEM (two different
                               translations, one by Percy Dearmer
                               [1867-1936], the other by Elizabeth
                               Poston [1905-   ]); A BOY IS BORN IN
                               BETHLEHEM (three different transla-
                               tions, one by H.J.D. Ryder, another
                               by George K. Evans, another by John
                               O'Connor [1870-1952]); A BABE IS BORN
                               IN BETHLEHEM; IN BETHLEHEM A BABE IS
                               BORN (translated by William Glass);
                               others.
Music: COMPOSER--anonymous.
            PLACE--Europe (possibly Germany or Bohemia,
                 Czechoslovakia).
            DATE--probably created 14th century; supplanted by
                 its descant by 16th century.
            VARIANT TUNES--much-used harmonization by Johann
                               Sebastian Bach (1685-1750); other
                               tunes.
Found: OXF, INT, COF, PEN, THF
Notes: There are two main variations of the lyrics, both
            similar; for a German version, see EIN KIND GEBORN
            ZU BETHLEHEM; for a Danish derivative, see ET BARN ER
            FØDT I BETLEHEM; for a Dutch derivative, see EEN KINT
            GHEBOREN IN BETHLEHEM; the tune is also used for the
            carol QUAE STELLA SOLE PULCHRIOR.

593.   PUER NOBIS NASCITUR

      Lyrics: AUTHOR--anonymous.
                PLACE--probably Germany.
                DATE--probably created 15th century.
                VARIANT VERNACULAR TITLE--PUER NOBIS.
                ENGLISH TITLES--UNTO US A BOY IS BORN! (translated by
                                Percy Dearmer [1867-1936]); UNTO US
                                IS BORN A SON (translated by George
                                Ratcliffe Woodward [1848-1934]);
                                UNTO US A BOY WAS BORN (paraphrase
                                by Willys Peck Kent [1877-   ]); TO
                                ALL MEN A CHILD IS COME (translated
                                by John O'Connor [1870-1952]).
      Music: COMPOSER--anonymous.
                PLACE--probably Germany.
                DATE--probably created 15th century.
                VARIANT TUNE--tune by Michael Praetorius (1571-1621).
      Found: OXF, PEN, COF, SIM, THF
      Notes: The main tune is also used for the carol TO US A
                CHILD OF ROYAL BIRTH.

594.   PUJDEM SPOLU DO BETLEMA

      Lyrics: AUTHOR--folk.
                PLACE--Bohemia, Czechoslovakia.
                DATE--possibly created 15th-17th century?
                ENGLISH TITLES--WE ARE GOING TO THE STABLE (trans-
                                lated by George K. Evans); COME TO
                                BETHLEHEM; BAGPIPE CAROL.
                DIFFERING FIRST LINE--COME TO BETHL'EM.
      Music: COMPOSER--folk.
                PLACE--Bohemia, Czechoslovakia.
                DATE--possibly created 15th-17th century?
      Found: INT, OBE, ZPE

595.   QUAE STELLA SOLE PULCHRIOR

      Lyrics: AUTHOR--Charles Coffin (1676-1740).
                PLACE--France.
                DATE--published 1736.
                ENGLISH TITLE--WHAT STAR IS THIS WITH BEAMS SO BRIGHT
                                  (translated by John Chandler [1806-
                                1876]).
      Music: COMPOSER--anonymous.
                PLACE--Europe (possibly Germany or Bohemia,
                    Czechoslovakia).
                DATE--probably created 14th century; supplanted by
                    its descant by 16th century.
      Found: CAT
      Notes: The tune is also used for the carols PUER NATUS IN
                BETHLEHEM and EIN KIND GEBORN ZU BETHLEHEM.

596. QUAND LA MIEJONUE SOUNAVO

    Lyrics: AUTHOR--folk.
              PLACE--Provence, France.
              DATE--possibly created 16th-18th century?
              ENGLISH TITLE--I WOKE, FROM MY COUCH UPRISING (trans-
                           lated by K.W. Simpson).
              DIFFERING FIRST LINE--I WOKE, FROM MY COUCH
                           UPSPRINGING.
    Music: COMPOSER--folk.
              PLACE--Provence, France.
              DATE--possibly created 16th-18th century?
              VARIANT TUNE--another French folk song.
    Found: THF, SMI

597. QUELLE EST CETTE ODEUR AGRÉABLE?

    Lyrics: AUTHOR--folk.
              PLACE--France (possibly Lorraine).
              DATE--possibly created 17th century.
              ENGLISH TITLES--WHENCE IS THAT GOODLY FRAGRANCE
                         and WHENCE IS THAT GOODLY FRAGRANCE
                         FLOWING? (two titles for the same
                         translation by Allen Beville Ramsay
                         [1872-   ]); WHAT IS THIS PERFUME
                         SO APPEALING? (translated by George
                         K. Evans); WHAT IS THIS FRAGRANCE?
                         (translated by K.W. Simpson).
              DIFFERING FIRST LINE--WHAT IS THIS FRAGRANCE SOFTLY
                         STEALING?
    Music: COMPOSER--folk.
              PLACE--France (possibly Lorraine).
               DATE--possibly created 17th century.
              VARIANT TUNE--tune by Patrick Forbes.
    Found: INT, REE, CCT, THF, UNI
    Notes: The main tune appeared in THE BEGGAR'S OPERA (1728),
             by John Gay (1685-1732).

598. QUEM PASTORES LAUDAVERE

    Lyrics: AUTHOR--anonymous.
              PLACE--Germany.
               DATE--created 14th century.
               VARIANT VERNACULAR TITLE--QUEM PASTORES.
              ENGLISH TITLES--SHEPHERDS LEFT THEIR FLOCKS A-
                         STRAYING (translated by Imogen Holst
                         [1907-   ]); SHEPHERDS CAME, THEIR
                         PRAISES BRINGING (translated by
                         G.B. Caird); WHOM OF OLD THE SHEPHERDS
                         PRAISED (translated by George Ratcliffe
                         Woodward [1848-1934]); HE, WHOM
                         JOYOUS SHEPHERDS PRAISED; HE WHOM
                         SHEPHERDS APPREHENDED (translated by
                         Elizabeth Poston [1905-   ]);

SHEPHERDS TELL YOUR BEAUTEOUS STORY
(translated by John O'Connor [1870-
1952]).
Music: COMPOSER--anonymous.
PLACE--Germany.
DATE--created 14th century.
VARIANT TUNE--another medieval tune.
Found: OXF, INT, CCT, PEN, THF
Notes: The first known text of the words and music is from
the 15th century.

599. QUEM VIDISTIS, PASTORES

Lyrics: AUTHOR--anonymous.
PLACE--Europe.
DATE--created medieval period.
ENGLISH TITLES--AS I WENT TO BETHLEHEM and SHEPHERDS,
IN THE FIELD ABIDING (the first a
translation, the second a derivative,
both by George Ratcliffe Woodward
[1848-1934]).
Music: COMPOSER--folk.
PLACE--England.
DATE--created 14th or 15th century.
Found: CCB, COS
Notes: The tune is the melody AS I WENT TO WALSINGHAM.

600. QUI CREAVIT COELUM

Lyrics: AUTHOR--anonymous.
PLACE--probably Chester, England.
DATE--probably created 14th or early 15th century.
ENGLISH TITLES--CHESTER CAROL (translated by Irene
Gass); SONG OF THE NUNS OF CHESTER
(two different translations, one by
Denis Stevens [1922-   ] and John A.
Parkinson [1920-   ], the other
anonymous); CAROL OF THE NUNS OF
SAINT MARY'S, CHESTER; HE BY WHOM THE
HEAVENS WERE MADE (translated by Ronald
Arbuthnott Knox [1888-1957]); LULLY,
LULLY, LU (translated by Anne Shaw
Faulkner Oberndorfer [1877-   ]).
DIFFERING FIRST LINES--QUI CREAVIT CAELUM; HE WHO
MADE THE STARRY SKIES; HE WHO
CREATED HEAVEN; HE WHO HEAV'N
CREATED; HEAV'N CREATED HIM
FOR ALL; HE WHO MADE THE EARTH
SO FAIR.
Music: COMPOSER--anonymous.
PLACE--probably Chester, England.
DATE--probably created 14th or early 15th century.
Found: OXF, PEN, UNI, OBE, THF
Notes: The song's first text was probably written around
1425.

601. QU'IL EST AMIABLE

Lyrics: AUTHOR--folk.
PLACE--Gascony, France.
DATE--possibly created 15th-17th century?
ENGLISH TITLE--INFANT SO GENTLE.
DIFFERING FIRST LINE--INFANT SO GENTLE, SO PURE AND
SO SWEET.
Music: COMPOSER--folk.
PLACE--Gascony, France.
DATE--possibly created 15th-17th Century?
Found: OBE, HUT, PRE, HEL

602. QUITTEZ, PASTEURS

Lyrics: AUTHOR--folk.
PLACE--France (possibly Anjou).
DATE--probably created 17th or 18th century;
probably first published 1728.
VARIANT VERNACULAR TITLE--QUITTEZ, PASTEURS, ET
BREBIS ET HOULETTES.
ENGLISH TITLES--O COME AWAY, YE SHEPHERDS (trans-
lated by George K. Evans); COME
LEAVE YOUR SHEEP (translated by John
Rutter); O LEAVE YOUR SHEEP (trans-
lated by Alice Raleigh); LEAVE,
SHEPHERDS, LEAVE (translated by
Edward Bliss Reed [1872-1940]);
LEAVE, SHEPHERDS, LEAVE YOUR PEACEFUL
FLOCKS (translated by K.W. Simpson);
LAY DOWN YOUR STAFFS, O SHEPHERDS.
DIFFERING FIRST LINE--NOW QUIT YOUR CARE.
Music: COMPOSER--folk.
PLACE--France (possibly Anjou).
DATE--probably created around 1875.
VARIANT TUNE--earlier folk tune from Besancon region,
France.
Found: INT, CCT, CFO, THF, REE
Notes: The variant tune is the air NANON DORMAIT, and the
ca. 1875 tune is a different version of that melody.

603. QUOI, MA VOISINE, EST-TU FÂCHÉE?

Lyrics: AUTHOR--probably folk, possibly Francois Colletet
(1628-1680).
PLACE-- probably Anjou, France.
DATE--probably created 17th century; probably
first published 1664.
VARIANT VERNACULAR TITLE--QUOI, MA VOISINE.
ENGLISH TITLES--NEIGHBOR, WHAT HAS YOU SO EXCITED?
(two different translations, one by
Bernard Gasso [1926-   ], the other
by George K. Evans); THE KINGDOM

(paraphrased by Patrick Reginald
Chalmers [1872-   ]); WHERE GO YE NOW?
(translated by W.B. Lindsay and Ruth
Heller [1920-   ]); THE SHEPHERDESSES
(translated by Edward Bliss Reed
[1872-1940]).
DIFFERING FIRST LINE--WHAT! MY GOOD NEIGHBOUR, ARE
                                    YOU ANGRY?

Music: COMPOSER--folk.
             PLACE--probably Anjou, France.
             DATE--probably created 17th or early 18th century.
Found: INT, OXF, HEL, ONT, CTW

604. QUOIQUE SOYEZ PETIT ENCORE

Lyrics: AUTHOR--folk.
             PLACE--France.
             DATE--probably created 18th century.
             ENGLISH TITLES--ALTHOUGH YOU STILL ARE WEAK AND
                   HELPLESS (translated by George K.
                   Evans); ALTHOUGH YOU ARE SO TINY;
                   THOUGH NOW A BABE (translated by
                   Edward Bliss Reed [1872-1940]).
             DIFFERING FIRST LINE--ALTHOUGH YOU STILL ARE BUT AN
                                    INFANT.
Music: COMPOSER--folk.
             PLACE--France.
             DATE--probably created 18th century.
Found: INT, CCM, CTT

605. REJOICE AND BE MERRY

Lyrics: AUTHOR--anonymous.
             PLACE--probably Dorsetshire, England.
             DATE--possibly created 17th-19th century?
             VARIANT VERNACULAR TITLE--A GALLERY CAROL.
             DIFFERING FIRST LINE--REJOICE AND BE MERRY IN SONGS
                                    AND IN MIRTH!
Music: COMPOSER--anonymous.
             PLACE--probably Dorsetshire, England.
             DATE--possibly created 17th-19th century?
Found: OXF, UNI, REF, CFS, CAT

606. REMEMBER, O THOU MAN

Lyrics: AUTHOR--anonymous.
             PLACE--England.
             DATE--probably created 16th century; probably first
                   published 1611.
             VARIANT VERNACULAR TITLES--REMEMBER; REMEMBER, MORTAL
                                    MAN (adaptation by Anthony
                                    G. Petti); REMEMBER LIFE

IS SHORT (modification by
William Josiah Irons
[1812-1883]).

Music: COMPOSER--probably Thomas Ravenscroft (1582-1635).
PLACE--England.
DATE--published 1611.

Found: OXF, CAT, CHO, UNI, HUS

607. REPOUSA TRANQUILO O MEIGO JESUS

Lyrics: AUTHOR--folk.
PLACE--Brazil.
DATE--possibly created 17th-19th century?
ENGLISH TITLE--LULLABY FOR BABY JESUS (translated by
Ruth Heller [1920-   ]).
DIFFERING FIRST LINE--SLEEP QUIETLY, MY JESUS.

Music: COMPOSER--folk.
PLACE--Brazil.
DATE--possibly created 17th-19th century?

Found: HEL

608. RESONET IN LAUDIBUS

Lyrics: AUTHOR--anonymous.
PLACE--Germany.
DATE--created 13th or 14th century.
VARIANT VERNACULAR TITLE--RESONEMUS LAUDIBUS.
ENGLISH TITLES--LONG AGO AND FAR AWAY (translated by
Edward Traill Horn [1909-   ]);
CHRIST WAS BORN ON CHRISTMAS DAY
(two different translations, one by
John Mason Neale [1818-1866], one by
Elizabeth Poston [1905-   ]); NOW
WITH GLADNESS CAROL WE (translated by
Ronald Arbuthnott Knox [1888-   ]).

Music: COMPOSER--anonymous.
PLACE--Germany.
DATE--probably created 14th century.

Found: SIM, LUT, CCT, PEN, THF

Notes: The translation by Neale is also used with three
different tunes to form another carol and its two
variants, all under the title CHRIST WAS BORN ON
CHRISTMAS DAY; the tune is also used for the carol
JOSEPH, LIEBER JOSEPH MEIN.

609. RING, CHRISTMAS BELLS

Lyrics: AUTHOR--M.L. Hohman.
PLACE--United States.
DATE--published 1947.

Music: COMPOSER--Mykola Dmytrovich Leontovych (1877-1921).
PLACE--Ukraine.
DATE--written early 20th century.

Found: PRE
Notes: The tune is also used for the carols CAROL OF THE
BELLS (both versions) and COME, DANCE AND SING.

610. RING OUT, WILD BELLS

Lyrics: AUTHOR--Alfred Tennyson (1809-1892).
PLACE--England.
DATE--published 1850.
DIFFERING FIRST LINE--RING OUT, WILD BELLS, TO THE
WILD SKY.
Music: COMPOSER--Edgar Leslie Bainton (1880-   ).
PLACE--England.
DATE--published 1900-1909.
Found: REE

611. RISE UP, SHEPHERD, AND FOLLOW

Lyrics: AUTHOR--folk (Black spiritual).
PLACE--United States.
DATE--probably created 18th or 19th century;
published 1867.
VARIANT VERNACULAR TITLES--RISE UP, SHEPHERD, AN'
FOLLER; RISE UP, SHEPHERD.
DIFFERING FIRST LINES--THERE'S A STAR IN THE EAST ON
CHRISTMAS MORN; DERE'S A STAR
IN DE EAS' ON CHRISTMAS
MORN.
Music: COMPOSER--folk (Black spiritual).
PLACE--United States.
DATE--probably created 18th or 19th century;
published 1867.
Found: INT, SIM, SHE, OBE, LOM

612. RITSCH, RATSCH, FILIBOM!

Lyrics: AUTHOR--folk.
PLACE--Sweden.
DATE--possibly created 16th-18th century?
ENGLISH TITLE--RITSCH, RATSCH, FILIBOM!
DIFFERING FIRST LINE--RITSCH, RATSCH, FILIBOM BOM
BOM.
Music: COMPOSER--folk.
PLACE--Sweden.
DATE--possibly created 16th-18th century?
Found: SHE, JUL, GLA

613. ROCKIN' AROUND THE CHRISTMAS TREE

Lyrics: AUTHOR--John D. Marks (1909-   ).
PLACE--United States.
DATE--published 1958.

Music: COMPOSER--John D. Marks (1909-   ).
       PLACE--United States.
       DATE--published 1958.
Found: NOR, POP, ULT, ONS, ONT

614. ROEDD YN Y WLAD HONNO

Lyrics: AUTHOR--folk.
        PLACE--Wales.
        DATE--possibly created 15th-17th century?
        ENGLISH TITLES--WELSH CAROL (paraphrase by K.E.
                    Roberts); ABIDING IN THE FIELDS
                    (translated by Marx E. Oberndorfer
                    [1876-   ]).
        DIFFERING FIRST LINE--AWAKE WERE THEY ONLY.
Music: COMPOSER--folk.
        PLACE--Wales.
        DATE--possibly created 15th-17th century?
Found: OXF, OBE

615. RORATE

Lyrics: AUTHOR--William Dunbar (ca. 1465-1530).
        PLACE--Scotland.
        DATE--written late 15th or early 16th century.
        DIFFERING FIRST LINES--RORATE COELI DESUPER!; RORATE
                          CAELI DESUPER!
Music: COMPOSER--folk.
        PLACE--Scotland.
        DATE--possibly created 16th-18th century?
        VARIANT TUNE--tune by John Sheeles (1688-1761).
Found: OXF, UNI
Notes: Despite the Latin first line, the words are mostly
        English.

616. RUDOLPH THE RED-NOSED REINDEER

Lyrics: AUTHOR--John D. Marks (1909-   ).
        PLACE--United States.
        DATE--published 1949.
        DIFFERING FIRST LINE--YOU KNOW DASHER AND DANCER AND
                          PRANCER AND VIXEN.
Music: COMPOSER--John D. Marks (1909-   ).
        PLACE--United States.
        DATE--published 1949.
Found: MANY
Notes: In 1939, Robert L. May created the story of Rudolph
        as part of an advertising promotion for Montgomery
        Ward stores; the story was published in book form in
        1947; in 1949, May's brother-in-law, Marks, adapted
        the story into song lyrics, wrote an accompanying
        tune, and published the resultant song.

617. SAINT STEPHEN WAS A HOLY MAN

    Lyrics: AUTHOR--folk.
            PLACE--England.
            DATE--possibly created 15th-17th century; probably
                first published 1823.
            VARIANT VERNACULAR TITLE--SAINT STEPHEN.
    Music: COMPOSER--folk.
            PLACE--England.
            DATE--possibly created 15th-17th century; probably
                first published 1833.
    Found: OXF, THF, GAS, SAN, YOU

618. SALTEN Y BALLEN

    Lyrics: AUTHOR--folk.
            PLACE--probably Roussillon region, France.
            DATE--possibly created 15th-17th century?
            VARIANT VERNACULAR TITLE--SALTEN I BALLEN.
            ENGLISH TITLE--LEAPING AND DANCING (translated by
                Elizabeth Poston [1905-   ]).
            DIFFERING FIRST LINE--SHEPHERDS AND LASSES, COME
                LEAPING AND DANCING.
    Music: COMPOSER--folk.
            PLACE--probably Roussillon region, France.
            DATE--possibly created 15th-17th century?
    Found: PEN, NPF

619. THE SALUTATION CAROL

    Lyrics: AUTHOR--folk.
            PLACE--England.
             DATE--created 15th century.
            VARIANT VERNACULAR TITLES--TIDINGS TRUE; THE SALUTA-
                        TION OF THE ANGEL; NOWEL,
                        THIS IS THE SALUTATION;
                        NOWELL, NOWELL: TIDINGS
                        TRUE.
            DIFFERING FIRST LINES--NOEL, NOEL, NOEL!; NOWELL,
                        NOWELL, NOWELL; NOWEL, NOWEL,
                        NOWEL; THIS IS THE SALUTATION
                        OF THE ANGEL GABRIEL; TIDINGS
                        TRUE THERE BE COME NEW; TIDINGS
                        TRUE I BRING TO YOU.
    Music: COMPOSER--folk.
            PLACE--England.
            DATE--created 15th century.
    Found: OXF, EAR, UNI, THF, MEC

620. SAN JOSÉ ERA CARPINTERO

    Lyrics: AUTHOR--folk.
              PLACE--Castille, Spain.
              DATE--possibly created 16th-18th century?
              VARIANT VERNACULAR TITLE--SAN JOSÉ.
    Music: COMPOSER--folk.
              PLACE--Castille, Spain.
              DATE--possibly created 16th-18th century?
              VARIANT TUNE--tune by Joaquín Nin y Castellanos
                            (1879-1949), composer from Cuba.
    Found: MON, CAN, NIN

621. SANS DAY CAROL

    Lyrics: AUTHOR--folk.
              PLACE--Cornwall, England.
              DATE--possibly created 16th-18th century?
               VARIANT VERNACULAR TITLE--ST. DAY CAROL.
              DIFFERING FIRST LINE--NOW THE HOLLY BEARS A BERRY AS
                              WHITE AS THE MILK.
    Music: COMPOSER--folk.
              PLACE--Cornwall, England.
              DATE--possibly created 16th-18th century?
    Found: OXF, CCT, UNI

622. SANT JOSEP I LA MARE DE DÉU

    Lyrics: AUTHOR--folk.
              PLACE--Catalonia, Spain.
               DATE--possibly created 16th-18th century?
               ENGLISH TITLE--HOLY JOSEPH AND MARY THE MAID
                            (translated by George K. Evans).
    Music: COMPOSER--folk.
              PLACE--Catalonia, Spain.
              DATE--possibly created 16th-18th century?
    Found: INT, SEA

623. SANTA BABY

    Lyrics: AUTHOR--Joan Javits Zeeman (1928-   ), Philip
                    Springer, and Tony Springer.
             PLACE--United States.
             DATE--written 1953.
    Music: COMPOSER--Joan Javits Zeeman (1928-   ), Philip
                    Springer, and Tony Springer.
             PLACE--United States.
             DATE--written 1953.

624. SANTA, BRING MY BABY BACK

    Lyrics: AUTHOR--Claude DeMetrius (1917-   ) and Aaron Harold
                      Schroeder (1926-   ).
              PLACE--United States.
              DATE--published 1957.
              DIFFERING FIRST LINE--DON'T NEED A LOT OF PRESENTS.
    Music: COMPOSER--Claude DeMetrius (1917-   ) and Aaron
                      Harold Schroeder (1926-   ).
              PLACE--United States.
              DATE--published 1957.
    Found: ULT

625. SANTA CLAUS BLUES

    Lyrics: AUTHOR--folk.
              PLACE--United States.
              DATE--created 20th century.
              DIFFERING FIRST LINE--SANTA CLAUS, SANTA CLAUS,
                                       LISTEN TO MY PLEA.
    Music: COMPOSER--folk.
              PLACE--United States.
              DATE--created 20th century.
    Found: SEA

626. SANTA CLAUS IS COMIN' TO TOWN

    Lyrics: AUTHOR--Haven Gillespie (1888-1975).
              PLACE--United States.
               DATE--written 1932.
               DIFFERING FIRST LINE--YOU BETTER WATCH OUT.
    Music: COMPOSER--John Frederick Coots (1897-   ).
              PLACE--United States.
               DATE--written 1932.
    Found: ONS, HAP

627. SCHLAF', MEIN KINDELEIN

    Lyrics: AUTHOR--folk.
              PLACE--Alsace, France.
              DATE--probably created 17th century; first known text
                    1697.
    Music: COMPOSER--folk.
              PLACE--Alsace, France.
              DATE--probably created 17th century.
    Found: INT, BUD, HFW
    Notes: This is the German version of DORS, MA COLOMBE.

628. SCHÖNSTER HERR JESU

      Lyrics: AUTHOR--folk.
               PLACE--Germany.
               DATE--probably created 16th or 17th century;
                     possibly first published 1677.
               ENGLISH TITLE--BEAUTIFUL SAVIOR (translated by
                     Joseph Augustus Seiss [1823-1904]).
      Music: COMPOSER--folk.
               PLACE--Germany.
               DATE--probably created 16th or 17th century;
                     possibly first published 1677.
               VARIANT TUNE--folk tune from Silesia, Germany.
      Found: PRE, BUD

629. THE SECRET OF CHRISTMAS

      Lyrics: AUTHOR--Sammy Cahn (1913-   ).
               PLACE--United States.
               DATE--written around 1959.
      Music: COMPOSER--Edward Chester Babcock (1913-   ).
               PLACE--United States.
               DATE--written around 1959.
      Found: ONS, ONT, HAP

630. SEE AMID THE WINTER'S SNOW

      Lyrics: AUTHOR--Edward Caswall (1814-1878).
               PLACE--England.
               DATE--published 1851.
               VARIANT VERNACULAR TITLE--WINTER'S SNOW.
      Music: COMPOSER--John Goss (1800-1880).
               PLACE--England.
               DATE--written 19th century.
               VARIANT TUNES--tunes by R.O. Morriss (1886-1948) and
                     R.A. Smith; tune from France.
      Found: OXF, CCO, HAW, HUT, YOU

631. SEL BYCH RÁD K BETLÉMU

      Lyrics: AUTHOR--folk.
               PLACE--Czechoslovakia.
               DATE--possibly created 16th-18th century?
               VARIANT VERNACULAR TITLE--JÁ BYCH RÁD K BETLÉMU.
               ENGLISH TITLES--I GO TO BETHLEHEM (translated by
                     George K. Evans); TO BETHL'EM I
                     WOULD GO (translated by Mary Cochrane
                     Vojácek); TO BETHLE'M I WOULD GO (a
                     different translation, anonymous);
                     I'LL GO TO BETHLEHEM (translated by
                     Edward Bliss Reed [1872-1940]).

Music: COMPOSER--folk.
           PLACE--Czechoslovakia.
           DATE--possibly created 16th-18th century?
Found: INT, SIM, SHE, SCC, CEI

632. SENHORA DONA SANCHA

Lyrics: AUTHOR--folk.
           PLACE--Brazil.
           DATE--possibly created 17th-19th century?
           ENGLISH TITLE--OH HEAR THE HEAV'NLY ANGELS (trans-
                          lated by Olga Paul).
Music: COMPOSER--folk.
           PLACE--Brazil.
           DATE--possibly created 17th-19th century?
Found: RTW

633. THE SEVEN BLESSINGS OF MARY

Lyrics: AUTHOR--folk.
           PLACE--Appalachian region.
           DATE--probably created 18th or 19th century.
           VARIANT VERNACULAR TITLES--THE BLESSINGS OF MARY;
                          THE SEVEN JOYS OF MARY.
           DIFFERING FIRST LINES--THE VERY FIRST BLESSING THAT
                          MARY HAD; THE VERY FIRST
                          BLESSING MARY HAD.
Music: COMPOSER--folk.
           PLACE--Appalachian region.
           DATE--probably created 18th or 19th century.
           VARIANT TUNES--two other Appalachian tunes.
Found: SEA, SEE, TCC, LOM
Notes: The lyrics are a derivative of the carol THE SEVEN
           JOYS OF MARY, with different tunes used.

634. THE SEVEN JOYS OF MARY

Lyrics: AUTHOR--folk.
           PLACE--England.
           DATE--created 15th century.
           VARIANT VERNACULAR TITLES--THE SEVEN REJOICES OF
                          MARY; THE SEVEN JOYS; THE
                          SEVEN GOOD JOYS; JOYS
                          SEVEN.
           DIFFERING FIRST LINES--THE FIRST GOOD JOY THAT MARY
                          HAD; THE FIRST REJOICE OUR
                          LADYE GOT.
Music: COMPOSER--folk.
           PLACE--England.
           DATE--probably created 18th century.
           VARIANT TUNE--another English folk song, probably
                          earlier than the above tune.

Found: OXF, INT, SIM, REE, THF
Notes: Reputedly, the song was used in 15th century mystery
           plays; for a United States derivative, see THE SEVEN
           BLESSINGS OF MARY.

635. SHAKESPEARE'S CAROL

   Lyrics: AUTHOR--William Shakespeare (1564-1616).
              PLACE--England.
              DATE--written around 1600.
              DIFFERING FIRST LINE--BLOW, BLOW, THOU WINTER WIND.
   Music: COMPOSER--Thomas Augustine Arne (1710-1778).
              PLACE--England.
              DATE--possibly first published 1750.
              VARIANT TUNE--tune by Richard John Samuel Stevens
                            (1757-1837).
   Found: OXF
   Notes: The lyrics are from AS YOU LIKE IT, Act II.

636. SHEPHERD, SHEPHERD

   Lyrics: AUTHOR--folk (Black spiritual).
              PLACE--United States.
              DATE--probably created 18th or 19th century.
   Music: COMPOSER--folk (Black spiritual).
              PLACE--United States.
              DATE--probably created 18th or 19th century.
   Found: SEE, ANS

637. SHEPHERD'S CAROL

   Lyrics: AUTHOR--William Billings (1746-1800).
              PLACE--probably Boston, Massachusetts area.
              DATE--published 1786.
              DIFFERING FIRST LINE--METHINKS I SEE A HEAVENLY HOST.
   Music: COMPOSER--William Billings (1746-1800).
              PLACE--probably Boston, Massachusetts area.
              DATE--published 1786.

638. SHEPHERD'S PIPE CAROL

   Lyrics: AUTHOR--John Rutter.
              PLACE--England.
              DATE--published 1967.
              DIFFERING FIRST LINE--GOING THROUGH THE HILLS ON A
                                    NIGHT SO STARRY.
   Music: COMPOSER--John Rutter.
              PLACE--England.
              DATE--published 1967.
   Found: CCT, CCF

639. THE SHEPHERDS WENT THEIR HASTY WAY

    Lyrics: AUTHOR--Samuel Taylor Coleridge (1772-1834).
              PLACE--England.
              DATE--published 1817.
    Music: COMPOSER--folk.
              PLACE--Alsace, France.
              DATE--possibly created 15th-17th century?
              VARIANT TUNE--tune by John Francis Barnett (1837-
                                   1916).
    Found: THF, STA
    Notes: The original title of Coleridge's poem was A CHRISTMAS
              CAROL.

640. SHOUT THE GLAD TIDINGS

    Lyrics: AUTHOR--William Augustus Muhlenberg (1796-1877).
              PLACE--probably Flushing, New York.
              DATE--published 1826.
              DIFFERING FIRST LINE--SHOUT THE GLAD TIDINGS,
                                     EXULTINGLY SING.
    Music: COMPOSER--Charles Avison (ca. 1710-1770).
              PLACE--England.
              DATE--written 18th century.
    Found: SIM, ONS, TRE, BAP
    Notes: The lyrics were written specifically for the tune.

641. SIGĒSATO PASA SARX BROTEIA

    Lyrics: AUTHOR--anonymous.
              PLACE--probably Palestine/Syria region.
               DATE--possibly created 5th century.
              ENGLISH TITLE--LET ALL MORTAL FLESH KEEP SILENCE
                                    (translated by Gerard Moultrie [1829-
                                    1885]).
    Music: COMPOSER--folk.
              PLACE--France (possibly Picardy region).
              DATE--probably created 17th century; possibly first
                      published 1860.
    Found: MET, OWE, PRA, HAR, MEN
    Notes: The lyrics are translated from the Liturgy of St.
              James of Jerusalem; the tune is also used as a variant
              for the carol LO, HE COMES WITH CLOUDS DESCENDING.

642. SILENCE CIEL! SILENCE TERRE!

    Lyrics: AUTHOR--folk.
              PLACE--France.
              DATE--probably created 16th-18th century.
              ENGLISH TITLE--BE SILENT HEAVEN! BE SILENT EARTH!
                                    (translated by K.W. Simpson).
    Music: COMPOSER--folk.

PLACE--France.
DATE--probably created 16th-18th century.
Found: THF, SMI
Notes: The song was possibly first published in 1867.

643. SILVER AND GOLD

Lyrics: AUTHOR--John D. Marks (1909-   ).
PLACE--United States.
DATE--published 1964.
Music: COMPOSER--John D. Marks (1909-   ).
PLACE--United States.
DATE--published 1964.
Found: ULT, ONS, ONT

644. SILVER BELLS

Lyrics: AUTHOR--Ray Evans (1915-   ).
PLACE--United States.
DATE--written around 1950.
DIFFERING FIRST LINES--CHRISTMAS MAKES YOU FEEL
EMOTIONAL; CITY SIDEWALKS,
BUSY SIDEWALKS, DRESSED IN
HOLIDAY STYLE.
Music: COMPOSER--Jay Livingston (1915-   ).
PLACE--United States.
DATE--written around 1950.
Found: NOR, SEV
Notes: The song was first presented in the 1951 movie THE
LEMON DROP KID.

645. SING-A-LAMB

Lyrics: AUTHOR--folk (Black spiritual).
PLACE--probably Texas or Louisiana.
DATE--probably created 19th century.
DIFFERING FIRST LINES--OH, THAT LAMB; BRING MARY AND
THE BABY.
Music: COMPOSER--folk (Black spiritual).
PLACE--probably Texas or Louisiana.
DATE--probably created 19th century.
Found: SEE

646. SING A SONG OF SANTA CLAUS

Lyrics: AUTHOR--Emanuel Kurtz (1911-   ).
PLACE--United States.
DATE--written around 1952.
Music: COMPOSER--Emanuel Kurtz (1911-   ).
PLACE--United States.
DATE--written around 1952.

647. SING, ALL MEN

    Lyrics: AUTHOR--folk.
            PLACE--probably Kentucky.
            DATE--probably created 18th or 19th century.
            DIFFERING FIRST LINE--SING, ALL MEN! 'TIS CHRISTMAS
                                  MORNING.
    Music: COMPOSER--folk.
            PLACE--probably Kentucky.
            DATE--probably created 18th or 19th century.
    Found: APP, TCC

648. SING HALLELU

    Lyrics: AUTHOR--folk (Black spiritual).
            PLACE--United States (possibly South Carolina).
            DATE--probably created 18th or 19th century.
            DIFFERING FIRST LINE--DOWN IN A VALLEY.
    Music: COMPOSER--folk (Black spiritual).
            PLACE--United States (possibly South Carolina).
            DATE--probably created 18th or 19th century.
    Found: SEE
    Notes: The lyrics are similar to those for MARY HAD A BABY.

649. SING, O SING THIS BLESSED MORN

    Lyrics: AUTHOR--Christopher Wordsworth (1807-1885).
            PLACE--England.
            DATE--published 1862.
    Music: COMPOSER--folk.
            PLACE--Germany.
            DATE--possibly created 16th-18th century?
            VARIANT TUNE--tune by Charles F. Roper.
    Found: ONT, HAP, PRS

650. THE SINNERS' REDEMPTION

    Lyrics: AUTHOR--folk.
            PLACE--England.
            DATE--probably created early 17th century; probably
                  first published 1631.
            VARIANT VERNACULAR TITLES--ALL YE WHO ARE TO MIRTH
                                INCLINED; THE BIRTH OF THE
                                SAVIOUR.
            DIFFERING FIRST LINES--ALL YOU THAT ARE TO MIRTH
                                INCLINED; ALL YOU THAT ARE UNTO
                                MIRTH INCLINED.
    Music: COMPOSER--folk.
            PLACE--England.
            DATE--probably created 17th or 18th century; possibly
                  first published 1775.
            VARIANT TUNES--tune by Erik Routley (1917-1982);
                        another English folk tune.

Found: OXF, UNI, ETE, SHA
Notes: For a carol with similar lyrics but a different tune,
            see LET ALL THAT ARE TO MIRTH INCLINED.

651. SIR CHRISTÈMAS

Lyrics: AUTHOR--probably Richard Smert.
            PLACE--probably Devonshire, England.
            DATE--probably written second half of 15th century.
            VARIANT VERNACULAR TITLES--SIR CHRISTMAS; WELCOME,
                              SIR CHRISTMAS; NOWELL,
                              NOWELL: DIEU VOUS GARDE.
            DIFFERING FIRST LINES--NOWELL, NOWELL, NOWELL,
                              NOWELL; NOEL, NOEL, NOEL, NOEL;
                              WHO IS THERE THAT SINGETH SO;
                              WHO IS THIS THAT SINGETH SO;
                              DIEU VOUS GARDE, BEAUX SIEURS;
                              DIEU VOUS GARDE, BEAU SIRE.
Music: COMPOSER--probably Richard Smert.
            PLACE--probably Devonshire, England.
            DATE--probably written second half of 15th century.
            VARIANT TUNE--tune by William Mathias (1934-   ).
Found: OXF, CCT, THF, EAR, MEC

652. SISTER MARY HAD-A BUT ONE CHILD

Lyrics: AUTHOR--folk (Black spiritual).
            PLACE--United States.
            DATE--probably created 18th or 19th century.
            VARIANT VERNACULAR TITLE--SISTER MARY HAD BUT ONE
                              CHILD.
Music: COMPOSER--folk (Black spiritual).
            PLACE--United States.
            DATE--probably created 18th or 19th century.
Found: REF, LAN

653. SLAVA

Lyrics: AUTHOR--folk.
            PLACE--Russia.
            DATE--possibly created 16th-18th century?
            VARIANT VERNACULAR TITLE--SLAWA.
            ENGLISH TITLE--LET US PRAISE THEE (translated by
                              Olga Paul).
            DIFFERING FIRST LINES--UZH KAK SLAVA TEBIE BOZHE NA
                              NEBESI!; LET US PRAISE THEE,
                              OH GOD IN THE HEAVENS.
Music: COMPOSER--folk.
            PLACE--Russia.
            DATE--possibly created 16th-18th century?
Found: RTW
Notes: The tune is similar to the one used for the carol
            SLAVA BOGU NA NEBE.

654. SLAVA BOGU NA NEBE

    Lyrics: AUTHOR--folk.
              PLACE--Russia.
              DATE--possibly created 16th-18th century?
              ENGLISH TITLES--PRAISE TO GOD IN THE HIGHEST!;
                          PRAISE TO GOD.
    Music: COMPOSER--folk.
              PLACE--Russia.
              DATE--possibly created 16th-18th century?
    Found: OXF, REE
    Notes: The song was possibly first published in 1815; the
              melody was used by Ludwig van Beethoven (1770-1827)
              in his quartet, Opus 59, No. 2 (1808), by Nicolai
              Rimsky-Korsakov (1844-1908) in his cantata SLAVA
              (ca. 1890); and by Modest Mussorgsky (1839-1881) in
              his opera BORIS GODUNOV (1868-1869); the tune is
              similar to the one used for the carol SLAVA.

655. SLEEP, HOLY BABE!

    Lyrics: AUTHOR--Edward Caswall (1814-1878).
              PLACE--England.
              DATE--published 1850.
    Music: COMPOSER--John Bacchus Dykes (1823-1876).
              PLACE--England.
              DATE--possibly first published 1871.
              VARIANT TUNES--tunes by Herbert Stephen Irons (1834-
                          1905) and others.
    Found: INT, OBE, HUT, CHO, ULT

656. SLEEP, MY LITTLE JESUS

    Lyrics: AUTHOR--William Channing Gannett (1840-1923).
              PLACE--Minnesota.
              DATE--written 1882; published 1894.
    Music: COMPOSER--Adam Geibel (1855-1933).
              PLACE--probably Philadelphia, Pennsylvania.
              DATE--written late 19th or early 20th century.
    Found: SIM, TRE

657. SLEEP, MY SAVIOUR, SLEEP

    Lyrics: AUTHOR--Sabine Baring-Gould (1834-1924).
              PLACE--England.
              DATE--probably first published 1875.
              VARIANT VERNACULAR TITLE--SLEEP, MY SAVIOR.
    Music: COMPOSER--Luise Reichardt (1780?-1826).
              PLACE--Germany.
              DATE--probably written early 19th century.
              VARIANT TUNE--folk tune from Bohemia, Czechoslovakia.
    Found: SIM, HUT, CHO, UNI, HEL

658. SLEIGH BELL SERENADE

　　　Lyrics: AUTHOR--Paul Francis Webster (1907-1984).
　　　　　　　PLACE--United States.
　　　　　　　DATE--probably written 1940's.
　　　Music: COMPOSER--Joseph Francis Burke (1914-1950).
　　　　　　　PLACE--United States.
　　　　　　　DATE--probably written 1940's.

659. SLEIGH RIDE

　　　Lyrics: AUTHOR--Mitchell Parish.
　　　　　　　PLACE--United States.
　　　　　　　DATE--written 1950.
　　　　　　　VARIANT VERNACULAR TITLE--SLEIGHRIDE.
　　　　　　　DIFFERING FIRST LINE--JUST HEAR THOSE SLEIGH BELLS
　　　　　　　　　　　　　　　　　JINGLEING, RINGTINGTINGLEING
　　　　　　　　　　　　　　　　　TOO.
　　　Music: COMPOSER--Leroy Anderson (1908-1975).
　　　　　　　PLACE--United States.
　　　　　　　DATE--written 1948.
　　　Found: ULT, HAP
　　　Notes: This was originally written as an instrumental piece,
　　　　　　　and is frequently performed that way.

660. SLICZNA PANIENKA

　　　Lyrics: AUTHOR--folk.
　　　　　　　PLACE--Poland.
　　　　　　　DATE--possibly created 15th-17th century?
　　　　　　　ENGLISH TITLE--CAROL OF THE HAY (translated by
　　　　　　　　　　　　　George K. Evans).
　　　　　　　DIFFERING FIRST LINE--MARY, THE MAIDEN.
　　　Music: COMPOSER--folk.
　　　　　　　PLACE--Poland.
　　　　　　　DATE--possibly created 15th-17th century?
　　　Found: INT

661. SLYSELI JSME V BETLEME

　　　Lyrics: AUTHOR--folk.
　　　　　　　PLACE--Czechoslovakia.
　　　　　　　DATE--possibly created 15th-17th century?
　　　　　　　ENGLISH TITLE--WE HAVE HEARD IN BETHLEHEM (translated
　　　　　　　　　　　　　by George K. Evans).
　　　Music: COMPOSER--folk.
　　　　　　　PLACE--Czechoslovakia.
　　　　　　　DATE--possibly created 15th-17th century?
　　　Found: INT, ZPE

662.   SNOOPY'S CHRISTMAS

    Lyrics: AUTHOR--Hugo Weiss, Luigi Weiss, and George David
                  Weiss.
              PLACE--United States.
              DATE--published 1967.
              DIFFERING FIRST LINE--THE NEWS HAD COME OUT.
    Music: COMPOSER--Hugo Weiss, Luigi Weiss, and George David
                  Weiss.
              PLACE--United States.
              DATE--published 1967.
    Found: POP

663.   SNOW IN THE STREET

    Lyrics: AUTHOR--William Morris (1834-1896).
              PLACE--England.
              DATE--probably written 1869.
              DIFFERING FIRST LINE--FROM FAR AWAY WE COME TO YOU.
    Music: COMPOSER--Ralph Vaughan Williams (1872-1958).
              PLACE--England.
              DATE--published 1928.
    Found: OXF, ECS

664.   THE SNOW LAY ON THE GROUND

    Lyrics: AUTHOR--folk.
              PLACE--probably West country, England.
              DATE--probably created 19th century.
    Music: COMPOSER--folk.
               PLACE--Ireland or England.
              DATE--possibly created 18th or 19th century?
              VARIANT TUNES--anonymous tune from Italy and TUNE OF
                  THE PIFFERARI.
    Found: INT, HUT, YAL, ULT, ONS
    Notes: The carol is also known by the title VENITE ADOREMUS
              (the beginning words of the refrain).

665.   THE SNOW LIES THICK

    Lyrics: AUTHOR--Selwyn Image (1849-1930).
              PLACE--England.
              DATE--probably written early 20th century.
              DIFFERING FIRST LINE--THE SNOW LIES THICK UPON THE
                  THE EARTH.
    Music: COMPOSER--Geoffrey Shaw (1879-1943).
              PLACE--England.
              DATE--probably written early 20th century.
    Found: OXF, HUT, ECF

666. SNOWBIRD

    Lyrics: AUTHOR--Gene MacLellan.
               PLACE--Canada.
               DATE--published 1970.
               DIFFERING FIRST LINE--BENEATH THIS SNOWY MANTLE
                                  COLD AND CLEAN.
    Music: COMPOSER--Gene MacLellan.
               PLACE--Canada.
               DATE--published 1970.
    Found: SEV

667. SOME CHILDREN SEE HIM

    Lyrics: AUTHOR--Wihla Hutson.
               PLACE--United States.
               DATE--published 1954.
               DIFFERING FIRST LINE--SOME CHILDREN SEE HIM LILY
                                  WHITE.
    Music: COMPOSER--Alfred Burt (1919 or 1920-1954).
               PLACE--United States.
               DATE--published 1954.
    Found: BUR, ULT

668. SOMERSET WASSAIL

    Lyrics: AUTHOR--folk.
               PLACE--probably Somerset, England.
               DATE--possibly created 18th century.
               DIFFERING FIRST LINE--WASSAIL AND WASSAIL ALL OVER
                                  THE TOWN!
    Music: COMPOSER--folk.
               PLACE--probably Somerset, England.
               DATE--possibly created 18th century.
    Found: OXF, CFS
    Notes: The lyrics are somewhat similar to GLOUCESTERSHIRE
               WASSAIL, but the melody is different.

669. SONGS OF THANKFULNESS AND PRAISE

    Lyrics: AUTHOR--Christopher Wordsworth (1807-1885).
               PLACE--England.
               DATE--published 1862.
    Music: COMPOSER--Charles Stegall (1826-1905).
               PLACE--England.
               DATE--probably written second half of 19th century.
               VARIANT TUNE--tune by John Richardson (1816-1879).
    Found: LUT, ENG

670. SPĒLAIŌ PAROKĒSAS

    Lyrics: AUTHOR--St. Anatolius (ca. 400-458).
               PLACE--probably Constantinople, Byzantine Empire.
               DATE--probably written mid-5th century.
               ENGLISH TITLE--IN A CAVERN OXEN-TROD (translated by
                                 George Ratcliffe Woodward [1848-1934]).
    Music: COMPOSER--folk.
               PLACE--Netherlands.
               DATE--possibly created 16th-18th century?
    Found: UNI, CCB
    Notes: The tune is the melody EEN SOUDAEN HAD EEN DOCHTERKEN.

671. STAFFAN VAR EN STALLEDRÄNG

    Lyrics: AUTHOR--folk.
               PLACE--Sweden.
               DATE--probably created medieval period.
               ENGLISH TITLES--STEFAN WAS A STABLE BOY; CAROL OF
                                   SAINT STAFFAN (translated by Anna M.
                                   Monrad and Edward Bliss Reed [1872-
                                   1940]).
               DIFFERING FIRST LINE--STAFFAN WAS A STABLE BOY.
    Music: COMPOSER--folk.
               PLACE--Sweden.
               DATE--probably created medieval period.
               VARIANT TUNE--another Swedish folk song.
    Found: SHE, CEL, GLA, JUL

672. STAND BENEATH THE MISTLETOE

    Lyrics: AUTHOR--Louis Hollingsworth (1920-   )
               PLACE--Florida.
                DATE--written 1953.
               DIFFERING FIRST LINE--CHRISTMAS LIGHTS, MISTLETOE.
    Music: COMPOSER--Louis Hollingsworth (1920-   ).
               PLACE--Florida.
               DATE--written 1953.
    Found: ONT

673. THE STAR CAROL

    Lyrics: AUTHOR--Wihla Hutson.
               PLACE--United States.
               DATE--published 1954.
               DIFFERING FIRST LINE--LONG YEARS AGO ON A DEEP WINTER
                                   NIGHT.
    Music: COMPOSER--Alfred Burt (1919 or 1920-1954).
               PLACE--United States.
               DATE--published 1954.
    Found: BUR, ULT, HAP

674. STAR CAROL

    Lyrics: AUTHOR--John Rutter.
                PLACE--England.
                DATE--published 1976.
                DIFFERING FIRST LINE--SING THIS NIGHT, FOR A BOY IS
                                    BORN IN BETHLEHEM.
    Music: COMPOSER--John Rutter.
                PLACE--England.
                DATE--published 1976.
    Found: CCF

675. STAR IN THE EAST

    Lyrics: AUTHOR--folk.
                PLACE--probably Southern States.
                DATE--probably created 19th century.
                DIFFERING FIRST LINES--HAIL, BLESSED MORN!; HAIL THE
                                    BLEST MORN.
    Music: COMPOSER--folk.
                PLACE--probably Southern States.
                DATE--probably created 19th century.
                VARIANT TUNE--another folk tune, probably of similar
                                    origins.
    Found: LAN, SEE
    Notes: The lyrics are similar to those for the English carol
                BRIGHTEST AND BEST; almost surely, the mainstream
                English song preceded this song; the United States
                folk tune used with the English carol is also used
                with this carol.

676. STAR OF BETHLEHEM, STAR ABOVE

    Lyrics: AUTHOR--Harry Robert Wilson (1901-1968).
                PLACE--United States.
                DATE--published 1959.
    Music: COMPOSER--Miklós Rózsa (1907-   ).
                PLACE--United States.
                DATE--published 1959.
    Found: HAP

677. STAR OF THE EAST

    Lyrics: AUTHOR--George Cooper (1840-1927).
                PLACE--United States.
                DATE--published 1890.
                DIFFERING FIRST LINE--STAR OF THE EAST, O BETHLEHEM'S
                                    STAR.
    Music: COMPOSER--Amanda Kennedy.
                PLACE--United States.
                DATE--published 1890.
    Found: SEV, ONS, ONT, HAP

678.   STARS IN THE HEAVEN

      Lyrics: AUTHOR--folk (Black spiritual).
              PLACE--probably Louisiana.
              DATE--probably created 19th century.
              VARIANT VERNACULAR TITLE--BYE AND BYE.
      Music: COMPOSER--folk (Black spiritual).
              PLACE--probably Louisiana.
              DATE--probably created 19th century.
      Found: SEE

679.   STILL, O HIMMEL! STILL, O ERDE!

      Lyrics: AUTHOR--folk.
              PLACE--probably Tyrol, Austria.
              DATE--possibly created 16th-18th century?
              ENGLISH TITLE--HUSH, O HEAVEN (translated by Edward
                                Bliss Reed [1872-1940]).
      Music: COMPOSER--folk.
              PLACE--probably Tyrol, Austria.
              DATE--possibly created 16th-18th century?
      Found: CFF

680.   STILL, STILL, STILL

      Lyrics: AUTHOR--folk.
              PLACE--Austria (possibly Salzburg region).
              DATE--probably created 18th or 19th century.
              ENGLISH TITLE--STILL, STILL, STILL (three different
                                translations, one anonymous, one by
                                Bernard Gasso [1926-   ], one by
                                George K. Evans).
      Music: COMPOSER--folk.
              PLACE--Austria (possibly Salzburg region).
              DATE--probably created 18th or 19th century.
      Found: INT, BUD, ULT, ONT

681.   STILLE NACHT, HEILIGE NACHT

      Lyrics: AUTHOR--Joseph Mohr (1792-1848).
              PLACE--Oberndorf, Austria.
              DATE--written December 1818.
              VARIANT VERNACULAR TITLES--STILLE NACHT; WEIHNACHTSLIED.
              ENGLISH TITLES--SILENT NIGHT, HOLY NIGHT, SILENT
                                NIGHT, and HOLY NIGHT (three titles for
                                the same well-known translation by John
                                Freeman Young [1820-1885]); another
                                lesser-known translation under the
                                title SILENT NIGHT, HOLY NIGHT is by
                                Elizabeth Poston [1905-   ], and
                                another lesser-known translation
                                under the title SILENT NIGHT is by
                                David Willcocks; HOLY NIGHT! PEACEFUL
                                NIGHT!

Music: COMPOSER--Franz Gruber (1787-1863).
           PLACE--Oberndorf, Austria.
           DATE--written December 1818.
Found: MANY
Notes: The song was specially written for a Christmas Eve
           service, probably because the church organ had a
           breakdown, and was set for two solo voices, chorus,
           and guitar; the organ repairman secured a copy of the
           song and soon it was in the possession of a singing
           troupe, the Strasser Family, who quickly popularized
           it; manuscripts of the song were also distributed
           throughout the region and a first printing was made
           in 1838; for some years the song was considered to be
           an anonymous Tyrolean folksong, and also it was
           attributed to Johann Michael Haydn (1737-1806), the
           younger brother of the great composer Franz Joseph
           Haydn (1732-1809); in 1854 a government investigation
           discovered the truth; it is the best-known German
           language carol and probably the best-known carol
           internationally.

682. SU LEVATE PASTORI

Lyrics: AUTHOR--folk.
           PLACE--Italy.
           DATE--probably created 16th or 17th century.
           ENGLISH TITLE--DARK IS THE EVEN (translated by K.W.
                          Simpson).
Music: COMPOSER--folk.
           PLACE--Italy.
           DATE--probably created 16th or 17th century.
Found: THF, ICC, UNI
Notes: The words and melody were possibly first published
           in 1674; the tune is the melody LA ROSELLINA.

683. SUMMER IN WINTER

Lyrics: AUTHOR--Richard Crashaw (1612?-1649).
           PLACE--probably Italy.
           DATE--published 1648.
           VARIANT VERNACULAR TITLE--AT THE NATIVITY.
           DIFFERING FIRST LINE--GLOOMY NIGHT EMBRACED THE
                                 PLACE.
Music: COMPOSER--folk.
           PLACE--Alsace, France.
           DATE--probably created 16th or 17th century;
                 probably first published 1697.
Found: OXF, THF, UNI

684. SUS ÎN POARTA RAIULUI

Lyrics: AUTHOR--folk.
           PLACE--Romania.

DATE--possibly created 17th-19th century?
ENGLISH TITLE--AT THE GATES OF HEAVEN ABOVE (trans-
                    lated by George K. Evans).
Music: COMPOSER--folk.
           PLACE--Romania.
           DATE--possibly created 17th-19th century?
Found: INT

685. SUSANI

Lyrics: AUTHOR--folk.
           PLACE--Germany.
           DATE--probably created 14th century.
           VARIANT VERNACULAR TITLES--SUSANI, SUSANI; SUSANNI;
                                 VOM HIMMEL HOCH, O ENGLEIN
                                 KOMMT!
           ENGLISH TITLES--the same as the German, with trans-
                       lations by George K. Evans, Marx E.
                       Oberndorfer (1876-   ), and others;
                       CHRIST CHILD'S SLUMBER SONG (trans-
                       lated by Ruth Heller [1920-   ]);
                       SUSANI! SUSANI! (translated by Edward
                       Bliss Reed [1872-1940]).
           DIFFERING FIRST LINES--FROM HEAV'N ON HIGH, O ANGELS
                               SING!; FROM HEAV'N, O ANGELS
                               COME BELOW; FROM HEAVEN HIGH,
                               THE ANGELS CAME; FROM HIGHEST
                               HEAVEN COME, ANGELS COME!;
                               FROM HEAVEN ABOVE, O ANGELS
                               DRAW NIGH.
Music: COMPOSER--folk.
           PLACE--Germany.
           DATE--probably created 14th century.
Found: INT, OBE, THF, CSI, UNI
Notes: The same tune is used for the similar carol SUSANNI.

686. SUSANNI

Lyrics: AUTHOR--folk.
           PLACE--England.
           DATE--probably created 15th century.
           VARIANT VERNACULAR TITLE--A LITTLE CHILD THERE IS
                               YBORE.
           DIFFERING FIRST LINE--A LITTLE CHILD THERE IS YBORN.
Music: COMPOSER--folk.
           PLACE--Germany.
           DATE--probably created 14th century.
Found: OXF, PEN
Notes: The same tune is used for the similar carol SUSANI.

687. SÜSSER DIE GLOCKEN NIE KLINGEN

      Lyrics: AUTHOR--folk.
              PLACE--Germany.
              DATE--possibly created 17th-19th century?
              ENGLISH TITLES--CHRISTMAS BELLS (translated by
                                Donald Franklin Malin [1896-   ]);
                                NEVER DO BELLS RING MORE SWEETLY
                                (translated by Ruth Heller [1920-
                                    ]).
              DIFFERING FIRST LINE--NEVER DO BELLS RING SO SWEETLY.
      Music: COMPOSER--folk.
              PLACE--Germany.
              DATE--possibly created 17th-19th century?
      Found: MAL, HEL

688. SUZY SNOWFLAKE

      Lyrics: AUTHOR--Sid Tepper (1918-   ) and Roy C. Bennett
                  (1918-   ).
              PLACE--United States.
              DATE--published 1951.
              DIFFERING FIRST LINE--HERE COMES SUZY SNOWFLAKE.
      Music: COMPOSER--Sid Tepper (1918-   ) and Roy C. Bennett
                  (1918-   ).
              PLACE--United States.
              DATE--published 1951.
      Found: ULT, ONS, ONT
      Notes: "Roy Brodsky" has been indicated as Tepper's
              collaborator.

689. SWEET WAS THE SONG THE VIRGIN SANG

      Lyrics: AUTHOR--William Ballet.
              PLACE--England.
              DATE--published around 1600.
              VARIANT VERNACULAR TITLES--SWEET WAS THE SONG THE
                                  VIRGIN SUNG; SWEET WAS THE
                                SONG; LUTE-BOOK LULLABY;
                                VIRGIN'S LULLABY.
      Music: COMPOSER--William Ballet.
              PLACE--England.
              DATE--published around 1600.
              VARIANT TUNE--tune by Stanley Taylor (1902-1972).
      Found: OXF, COF, UNI, APP, REE

690. THAT CHRISTMAS FEELING

      Lyrics: AUTHOR--Bennie Benjamin (1907-   ) and George David
                  Weiss.
              PLACE--United States.
              DATE--published 1946.

DIFFERING FIRST LINE--HOW I LOVE THAT CHRISTMAS
FEELING.
Music: COMPOSER--Bennie Benjamin (1907-   ) and George
David Weiss.
PLACE--United States.
DATE--published 1946.
Found: ULT

691. THAT'S WHAT I WANT FOR CHRISTMAS

Lyrics: AUTHOR--Irving Caesar (1895-   ).
PLACE--United States.
DATE--written 1936.
Music: COMPOSER--Gerald Marks (1900-   ).
PLACE--United States.
DATE--written 1936.

692. THAT'S WHAT I WANT FOR CHRISTMAS

Lyrics: AUTHOR--E.E. Lawrence.
PLACE--United States.
DATE--published 1963.
DIFFERING FIRST LINE--WHEN YOU SAID YESTERDAY THAT
IT'S NEARLY CHRISTMAS.
Music: COMPOSER--E.E. Lawrence.
PLACE--United States.
DATE--published 1963.
Found: SEV

693. THERE IS NO CHRISTMAS LIKE A HOME CHRISTMAS

Lyrics: AUTHOR--Carl Sigman (1909-   ).
PLACE--United States.
DATE--published 1950.
Music: COMPOSER--Mickey J. Addy.
PLACE--United States.
DATE--published 1950.
Found: POP, ULT, ONS, ONT, HAP

694. THERE IS NO ROSE OF SUCH VIRTUE

Lyrics: AUTHOR--anonymous.
PLACE--England.
DATE--probably created 14th or early 15th century.
VARIANT VERNACULAR TITLES--THERE IS NO ROSE; NO ROSE
OF SUCH VIRTUE.
DIFFERING FIRST LINE--THERE IS NO ROSE OF SUCH VERTU.
Music: COMPOSER--anonymous.
PLACE--England.
DATE--probably created 14th or early 15th century.
VARIANT TUNE--tune by Benjamin Britten (1913-1976).

       Found: CCT, BRI, UNI, EAR, MEC
       Notes: The first known text of words and music was written
                  around 1420.

695.   THERE'S A SONG IN THE AIR

       Lyrics: AUTHOR--Josiah Gilbert Holland (1819-1881).
                 PLACE--United States.
                 DATE--published 1872.
       Music: COMPOSER--Karl P. Harrington (1861-1953).
                 PLACE--North Woodstock, New Hampshire.
                 DATE--written July 1904; published 1905.
                 VARIANT TUNES--tune by George Edward Martin (1851-
                                 ); anonymous tune; 1879 tune by
                               George Frederick Root (1820-1895).
       Found: INT, HUT, MET, CHW, HAP

696.   THIRTY-TWO FEET AND EIGHT LITTLE TAILS

       Lyrics: AUTHOR--John Redmond (1906-   ), James Cavanaugh
                      (d. 1967), and Frank Weldon (d. 1970).
                 PLACE--United States.
                 DATE--published 1951.
                 VARIANT VERNACULAR TITLE--DASHER, DANCER, PRANCER,
                                   VIXEN, COMET, CUPID, DONNER,
                                   BLITZEN.
       Music: COMPOSER--John Redmond (1906-   ), James Cavanaugh
                      (d. 1967), and Frank Weldon (d. 1970).
                 PLACE--United States.
                 DATE--published 1951.
       Found: ONS, ONT, HAP

697.   THIS ENDRIS NIGHT

       Lyrics: AUTHOR--folk.
                 PLACE--England.
                 DATE--created 15th century.
                 VARIANT VERNACULAR TITLES--THIS ENDERS NIGHT; THIS
                                   ENDERS NYZGT.
                 DIFFERING FIRST LINE--THE OTHER NIGHT.
       Music: COMPOSER--folk.
                 PLACE--England.
                 DATE--created 15th or 16th century.
       Found: OXF, INT, PEN, UNI, THF
       Notes: The tune is also used for the carol BEHOLD THE
                 GREAT CREATOR MAKES.

698.   THIS LITTLE BABE

       Lyrics: AUTHOR--Robert Southwell (ca. 1561-1595).
                 PLACE--England.
                 DATE--written late 16th century.

                    VARIANT VERNACULAR TITLE--THIS LITTLE BABE SO FEW
                                                    DAYS OLD.
      Music: COMPOSER--Benjamin Britten (1913-1976).
                    PLACE--England.
                    DATE--written 1942
                    VARIANT TUNE--tune by Melchior Vulpius (ca. 1560-
                                            1615).
      Found: BRI, SIG

699.   THIS NEW CHRISTMAS CAROL

      Lyrics: AUTHOR--folk.
                    PLACE--probably West country, England.
                    DATE--possibly created 16th-18th century; probably
                            first published 1823.
      Music: COMPOSER--folk.
                    PLACE--probably West country, England.
                    DATE--possibly created 16th-18th century; probably
                            first published 1833.
                    VARIANT TUNE--folk tune from Brittany, France.
      Found: OXF, THF, SAO, GAS, UNI
      Notes: The Brittany tune, ME ANVEZ EUR GOULMIK, and the West
                    country tune may have a common origin.

700.   THOU DIDST LEAVE THY THRONE

      Lyrics: AUTHOR--Emily Elizabeth Steele Elliott (1836-1897).
                    PLACE--England.
                    DATE--written second half of 19th century.
      Music: COMPOSER--Timothy Richard Matthews (1826-1910).
                    PLACE--England.
                    DATE--published 1876.
                    VARIANT TUNE--tune by James Baden Powell (1842-   ).
      Found: YAL, HUT, PRA

701.   THOU MUST LEAVE THY LOWLY DWELLING

      Lyrics: AUTHOR--Paul England.
                    PLACE--England.
                    DATE--probably written first half of 20th century.
                    VARIANT VERNACULAR TITLES--THE SHEPHERDS' FAREWELL
                                                TO THE HOLY FAMILY; THE
                                                SHEPHERDS' FAREWELL.
      Music: COMPOSER--Hector Berlioz (1803-1869).
                    PLACE--France.
                    DATE--published 1855.
      Found: REE, CCO, UNI
      Notes: The tune is from Berlioz's L'ENFANCE DU CHRIST.

702. THE THREE DROVERS

    Lyrics: AUTHOR--John Wheeler.
               PLACE--Australia.
               DATE--written 20th century.
               DIFFERING FIRST LINE--ACROSS THE PLAINS ONE
                                     CHRISTMAS NIGHT.
    Music: COMPOSER--William Garnet James (1895-   ).
               PLACE--Australia.
               DATE--written 20th century.
    Found: UNI

703. THE THREE SHIPS

    Lyrics: AUTHOR--Alfred Noyes (1880-1958).
               PLACE--England.
               DATE--published 1908.
               DIFFERING FIRST LINE--AS I WENT UP THE MOUNTAINSIDE.
    Music: COMPOSER--Colin Taylor (1881-   ).
               PLACE--South Africa.
                DATE--published 1955.
    Found: SIM, TRE
    Notes: The tune was derived, by the composer, from a work
               published by him almost a half century earlier; for
               two carols with somewhat similar lyrics, see I SAW
               THREE SHIPS (both versions).

704. TO US A CHILD OF ROYAL BIRTH

    Lyrics: AUTHOR--Charles Wesley (1707-1788).
               PLACE--England.
               DATE--written 18th century; possibly first published
                    1830.
    Music: COMPOSER--anonymous.
               PLACE--probably Germany.
               DATE--probably created 15th century.
    Found: CAT
    Notes: The tune is also used for the carol PUER NOBIS
               NASCITUR.

705. TOMORROW SHALL BE MY DANCING DAY

    Lyrics: AUTHOR--folk.
               PLACE--probably West country, England.
               DATE--possibly created 16th century.
               VARIANT VERNACULAR TITLE--MY DANCING DAY.
    Music: COMPOSER--folk.
               PLACE--probably West country, England.
               DATE--possibly created 16th century.
    Found: PEN, OXF, CCT, APP, UNI
    Notes: The carol has three sections--Christmas, Lent and
               Passiontide, Easter and Ascension; the song was
               possibly first published in 1833.

706.   TOO FAT FOR THE CHIMNEY

    Lyrics: AUTHOR--Irving Gordon (1915-   ).
              PLACE--United States.
              DATE--published 1953.
              DIFFERING FIRST LINE--WAKE UP, WAKE UP, MOMMY DEAR.
    Music: COMPOSER--Irving Gordon (1915-   ).
              PLACE--United States.
              DATE--published 1953.
    Found: NOR, SEV

707.   TOURO-LOURO-LOURO!

    Lyrics: AUTHOR--folk.
              PLACE--Provence, France.
              DATE--probably created 17th century.
              ENGLISH TITLES--TOURO-LOURO-LOURO (translated by
                            George K. Evans); THE PEASANT'S
                            PILGRIMAGE (translated by Richard
                            Runciman Terry [1865-1938]).
              DIFFERING FIRST LINE--TU-RE-LU-RE-LU!
    Music: COMPOSER--folk.
              PLACE--Provence, France.
              DATE--probably created 17th century.
    Found: INT, THF
    Notes: This carol is sometimes attributed to Nicholas
              Saboly (1614-1675).

708.   TOYLAND

    Lyrics: AUTHOR--Glen MacDonough (1870-1924).
              PLACE--United States.
               DATE--probably written 1903.
    Music: COMPOSER--Victor Herbert (1859-1924).
              PLACE--United States.
              DATE--probably written 1903.
    Found: ULT, ONS, HAP
    Notes: This is from the operetta BABES IN TOYLAND.

709.   TRES MAGI DE GENTIBUS

    Lyrics: AUTHOR--anonymous.
              PLACE--probably Germany.
               DATE--created 15th century; probably first published
                  1567.
              ENGLISH TITLE--EASTERN MONARCHS, SAGES THREE.
    Music: COMPOSER--anonymous.
              PLACE--probably Germany.
               DATE--probably created 15th or 16th century;
                  probably first published 1608.
    Found: COF, OBE, HUT

710. TRÖSTET, TRÖSTET MEINE LEBEN

    Lyrics: AUTHOR--Johann Olearius (1611-1684).
               PLACE--Germany.
               DATE--published 1671.
               ENGLISH TITLE--COMFORT, COMFORT YE MY PEOPLE (trans-
                       lated by Catherine Winkworth [1827-
                       1878]).
    Music: COMPOSER--anonymous.
               PLACE--probably Switzerland.
               DATE--published 1551.
    Found: HAR, LUT, MEN

711. THE TRUTH FROM ABOVE

    Lyrics: AUTHOR--folk.
               PLACE--probably Herefordshire, England.
               DATE--possibly created 16th-18th century?
               VARIANT VERNACULAR TITLES--THIS IS THE TRUTH SENT
                       FROM ABOVE; THE TRUTH SENT
                       FROM ABOVE.
    Music: COMPOSER--folk.
               PLACE--probably Herefordshire, England.
               DATE--possibly created 16th-18th century?
    Found: OXF, CCT, REE, CFS, ETE

712. TU QUE CERQUES TEI DELICE

    Lyrics: AUTHOR--folk.
               PLACE--Provence, France.
               DATE--possibly created 16th-18th century?
               ENGLISH TITLE--YOU THAT MAKE A TOIL OF PLEASURE
                       (translated by John O'Connor [1870-
                       1952]).
    Music: COMPOSER--folk.
               PLACE--Provence, France.
               DATE--possibly created 16th-18th century?
    Found: THF, SMI

713. TU SCENDI DALLE STELLE

    Lyrics: AUTHOR--Alphonsus Liguori (1696-1787).
               PLACE--Italy.
               DATE--written 18th century.
               ENGLISH TITLES--FROM STARRY SKIES THOU COMEST
                       (translated by George K. Evans);
                       FROM STARRY SKIES DESCENDING.
    Music: COMPOSER--Alphonsus Liguori (1696-1787).
               PLACE--Italy.
               DATE--written 18th century.
    Found: INT, TRA, NAT
    Notes: The Italian lyrics have been attributed to Pope Pius
               IX (1846-1878).

714. 'TWAS THE NIGHT BEFORE CHRISTMAS

   Lyrics: AUTHOR--Clement Clarke Moore (1779-1863).
       PLACE--probably New York City.
       DATE--written 1822.
       VARIANT VERNACULAR TITLE--THE NIGHT BEFORE CHRISTMAS
               SONG.
       DIFFERING FIRST LINE--'TWAS THE NIGHT BEFORE CHRISTMAS
               AND ALL THROUGH THE HOUSE.
   Music: COMPOSER--Ken Darby.
       PLACE--United States.
       DATE--published 1942.
       VARIANT TUNES--1951 tune by Frank Henri Klickman
             (1885-1966); 1952 tune by John D.
             Marks (1909-   ).
   Found: TWA, NOR, SEV, POP, ULT
   Notes: Moore's poem was first published in Troy, New York
       on December 23, 1823.

715. THE TWELVE DAYS OF CHRISTMAS

   Lyrics: AUTHOR--folk.
       PLACE--England.
       DATE--probably created 17th or 18th century;
          probably first published around 1780.
       VARIANT VERNACULAR TITLES--ON THE FIRST DAY OF
                  CHRISTMAS; THE FIRST DAY
                  OF CHRISTMAS.
   Music: COMPOSER--folk.
       PLACE--England.
       DATE--probably created 17th or 18th century.
       VARIANT TUNE--United States folk song, possibly from
             Florida.
   Found: MANY
   Notes: A similar folksong is also known in France, indicat-
       ing possible original French creation; there are
       several versions of the lyrics, including at least
       one created in the United States.

716. TYRLEY, TYRLOW

   Lyrics: AUTHOR--folk.
       PLACE--England.
       DATE--probably created 15th century; first-known text
          second half of 15th century.
       DIFFERING FIRST LINE--ABOUT THE FIELD THEY PIPED FULL
                 RIGHT.
   Music: COMPOSER--Peter Warlock (1894-1930).
       PLACE--England.
       DATE--probably written around 1925.
   Found: OXF

717. UN FLAMBEAU, JEANETTE, ISABELLE

    Lyrics: AUTHOR--folk.
              PLACE--Provence, France.
              DATE--probably created 17th century.
              ENGLISH TITLES--BRING A TORCH, JEANNETTE, ISABELLA
                        and JEANNETTE, ISABELLA (two varia-
                        tions of the same translation by
                        Edward Cuthbert Nunn [1868-1914]);
                        the first title also used for two
                        other translations, one by Ruth
                        Heller (1920-   ), the other by
                        Marx E. Oberndorfer (1876-   ); HERE
                        A TORCH (translated by Charles
                        Fonteyn Manney [1872-1951]); BRING
                        YOUR TORCHES, JEANNETTE, ISABELLA;
                        BRING YOUR TORCHES.
              DIFFERING FIRST LINE--HERE A TORCH, JEANNETTE,
                              ISABELLA.
    Music: COMPOSER--folk.
              PLACE--Provence, France.
               DATE--probably created 17th century.
    Found: INT, SIM, SHE, TRA, YAL
    Notes: The carol is sometimes attributed to Nicholas Saboly
              (1614-1675).

718. UNE VAINE CRAINTE

    Lyrics: AUTHOR--folk.
              PLACE--France.
              DATE--possibly created 15th-17th century?
              ENGLISH TITLE--GLAD TIDINGS (translated by K.W.
                        Simpson).
              DIFFERING FIRST LINE--FEARFULNESS AND SADNESS.
    Music: COMPOSER--folk.
              PLACE--France.
              DATE--possibly created 15th-17th century?
    Found: OXF, THF

719. UP ON THE HOUSETOP

    Lyrics: AUTHOR--Benjamin R. Hanby (1833-1867).
              PLACE--probably Ohio.
              DATE--written 1850's or 1860's.
              VARIANT VERNACULAR TITLES--SANTA CLAUS, OR UP ON THE
                                HOUSE TOP; UP ON THE
                                HOUSE-TOP.
    Music: COMPOSER--Benjamin R. Hanby (1833-1867).
              PLACE--probably Ohio.
              DATE--written 1850's or 1860's.
    Found: INT, SEV, POP, ULT, CCC

720. VAMOS A BELÉN

    Lyrics: AUTHOR--folk.
             PLACE--Chile.
             DATE--possibly created 18th or 19th century?
             ENGLISH TITLE--GOING TO BETHLEHEM (translated by
                      George K. Evans).
             DIFFERING FIRST LINES--BUENAS NOCHES, MARIAQUITA;
                      GOOD EVENING, DEAR LITTLE MARY.
    Music: COMPOSER--folk.
             PLACE--Chile.
             DATE--possibly created 18th or 19th century?
    Found: INT

721. VAMOS, PASTORCITOS

    Lyrics: AUTHOR--folk.
             PLACE--Colombia.
             DATE--possibly created 18th or 19th century?
             ENGLISH TITLES--HASTEN NOW, O SHEPHERDS (translated by
                  George K. Evans); LET US GO, O
                  SHEPHERDS.
    Music: COMPOSER--folk.
             PLACE--Colombia.
             DATE--possibly created 18th or 19th century?
    Found: INT, ONS, ONT, HAP

722. VELKOMIN VERTU

    Lyrics: AUTHOR--folk.
             PLACE--Iceland.
             DATE--probably created medieval period.
             ENGLISH TITLE--WE WELCOME THEE TONIGHT (translated by
                  John Morrison).
    Music: COMPOSER--folk.
             PLACE--Iceland.
             DATE--probably created medieval period.
    Found: REF

723. VENI, EMMANUEL

    Lyrics: AUTHOR--anonymous.
             PLACE--Europe.
             DATE--probably created 12th century.
             VARIANT VERNACULAR TITLES--VENI, VENI, EMMANUEL; VENI
                  IMMANUEL.
             ENGLISH TITLE--O COME, O COME, EMMANUEL (one trans-
                  lation by John Mason Neale [1818-
                  1866]) with partial translation by
                  Henry Sloane Coffin [1877-1954],
                  another translation by Thomas Alexander
                  Lacey [1853-1931]).

Music: COMPOSER--anonymous.
　　　　　PLACE--Europe (possibly France).
　　　　　DATE--possibly created 12th or 13th century.
Found: MANY
Notes: Thomas Helmore (1811-1890) adapted the music for
　　　　　use with Neale's 1851 translation and the adaptation
　　　　　was published in 1854; the adaptation was made from
　　　　　one or more medieval plainsongs (possibly from a
　　　　　tune set to a 15th century processional used by
　　　　　Franciscan nuns); Neale's translation has been
　　　　　printed as O COME, O COME IMMANUEL.

724. VENI, REDEMPTOR GENTIUM

Lyrics: AUTHOR--probably St. Ambrose (340?-397).
　　　　　PLACE--probably Milan, Italy.
　　　　　DATE--written late 4th century.
　　　　　ENGLISH TITLES--SAVIOR OF THE NATIONS, COME (trans-
　　　　　　　　　　　　lated by William Morton Reynolds
　　　　　　　　　　　　[1812-1876] and Martin L. Seltz
　　　　　　　　　　　　[1909-1967]); COME, THOU REDEEMER OF
　　　　　　　　　　　　THE EARTH (translated by John Mason
　　　　　　　　　　　　Neale [1818-1866] and others).
Music: COMPOSER--anonymous.
　　　　　PLACE--Germany.
　　　　　DATE--published 1524.
　　　　　VARIANT TUNE--pre-17th century German folk song.
Found: CCT, HAR, SIG
Notes: The main tune is the melody NUN KOMM, DER HEIDEN
　　　　　HEILAND.

725. VESELÉ VÁNOCNÍ HODY

Lyrics: AUTHOR--folk.
　　　　　PLACE--Czechoslovakia.
　　　　　DATE--possibly created 16th-18th century?
　　　　　ENGLISH TITLE--SING WE MERRILY THIS HAPPY DAY
　　　　　　　　　　　　(translated by Mary Cochrane Vojácek).
Music: COMPOSER--folk.
　　　　　PLACE--Czechoslovakia.
　　　　　DATE--possibly created 16th-18th century?
Found: ZPE, SCC

726. VILLANCICO DE NAVIDAD

Lyrics: AUTHOR--folk.
　　　　　PLACE--Galicia, Spain.
　　　　　DATE--possibly created 16th-18th century?
　　　　　ENGLISH TITLE--TORCHES (translated by John Brande
　　　　　　　　　　　　Trend [1887-1958]).
　　　　　DIFFERING FIRST LINE--TORCHES, TORCHES, RUN WITH
　　　　　　　　　　　　TORCHES.

    Music: COMPOSER--folk.
             PLACE--Galicia, Spain.
             DATE--possibly created 16th-18th century?
             VARIANT TUNE--tune by John Joubert (1927-   ), a
                              composer from England.
    Found: OXF, CCO

727. THE VIRGIN MARY HAD A BABY BOY

    Lyrics: AUTHOR--folk.
             PLACE--West Indies.
             DATE--probably created 19th or early 20th century.
             DIFFERING FIRST LINE--DE VIRGIN MARY HAD A BABY BOY.
    Music: COMPOSER--folk.
             PLACE--West Indies.
             DATE--probably created 19th or early 20th century.
    Found: REF, APP

728. THE VIRGIN'S CRADLE HYMN

    Lyrics: AUTHOR--Samuel Taylor Coleridge (1772-1834).
             PLACE--England.
             DATE--published 1801.
             DIFFERING FIRST LINE--SLEEP, SWEET BABE! MY CARES
                             BEGUILING.
    Music: COMPOSER--Edmund Rubbra (1901-   ).
             PLACE--England.
             DATE--possibly written 1925.
             VARIANT TUNE--tune by F.T. Durrant.
    Found: OXF, REE
    Notes: The lyrics were derived from a Latin poem, DORMI,
             JESU!, which possibly originated in Germany.

729. VOISIN, D'OU VENAIT?

    Lyrics: AUTHOR--folk.
             PLACE--France (possibly Anjou).
             DATE--possibly created 17th or 18th century?
             ENGLISH TITLE--WAKING-TIME (paraphrase by Eleanor
                      Farjeon [1881-]).
             DIFFERING FIRST LINES--VOISIN, D'OU VENAIT CE GRAND
                            BRUIT; NEIGHBOUR, WHAT WAS THE
                            SOUND, I PRAY.
    Music: COMPOSER--folk.
             PLACE--France (possibly Anjou).
             DATE--possibly created 17th or 18th century; possibly
               first published 1766.
    Found: OXF, SMI

730. VOM HIMMEL HOCH, DA KOMM ICH HER

Lyrics: AUTHOR--Martin Luther (1483-1546).
PLACE--Germany.
DATE--probably written 1534; published 1535.
VARIANT VERNACULAR TITLE--VOM HIMMEL HOCH.
ENGLISH TITLES--FROM HEAVEN ABOVE TO EARTH I COME,
FROM HEAVEN HIGH, FROM HEAVEN ABOVE,
and LUTHER'S CAROL (four titles for
the same translation by Catherine
Winkworth [1827-1878]); FROM HEAVEN
HIGH I COME TO YOU; others.
DIFFERING FIRST LINE--FROM HEAVEN HIGH I COME TO
EARTH.

Music: COMPOSER--probably Martin Luther (1483-1546).
PLACE--Germany.
DATE--published 1539.
VARIANT TUNE--folk tune from Scotland, probably 16th
century.

Found: MANY

Notes: The words for the carol VOM HIMMEL KAM DER ENGEL
SCHAR (1543) were written by Luther with the intention of providing a shorter substitute for VOM HIMMEL
HOCH; the tune is sometimes used for VOM HIMMEL KAM,
is used for the carol THE HOLY SON OF GOD, and was
also used by Johann Sebastian Bach (1685-1750), in
three different harmonizations, in his CHRISTMAS
ORATORIO (1734); this carol is perhaps the best-
known carol from Germany; for an English derivative,
see the carol BALULALOW.

731. VOM HIMMEL KAM DER ENGEL SCHAR

Lyrics: AUTHOR--Martin Luther (1483-1546).
PLACE--Germany.
DATE--published 1543.

Music: COMPOSER--anonymous.
PLACE--Germany.
DATE--published 1588.
VARIANT TUNE--tune used for VOM HIMMEL HOCH, DA
KOMM ICH HER.

Found: BUD

Notes: The lyrics were written by Luther with the intention
of providing a shorter substitute for his 1535 carol,
VOM HIMMEL HOCH, DA KOMM ICH HER; at first Luther's
tune for the earlier carol was used for this one,
but in 1588 another tune, derived from the carol
A SOLIS ORTUS CARDINE, was also attached to this
carol.

732. VOX CLARA ECCE INTONAT

      Lyrics: AUTHOR--anonymous.
                  PLACE--Europe.
                  DATE--probably written 5th or 6th century.
                  ENGLISH TITLES--HARK! A THRILLING VOICE IS SOUNDING,
                              HARK! A HERALD VOICE IS CALLING, and
                              HEAR THE HERALD VOICE RESOUNDING
                              (three variations of the same trans-
                              lation by Edward Caswall [1814-
                              1878]).
      Music: COMPOSER--William Henry Monk (1823-1889).
                  PLACE--England.
                  DATE--written 19th century.
                  VARIANT TUNE--tune by Michael Weisse (ca. 1480-1534).
      Found: CAT, LUT, ENG, SIG

733. W ZLOBIE LEZY

      Lyrics: AUTHOR--folk.
                  PLACE--Poland.
                  DATE--probably created 13th or 14th century.
                  ENGLISH TITLES--JESUS HOLY, BORN SO LOWLY (translated
                              by George K. Evans); BABY JESUS, IN A
                              MANGER; INFANT HOLY, INFANT LOWLY
                              (paraphrased by Edith Margaret
                              Cellibrand Reed [1885-1933]); HE IS
                              SLEEPING IN A MANGER; HE IS BORN;
                              TELL, O SHEPHERDS.
                  DIFFERING FIRST LINE--IN A MANGER HE IS LYING.
      Music: COMPOSER--folk.
                  PLACE--Poland.
                  DATE--probably created 13th or 14th century.
      Found: INT, SHE, THF, MET, OBE
      Notes: This is perhaps the best-known Polish carol.

734. WACHET AUF! RUFT UNS DIE STIMME

      Lyrics: AUTHOR--Philipp Nicolai (1556-1608).
                  PLACE--Germany.
                  DATE--published 1599.
                  VARIANT VERNACULAR TITLE--WACHET AUF.
                  ENGLISH TITLE--WAKE, AWAKE, FOR NIGHT IS FLYING
                              (translated by Catherine Winkworth
                              [1827-1878]).
      Music: COMPOSER--Philipp Nicolai (1556-1608).
                  PLACE--Germany.
                  DATE--published 1599.
      Found: SIM, YAL, MET, HAR, LUT
      Notes: Johann Sebastian Bach (1685-1750) used Nicolai's
                  lyrics and melody as the foundation for his Cantata
                  No. 140 (ca. 1731).

735. WASN'T THAT A MIGHTY DAY

    Lyrics: AUTHOR--folk (Black spiritual).
               PLACE--United States.
               DATE--probably created 18th or 19th century.
    Music: COMPOSER--folk (Black spiritual).
               PLACE--United States.
               DATE--probably created 18th or 19th century.
    Found: ANS, SEA, SEE, LAN

736. WASSAIL SONG

    Lyrics: AUTHOR--folk.
               PLACE--probably Yorkshire, England.
               DATE--probably created 17th century.
               VARIANT VERNACULAR TITLES--HERE WE GO A-CAROLING;
                                        HERE WE COME A-CAROLING;
                                        HERE WE COME A-WASSAILING.
               DIFFERING FIRST LINE--HERE WE COME AWASSAILING.
    Music: COMPOSER--folk.
               PLACE--probably Yorkshire, England.
               DATE--probably created 17th century.
               VARIANT TUNE--folk tune probably from Leeds, England;
                             probably created in 17th or 18th
                             century.
    Found: MANY
    Notes: Sometimes two verses of this song are treated as a
               separate carol, GOOD-BYE; despite the compatibility
               of the lyrics of WASSAIL SONG and GOOD-BYE, they
               appear to be from different sources; the same music
               is used for both; for a carol with lyrics similar to
               WASSAIL SONG but with a different tune, see WE'VE
               BEEN AWHILE A-WANDERING.

737. WATCHMAN, TELL US OF THE NIGHT

    Lyrics: AUTHOR--John Bowring (1792-1872).
               PLACE--England.
               DATE--published 1825.
    Music: COMPOSER--probably Jakob Hintze (1622-1702).
               PLACE--Germany.
               DATE--published 1678.
               VARIANT TUNES--1879 tune by Joseph Parry (1841-1903),
                                composer from Wales; tune by Lowell
                              Mason (1792-1872).
    Found: SIM, MET, ULT, HAR, LUT
    Notes: Parry's tune is also used for the hymn JESUS, LOVER
               OF MY SOUL.

738.   WE NEED A LITTLE CHRISTMAS

    Lyrics: AUTHOR--Jerry Herman (1933-   ).
              PLACE--United States.
              DATE--published 1966.
              DIFFERING FIRST LINE--HAUL OUT THE HOLLY.
    Music: COMPOSER--Jerry Herman (1933-   ).
              PLACE--United States.
              DATE--published 1966.
    Found: SEV
    Notes: This is from Herman's Broadway musical MAME.

739.   WE THREE KINGS OF ORIENT ARE

    Lyrics: AUTHOR--John Henry Hopkins (1820-1891).
              PLACE--probably New York City.
              DATE--written 1857.
              VARIANT VERNACULAR TITLES--KINGS OF ORIENT; THE THREE
                                          KINGS.
    Music: COMPOSER--John Henry Hopkins (1820-1891).
              PLACE--probably New York City.
               DATE--written 1857.
    Found: MANY
    Notes: It was possibly first published in 1859 and was
              definitely published in 1863; there is some contro-
              versy over the use of the phrase "We three kings"
              in the lyrics ("three kings" is not biblically
              supported); it is probably the best-known song having
              the visit of the wise men as its primary theme.

740.   WE WISH YOU A MERRY CHRISTMAS

    Lyrics: AUTHOR--folk.
              PLACE--West country, England.
              DATE--possibly created 16th century.
              VARIANT VERNACULAR TITLE--A MERRY CHRISTMAS.
              DIFFERING FIRST LINES--I WISH YOU A MERRY CHRISTMAS;
                                    NOW BRING US SOME FIGGY
                                    PUDDING.
    Music: COMPOSER--folk.
              PLACE--West country, England.
               DATE--possibly created 16th century.
    Found: INT, CCO, LEI, FCC, MAL
    Notes: There also is an unrelated United States carol of the
              same title.

741.   WE WOULD SEE JESUS, LO! HIS STAR IS SHINING.

    Lyrics: AUTHOR--John Edgar Park (1879-1956).
              PLACE--United States.
               DATE--published 1913.
               VARIANT VERNACULAR TITLE--WE WOULD SEE JESUS.

Music: COMPOSER--Herbert Barclay Turner (1852-1927).
PLACE--United States.
DATE--published 1907.
Found: PRS, MET, CHW

742. WELCOME CHRISTMAS

Lyrics: AUTHOR--Theodore Seuss Geisel (1904-   ).
PLACE--United States.
DATE--published 1966.
DIFFERING FIRST LINE--FAH WHO FORAZE.
Music: COMPOSER--Albert Hague (1920-   ).
PLACE--United States.
DATE--published 1966.
Found: HAP
Notes: This is from Dr. Seuss' television program HOW THE
GRINCH STOLE CHRISTMAS.

743. WELCOME YULE

Lyrics: AUTHOR--folk.
PLACE--England.
DATE--probably created 15th century.
DIFFERING FIRST LINES--WELCOME YULE, THOU MERRY MAN;
WELCOME BE THOU, HEAVENKING.
Music: COMPOSER--Sydney Hugo Nicholson (1875-1947).
PLACE--England.
DATE--probably written early 20th century.
VARIANT TUNES--tune by Percy M. Young (1912-   );
anonymous tune published 1609.
Found: OXF, HUT, UNI, YOU, ECS
Notes: The lyrics are very similar to those for WOLCUM
YOLE!

744. WE'LL DRESS THE HOUSE

Lyrics: AUTHOR--Wihla Hutson.
PLACE--United States.
DATE--published 1954.
DIFFERING FIRST LINE--WE'LL DRESS THE HOUSE WITH
HOLLY BRIGHT.
Music: COMPOSER--Alfred Burt (1919 or 1920-1954).
PLACE--United States.
DATE--published 1954.
Found: BUR

745. WE'VE BEEN AWHILE A-WANDERING

Lyrics: AUTHOR--folk.
PLACE--probably Yorkshire, England.
DATE--probably created 17th century.
VARIANT VERNACULAR TITLE--WASSAIL SONG.
Music: COMPOSER--folk.

PLACE--probably Yorkshire, England.
DATE--possibly created 17th century.
Found: CCO, ETE
Notes: For a carol with similar lyrics but a different tune,
             see WASSAIL SONG.

746. WEXFORD CAROL

     Lyrics: AUTHOR--folk.
                  PLACE--probably England and Wexford region, Ireland.
                  DATE--probably created 17th or 18th century.
                  DIFFERING FIRST LINE--GOOD PEOPLE ALL, THIS
                                        CHRISTMASTIME.
     Music: COMPOSER--folk.
                  PLACE--probably Wexford region, Ireland.
                  DATE--probably created 17th or 18th century.
     Found: OXF

747. WHAT CAN I GIVE HIM

     Lyrics: AUTHOR--Paul Francis Webster (1909-1984).
                  PLACE--United States.
                  DATE--published 1963.
                  DIFFERING FIRST LINE--WHAT CAN I GIVE HIM, POOR AS I
                                        AM?
     Music: COMPOSER--Ben Weisman (1921-   ).
                  PLACE--United States.
                  DATE--published 1963.
     Found: ONS, HAP

748. WHAT CHEER?

     Lyrics: AUTHOR--folk.
                  PLACE--England.
                  DATE--probably created 15th century.
     Music: COMPOSER--William Walton (1902-1983).
                  PLACE--England.
                  DATE--published 1961.
     Found: CCO

749. WHAT CHILD IS THIS?

     Lyrics: AUTHOR--William Chatterton Dix (1837-1898).
                  PLACE--England.
                  DATE--written around 1865.
     Music: COMPOSER--folk.
                  PLACE--England.
                  DATE--created 16th century.
                  VARIANT TUNE--tune by James T. Field.
     Found: MANY
     Notes: The 16th century tune is the well-known melody
                  GREENSLEEVES; it is also used for the carol THE OLD
                  YEAR NOW AWAY IS FLED.

750. WHAT SWEETER MUSIC

     Lyrics: AUTHOR--Robert Herrick (1591-1674).
                PLACE--probably Devonshire, England.
                DATE--published 1648.
                VARIANT VERNACULAR TITLE--HERRICK'S CAROL.
                DIFFERING FIRST LINE--WHAT SWEETER MUSIC CAN WE
                                  BRING.
     Music: COMPOSER--Johannes Brahms (1833-1897).
                PLACE--Germany.
                DATE--written 1882; published 1883.
                VARIANT TUNE--German folk tune, probably 16th
                                  century.
     Found: SIM, OXF
     Notes: Brahm's tune is from his string quintet, Opus 88;
                the folk tune is also used for the carol ALS ICH BEI
                MEINEN SCHAFEN WACHT.

751. WHAT TIDINGS BRINGEST THOU, MESSENGER?

     Lyrics: AUTHOR--folk.
                PLACE--England.
                DATE--created 15th century.
                VARIANT VERNACULAR TITLES--WONDER TIDINGS; WHAT
                                  TIDINGS BRINGEST THOU?;
                                  WHAT TIDINGS BRING'ST US,
                                MESSENGER?
                DIFFERING FIRST LINE--A BABE IS BORN OF HIGH NATURE.
     Music: COMPOSER--folk.
                PLACE--England.
                DATE--created 15th century.
                VARIANT TUNES--another 15th century English folk tune;
                              tune by John LaMontaine (1920-   ).
     Found: OXF, APP, MEC, WON, UNI

752. WHAT YOU GONNA CALL YO' PRETTY LITTLE BABY?

     Lyrics: AUTHOR--folk (Black spiritual).
                PLACE--United States.
                DATE--probably created 18th or 19th century.
     Music: COMPOSER--folk (Black spiritual).
                PLACE--United States.
                DATE--probably created 18th or 19th century.
     Found: OWE, LAN
     Notes: For carols with somewhat similar lyrics but different
                tunes, see MARY, WHAT ARE YOU GOING TO NAME THAT
                PRETTY LITTLE BABY? and GLORY TO THAT NEWBORN KING.

753. WHATEVER HAPPENED?

     Lyrics: AUTHOR--Jimmy Webb (1946-   ).
                PLACE--United States.
                DATE--published 1968.

                    DIFFERING FIRST LINE--WHATEVER HAPPENED TO CHRISTMAS?
          Music: COMPOSER--Jimmy Webb (1946-   ).
                    PLACE--United States.
                    DATE--published 1968.
          Found: SEV

754. WHEN CHRIST WAS BORN IN BETHLEHEM

          Lyrics: AUTHOR--Henry Wadsworth Longfellow (1807-1882).
                    PLACE--probably Massachusetts.
                    DATE--probably written mid-19th century.
          Music: COMPOSER--Ebenezer Beesley (1840-   ).
                    PLACE--probably Salt Lake City, Utah.
                    DATE--probably written second half of 19th century.
                    VARIANT TUNE--tune by W.F. Taylor.
          Found: LDS, HUT
          Notes: Longfellow's poem, originally entitled CHRISTMAS
                    CAROL, was a translation of a poem from the Naples,
                    Italy region.

755. WHEN CHRIST WAS BORN OF MARY FREE

          Lyrics: AUTHOR--folk.
                    PLACE--England.
                    DATE--probably created 15th century; first known text
                        1456.
                    VARIANT VERNACULAR TITLES--WHEN CHRIST WAS BORN;
                                            IN EXCELSIUS GLORIA; WHEN
                                            CHRIST WAS BORN OF PURE
                                            MARIE.
          Music: COMPOSER--Arthur Henry Brown (1830-1926).
                    PLACE--England.
                    DATE--published 1871.
                    VARIANT TUNES--tunes by Martin Shaw (1875-1958),
                                Reginald Jacques (1894-   ), William
                                Leonard Reed, Herbert Stephens Irons
                                (1834-1905), and Trevor Widdicombe.
          Found: OXF, HAW, REE, CCO, UNI
          Notes: The original tune (possibly 16th century) has been
                    lost.

756. WHEN JESUS CHRIST WAS TWELVE YEARS OLD

          Lyrics: AUTHOR--folk.
                    PLACE--England.
                    DATE--possibly created 16th-18th century; probably
                        first published 1823.
                    VARIANT VERNACULAR TITLE--WONDROUS WORKS.
          Music: COMPOSER--folk.
                    PLACE--England.
                    DATE--possibly created 16th-18th century; probably
                        first published 1833.

Found: OXF, THF, GAS, SAN, UNI
Notes: Only the first part of the song is affiliated with Christmas; the second part is associated with Easter.

757. WHEN JOSEPH WAS AN OLD MAN

Lyrics: AUTHOR--folk.
PLACE--probably Appalachian region.
DATE--probably created 18th or 19th century.
Music: COMPOSER--folk.
PLACE--probably Appalachian region.
DATE--probably created 18th or 19th century.
Found: RTW
Notes: This is another version of THE CHERRY TREE CAROL, with lyrics very similar to those for other versions, but with a different tune; look under THE CHERRY TREE CAROL in the index for all related carols.

758. WHEN RIGHTEOUS JOSEPH WEDDED WAS

Lyrics: AUTHOR--folk.
PLACE--Cornwall, England.
DATE--possibly created 16th-18th century.
VARIANT VERNACULAR TITLE--RIGHTEOUS JOSEPH.
Music: COMPOSER--folk.
PLACE--Cornwall, England.
DATE--possibly created 16th-18th century.
VARIANT TUNE--tune from Devonshire, England.
Found: OXF, THF, GAS, SAN, UNI
Notes: The carol was probably first published in 1822; this carol's first verse is similar to the first verse of one version of the carol O MORTAL MAN, REMEMBER WELL, but otherwise they are unrelated.

759. WHEN SANTA CLAUS GETS YOUR LETTER

Lyrics: AUTHOR--John D. Marks (1909-   ).
PLACE--United States.
DATE--published 1950.
DIFFERING FIRST LINE--CHRISTMAS COMES BUT ONCE A
YEAR.
Music: COMPOSER--John D. Marks (1909-   ).
PLACE--United States.
DATE--published 1950.
Found: POP, ULT, ONS, ONT

760. WHEN THE CRIMSON SUN HAD SET

Lyrics: AUTHOR--George Peirce Grantham.
PLACE--England.
DATE--probably written 1860-1875.

Music: COMPOSER--anonymous, possibly folk.
           PLACE--France.
           DATE--probably created 18th century.
Found: RSC, HUT, CHO
Notes: The tune is also used for the carol LES ANGES DANS
           NOS CAMPAGNES.

761. WHERE THE LITTLE JESUS SLEEPS

Lyrics: AUTHOR--Milton Theodore Okun (1923-   ), Robert
               Corman, and C.C. Carter.
           PLACE--United States.
           DATE--published 1958.
           DIFFERING FIRST LINE--COME TO BETHL'EM, COME TO
                                 BETHL'EM.
Music: COMPOSER--Milton Theodore Okun (1923-   ), Robert
               Corman, and C.C. Carter.
           PLACE--United States.
           DATE--published 1958.
Found: SEV

762. WHILE SHEPHERDS WATCHED THEIR FLOCKS

Lyrics: AUTHOR--Nahum Tate (1652-1715).
           PLACE--England.
           DATE--published 1700.
           VARIANT VERNACULAR TITLES--WHILE SHEPHERDS WATCHED;
                                      WHILE SHEPHERDS WATCHED
                                      THEIR FLOCKS BY NIGHT; THE
                                      VISION OF THE SHEPHERDS;
                                      SHEPHERD'S SONG.
Music: COMPOSER--anonymous, possibly Thomas Este (ca. 1540-
               1608), possibly George Kirbye (ca. 1560-
               1634).
           PLACE--England.
           DATE--created 16th century; first published in
               Este's THE WHOLE BOOK OF PSALMS (1592) with
               probable arrangement by Kirbye.
           VARIANT TUNES--tune by George Frederick Handel (1685-
               1759), adapted from his 1728 opera
               SIROE, KING OF PERSIA; tune by Richard
               Storrs Willis (1819-1900), also used
               for IT CAME UPON THE MIDNIGHT CLEAR;
               United States folk tune; tune by
               William Knapp (1698-1768); other tunes.
Found: MANY
Notes: The first known joining of Tate's words and the 16th
           century tune was in the 1861 collection HYMNS ANCIENT
           AND MODERN; the tune by Willis is also used for the
           carol CALM ON THE LISTENING EAR OF NIGHT.

763. WHITE CHRISTMAS

Lyrics: AUTHOR--Irving Berlin (1888-   ).
         PLACE--United States.
         DATE--written 1940.
         VARIANT VERNACULAR TITLE--I'M DREAMING OF A WHITE
                 CHRISTMAS.
Music: COMPOSER--Irving Berlin (1888-   ).
         PLACE--United States.
         DATE--written 1940.
Notes: The song was first presented in the 1942 movie
         HOLIDAY INN; this is the most successful of 20th
         century American popular Christmas songs.

764. THE WHITE WORLD OF WINTER

Lyrics: AUTHOR--Mitchell Parish.
         PLACE--United States.
         DATE--published 1965.
         DIFFERING FIRST LINE--IN THIS WONDERFUL WHITE WORLD
                 OF WINTER.
Music: COMPOSER--Hoagy Carmichael (1899-1981).
         PLACE--United States.
         DATE--published 1965.
Found: ULT, ONS, HAP

765. WHY ISN'T CHRISTMAS ALL THE YEAR ROUND?

Lyrics: AUTHOR--Harry Robert Wilson (1901-1968).
         PLACE--United States.
         DATE--published 1957.
Music: COMPOSER--Harry Robert Wilson (1901-1968).
         PLACE--United States.
         DATE--published 1957.
Found: WIL

766. WIE SCHÖN LEUCHTET DER MORGENSTERN

Lyrics: AUTHOR--Philipp Nicolai (1556-1608).
         PLACE--Germany.
         DATE--published 1599.
         VARIANT VERNACULAR TITLE--WIE SCHÖN LEUCHTET.
         ENGLISH TITLES--HOW BRIGHTLY SHINES THE MORNING STAR
                 (translated by William Mercer [1811-
                 1873]); O MORNING STAR, HOW FAIR AND
                 BRIGHT and HOW BRIGHTLY BEAMS THE
                 MORNING STAR (also called HOW BRIGHTLY
                 BEAMS), two different translations by
                 Catherine Winkworth (1827-1878);
                 others.

Music: COMPOSER--Philipp Nicolai (1556-1608).
          PLACE--Germany.
          DATE--published 1599.
Found: OXF, INT, SIM, OBE, MET
Notes: The first line originally was "Wie herlich strahlt
          der Morgenstern"; the first line and much of Nicolai's
          lyrics were rewritten in 1768 by Johann Adolf
          Schlegel (1721-1793); Johann Sebastian Bach (1685-
          1750) used the melody in his Cantata No. 1 (1725),
          and Bach's arrangement is used most often today;
          the tune is sometimes used as an accompaniment to
          the carol DIE KÖNIGE.

767. WIE SOLL ICH DICH EMPFANGEN?

Lyrics: AUTHOR--Paul Gerhardt (1607-1676).
          PLACE--Germany.
          DATE--published 1653.
          ENGLISH TITLES--O HOW SHALL I RECEIVE THEE; HOW
                          SHALL I FITLY MEET THEE?
Music: COMPOSER--Johann Georg Ebeling (1637-1676).
          PLACE--Germany.
          DATE--published 1667.
          VARIANT TUNES--tunes by Hans Leo Hassler (1564-1612)
                         and Melchior Teschner (1584-1635).
Found: SIM, BUD, LUT, MEN, NHW
Notes: The words have been erroneously attributed to
          Christian Friedrich Henrici (1700-1764), who under
          the pen name "Picander" collaborated with Johann
          Sebastian Bach (1685-1750) on Bach's CHRISTMAS
          ORATORIO (1734); the lyrics and Hassler's tune were
          used in that work.

768. WIEGENLIED DER HIRTEN

Lyrics: AUTHOR--Christian Friedrich Daniel Schubart (1739-
                 1791).
          PLACE--Germany.
          DATE--published 1786.
          VARIANT VERNACULAR TITLE--WIEGENLIED.
          ENGLISH TITLES--SHEPHERDS' CRADLE SONG (two differ-
                          ent translations, one by George K.
                          Evans, the other by John Davies);
                          THE SHEPHERDS' CRADLE SONG (trans-
                          lated by A. Foxton Ferguson); SLEEP
                          WELL, YOU HEAVENLY CHILD (translated
                          by Edward Bliss Reed [1872-1940]).
          DIFFERING FIRST LINES--SCHLAF WOHL, DU HIMMELSKNABE
                          DU; O SLEEP THOU HEAV'N-BORN
                          TREASURE, THOU; SLEEP WELL,
                          YOU HEAV'NLY CHILD SO FAIR;
                          SLEEP WELL, THOU LOVELY
                          HEAV'NLY BABE.

Music: COMPOSER--Karl Leuner.
PLACE--Germany.
DATE--published 1814.
VARIANT TUNE--tune by Joseph Anton Fehr (1761-1807).
Found: INT, CCT, CEL, UNI

769. WINTER WONDERLAND

Lyrics: AUTHOR--Richard B. Smith (1901-1935).
PLACE--United States.
DATE--published 1934.
DIFFERING FIRST LINES--OVER THE GROUND LIES A
MANTLE OF WHITE; SLEIGHBELLS
RING, ARE YOU LIST'NIN'?
Music: COMPOSER--Felix Bernard (1897-1944).
PLACE--United States.
DATE--published 1934.
Found: SEV, POP, HAP

770. WISE MEN SEEKING JESUS

Lyrics: AUTHOR--James Thomas East.
PLACE--United States.
DATE--published 1926.
Music: COMPOSER--Kenneth George Finlay.
PLACE--United States.
DATE--published 1925.
VARIANT TUNE--tune by Alonzo Potter Howard (1838-
1902).
Found: MEN, CHW

771. WITHER'S ROCKING HYMN

Lyrics: AUTHOR--George Wither (1588-1667).
PLACE--England.
DATE--published 1641.
VARIANT VERNACULAR TITLE--SWEET BABY, SLEEP!
DIFFERING FIRST LINE--SWEET BABY, SLEEP! WHAT AILS
MY DEAR?
Music: COMPOSER--Ralph Vaughan Williams (1872-1958).
PLACE--England.
DATE--published 1928.
Found: OXF, NOB, CFS

772. WOLCUM YOLE!

Lyrics: AUTHOR--anonymous, possibly John Wedderburn (1500?-1556)
and/or James Wedderburn (1495?-1553).
PLACE--England.
DATE--possibly written 16th century.
DIFFERING FIRST LINE--WOLCUM, WOLCUM.

Music: COMPOSER--Benjamin Britten (1913-1976).
          PLACE--England.
          DATE--written about 1948.
Found: BRI
Notes: The lyrics are very similar to those for WELCOME
          YULE.

773. WONDERFUL CHRISTMASTIME

Lyrics: AUTHOR--Paul McCartney (1942-   ).
          PLACE--England.
          DATE--published 1979.
          DIFFERING FIRST LINE--THE MOOD IS RIGHT.
Music: COMPOSER--Paul McCartney (1942-   ).
          PLACE--England.
          DATE--published 1979.

774. WONDERFUL COUNSELOR

Lyrics: AUTHOR--folk (Black spiritual).
          PLACE--United States.
          DATE--probably created 19th or early 20th century.
          DIFFERING FIRST LINE--TELL ME WHO DO YOU CALL THE
                              WONDERFUL COUNSELOR.
Music: COMPOSER--folk (Black spiritual).
          PLACE--United States.
          DATE--probably created 19th or early 20th century.

775. THE WONDERFUL WORLD OF CHRISTMAS

Lyrics: AUTHOR--Charles Tobias (1898-1970).
          PLACE--United States.
          DATE--published 1968.
Music: COMPOSER--Albert T. Frisch (1916-1976).
          PLACE--United States.
          DATE--published 1968.
Found: ULT, ONS, HAP

776. WONDROUS LOVE

Lyrics: AUTHOR--anonymous, possibly folk.
          PLACE--probably Southern States.
          DATE--published 1867.
          DIFFERING FIRST LINE--WHAT WONDROUS LOVE IS THIS.
Music: COMPOSER--folk.
          PLACE--Southern States.
          DATE--probably created 18th or 19th century.
          VARIANT TUNE--another folk tune, probably of similar
                       origins.
Found: APP, LAN

777. WORKERS' CAROL

    Lyrics: AUTHOR--Morris Martin (1910-   ).
             PLACE--England.
             DATE--possibly written 1949.
             DIFFERING FIRST LINE--COLDLY THE NIGHT WINDS WINGING.
    Music: COMPOSER--Paul Petrocokino (1910-   ).
             PLACE--England.
             DATE--possibly written 1949.
    Found: REE, GOL

778. THE WORLD'S DESIRE

    Lyrics: AUTHOR--Gilbert Keith Chesterton (1874-1936).
             PLACE--England.
             DATE--probably written early 20th century.
             VARIANT VERNACULAR TITLE--THE CHRIST-CHILD LAY.
             DIFFERING FIRST LINE--THE CHRIST-CHILD LAY ON MARY'S
                                  LAP.
    Music: COMPOSER--folk.
             PLACE--probably United States.
             DATE--probably created 18th or 19th century.
             VARIANT TUNES--folk tune from Austria, probably 16th
                            century; tune by Enid Richardson.
    Found: OXF, NOB, THF, UNI, REF
    Notes: The Austrian tune is also used for the carol EIN
             KINDLEIN IN DER WIEGEN.

779. WŚROD NOCNÉJ CISZY

    Lyrics: AUTHOR--folk.
             PLACE--Poland.
             DATE--possibly created 14th-16th century?
             ENGLISH TITLES--ECHOES ARE SOUNDING (translated by
                        Olga Paul); MIDST THE DEEP SILENCE
                        (translated by Alice Zienko and Ruth
                        Heller [1920-   ]); IN MIDNIGHT'S
                        SILENCE (translated by George K.
                        Evans); IN THE SILENCE OF THE NIGHT.
             DIFFERING FIRST LINE--IN THE SILENCE OF THAT NIGHT
                            SO BRIGHT.
    Music: COMPOSER--folk.
             PLACE--Poland.
             DATE--possibly created 14th-16th century?
    Found: INT, OBE, REB, RTW, HEL

780. YA VIENE LA VIEJA

    Lyrics: AUTHOR--folk.
             PLACE--Andalusia, Spain.
             DATE--possibly created 17th-19th century?

ENGLISH TITLE--COME, MY DEAR OLD LADY (translated by
          George K. Evans).
Music: COMPOSER--folk.
           PLACE--Andalusia, Spain.
           DATE--possibly created 17th-19th century?
Found: INT, MON

781. YE WATCHERS AND YE HOLY ONES

Lyrics: AUTHOR--Athelstan Riley (1858-1945).
           PLACE--England.
           DATE--published 1906.
Music: COMPOSER--anonymous.
           PLACE--Germany.
           DATE--published 1623.
Found: YAL, MET
Notes: The tune originally was written for an Easter song,
           LASST UNS ERFREUEN HERZLICH SEHR.

782. YEOMAN'S CAROL

Lyrics: AUTHOR--anonymous.
           PLACE--probably Dorsetshire, England.
           DATE--possibly created 17th-19th century?
           VARIANT VERNACULAR TITLE--A YEOMAN'S CAROL.
           DIFFERING FIRST LINE--LET CHRISTIANS ALL WITH JOYFUL
                                  MIRTH.
Music: COMPOSER--anonymous.
           PLACE--probably Dorsetshire, England.
           DATE--possibly created 17th-19th century?
Found: OXF, ECS

783. YOUNG AND OLD MUST RAISE THE LAY

Lyrics: AUTHOR--John Mason Neale (1818-1866).
           PLACE--England.
           DATE--published 1866.
Music: COMPOSER--anonymous.
           PLACE--Germany.
           DATE--probably created medieval period; possibly
                 first published 1609.
           VARIANT TUNE--another German tune, possibly from
                         medieval period.
Found: COF, HUT

784. YOU'RE ALL I WANT FOR CHRISTMAS

Lyrics: AUTHOR--Glen Moore and Seger Ellis (1904-   ).
           PLACE--United States.
           DATE--published 1948.

DIFFERING FIRST LINE--WHEN SANTA COMES AROUND AT
CHRISTMAS TIME.
Music: COMPOSER--Glen Moore and Seger Ellis (1904-   ).
PLACE--United States.
DATE--published 1948.
Found: NOR, POP

785. YULE RETURNS, COME, CHRISTIAN PEOPLE

Lyrics: AUTHOR--R. Watham.
PLACE--England.
DATE--probably created 19th or early 20th century.
Music: COMPOSER--Vernon Bryan Crowther-Beynon.
PLACE--England.
DATE--possibly written early 20th century.
Found: HAP, HUT

786. ZEZULKA Z LESA VYLÍTLA

Lyrics: AUTHOR--folk.
PLACE--Czechoslovakia.
DATE--possibly created 17th-19th century?
ENGLISH TITLES--FROM OUT THE FOREST A CUCKOO FLEW
(translated by George K. Evans);
CAROL OF THE BIRDS; THE BIRDS
(translated by Percy Dearmer [1867-
1936]).
DIFFERING FIRST LINES--ZEZULKA Z LESA VYLÍTLA, KUKU!;
CUCKOO, CUCKOO, CUCKOO; FROM
OUT OF A WOOD A CUCKOO DID
FLY; FROM OUT OF A WOOD DID A
CUCKOO FLY.
Music: COMPOSER--folk.
PLACE--Czechoslovakia.
DATE--possibly created 17th-19th century?
VARIANT TUNE--tune by John LaMontaine (1920-   ).
Found: INT, SHE, SON, NOB, OXF

787. ZU BETHLEHEM GEBOREN

Lyrics: AUTHOR--folk.
PLACE--Germany.
DATE--probably created 16th or 17th century.
VARIANT VERNACULAR TITLE--ZUM BETHLEHEM GEBOREN.
ENGLISH TITLES--IN BETHLEHEM SO LOWLY (translated by
George K. Evans); EIA, EIA; THERE'S
BORN IN BETHLEHEM'S MANGER (translated
by Edward Bliss Reed [1872-1940]).
DIFFERING FIRST LINE--TO US IN BETHLEM CITY.
Music: COMPOSER--folk.
PLACE--Germany.
DATE--probably created 16th or 17th century.

Found: INT, OXF, SIM, BUD, CTW
Notes: The carol was probably first published in 1638.

788. ZU MITTEN DER NACHT SIND HIRTER ERWACHT

   Lyrics: AUTHOR--folk.
         PLACE--probably Upper Palatinate, Germany.
         DATE--possibly created 17th-19th century; possibly
               first published 1880.
         VARIANT VERNACULAR TITLE--ZU MITTEN DER NACHT.
         ENGLISH TITLE--IN MIDNIGHT FROM SLEEP (translated by
               Edward Bliss Reed [1872-1940]).
   Music: COMPOSER--folk.
         PLACE--Germany.
         DATE--possibly created 16th-18th century?
         VARIANT TUNE--another German tune.
   Found: BUD, CFI

789. ZVIM NA ZEMLJI MIR

   Lyrics: AUTHOR--folk.
         PLACE--Croatia, Yugoslavia.
         DATE--probably created medieval period.
         ENGLISH TITLE--TO ALL THE EARTH (translated by Ruth
               Heller [1920-   ]).
   Music: COMPOSER--folk.
         PLACE--Croatia, Yugoslavia.
         DATE--probably created medieval period.
   Found: HEL

INDEXES

TITLE INDEX

PERSON AND GROUP INDEX

Brand, Oscar   108
Brébeuf, Jean de   389
Brewer, Alfred Herbert   352
Bridges, Matthew   430
Brimhall, John   164, 168
Britten, Benjamin   21, 30, 82,
   86, 356, 694, 698, 772
Broadhurst, Cecil   194
Brodsky, Roy   688
Brooks, Phillips   266, 535
Brossard de Montaney, Jacques
   Charles   510
Brown, Abbie Farwell   421
Brown, Arthur Henry   205, 372,
   557, 755
Brown, Herbert S.   344
Brownlie, John   414
Brueckner, H.   496
Bunnett, Edward   129
Burgess, Dave   499
Burke, Joseph Francis   483, 658
Burnap, Uzziah Christopher   378
Burns, Robert   70
Burt, Alfred   34, 43, 127, 130,
   181, 386, 528, 667, 673, 744
Burt, Bates Gilbert   34, 43,
   386
Byrd, William   564
Byrom, John   147

Caesar, Irving   691
Cahn, Sammy   161, 171, 176,
   435, 629
Caird, G. B.   598
Calkin, John Baptiste   352, 459
Campbell, Robert   376
Cappeau, Placide   118
Carmichael, Hoagy   764
Carpenter, Richard Lynn   481
Carson, Jenny Lou   109
Carter, C.C.   761
Castellanos, Joaquin Nin y
   see Nin y Castellanos,
   Joaquin
Caswell, Edward   544, 630, 655,
   732
Cates, George   482
Catrick, John   68
Catterick, John   68
Cavanaugh, James   156, 696
Cawood, John   324
Celerio, Levi   54
Cennick, John   447

Chalmers, Patrick Reginald   393,
   429, 603
Chandler, John   376, 595
Charles, Stephan   79
Chaucer, Geoffrey   1
Chesterton, Frances   348
Chesterton, Gilbert Keith   778
Chopin, Frédéric   455
Christierson, Frank von
   see Von Christierson, Frank
Clark, Tony   85
Coffin, Charles   376, 595
Coffin, Henry Sloane   723
Coleridge, Samuel Taylor   639,
   728
Coles, George   280
Colletet, Francois   603
Colum, Padraic   537
Conkey, Ithamar   183
Conley, Larry   437
Connor, Tommie   353
Cook, Joseph Simpson   290
Cooke, Arnold   537
Cooper, George   677
Coots, John Frederick   350,
   626
Corman, Robert   761
Cornelius, Peter   146, 212, 403
Corner, David Gregorius   86, 240
Coverdale, Miles   193
Cowdrey, Cecil   408
Crashaw, Richard   683
Crestot,   433
Croo, Robert   192
Crosby, Fanny
   see Van Alstyne, Frances Jane
   Crosby
Crowther-Beynon, Vernon Bryan
   785
Cruciger, Elizabeth   335
Cruger, Johann   314
Cummings, William Hayman   323
Custance, Arthur F.M.   186

d'Andichon, Henri   325
Darby, Ken   714
David, Hal   149, 219
Davies, Henry Walford   67, 98,
   160, 535
Davies, John   768
Davis, Henry W.   259
Davis, Katherine K.   444
Davis, Robert   278

Jacques, Reginald   354, 755
James, Mary   85
James, William Garnet   125,
    509, 702
Janzow, F. Samuel   289, 448
Jessel, Leon   570
Jesuits   389
Johnson, Jay W.   99
Johnson, Norman   385
Jones, J.D.   105
Jones, William   103, 414
Jonson, Ben   357
Joubert, John   726
Juncos, Manuel Fernandez   203

Katterjohn, Henry   526
Kennedy, Amanda   677
Kent, Willys Peck   126, 178,
    428, 593
Kielland, Gustava   532
Kindlemarsh, Francis   277
King, Oliver A.   536
King, Pete   456
Kirbye, George   762
Kirkpatrick, William James   76
Kletke, Gustav Hermann   52
Klickmann, Frank Henri   714
Kocher, Conrad   67
Kohler, Emmy   521
König, Johann Balthasar   376
Knapp, William   762
Knox, Ronald Arbuthnott   189,
    233, 600, 608
Knudsen, Peder   385
Krauth, Charles Porterfield
    208
Krohn, Johan Jacob   227
Krolik, Mary Stuart   90
Kunz, Jack   163
Kurtz, Emanuel   646

Lacey, Thomas Alexander   723
La Montaine, John   200, 315,
    525, 559, 751, 786
Large, Donald E.   339
Latino, Frank   342
Laub, Thomas Linnemann   206
LaVoie, Roger   293
Lawrence, E.E.   692
Ledbetter, Huddie   50
Lee, Lester   152
Le Moigne, Lucas   137

Leontovych, Mykola Dmytrovich
    122, 123, 180, 609
Leuner, Karl   768
Leven, Melville Abner   61
Levitt, Estelle   317
Liguori, Alphonsus   713
Linale, Frank   107
Lindsay, W.B.   137, 410, 603
Lissant, George B.   281, 440
Littledale, Richard Frederick
    132, 370
Livingston, Jay   644
Longfellow, Henry Wadsworth
    352, 754
Lonsdale, R.E.   303
Lombardo, Carmen   319
Luboff, Norman   16
Luna, Felix   452
Luther, Martin   76, 289, 345,
    730, 731

Macbean, Lachlan   431
MacDonald, Ballard   570
Macdonald, Mary   431
MacDonough, Glen   708
Machado, Antonio   243
MacLellan, Gene   666
Maconchy, Elizabeth   37, 114
MacWilliam, Margaret   188
Madan, Martin   323
Maier, Betty   449
Malin, Donald Franklin   687
Mann, Arthur Henry   281
Marks, Gerald   361, 691
Marks, John D.   3, 13, 19, 319,
    352, 398, 492, 613, 616, 643,
    714, 759
Marlatt, Earl Bowman   432
Martens, Frederick Herman   292
Martin, George Clement   357
Martin, George Edward   695
Martin, Hugh   326
Martin, Morris   131, 443, 777
Martin, Nicolas   381
Mason, Lowell   183, 324, 406,
    580, 737
Mathias, William   357, 651
Matthews, Timothy Richard   700
Maxwell, Robert   148, 327
May, Robert L.   616
McCartney, Paul   773
Mclennan, William   225
Mendelssohn, Arnold   553
Mendelssohn, Felix   323

Wadding, Luke 377
Wade, John Francis 31
Wagner, Roger 445
Wainwright, John 147
Waits of London 300
Wakefield, Samuel 40
Walton, William 44, 748
Warlock, Peter 30, 82, 716
Watham, R. 785
Watts, Isaac 349, 405, 406
Webb, George James 314
Webb, Jimmy 753
Weber, Lloyd 151
Webster, Paul Francis 456, 483,
 658, 747
Wedderburn, James 82, 772
Wedderburn, John 82, 772
Wedderburn, Robert 82
Weisberg, Steve 154
Weismann, Ben 747
Weiss, George David 662, 690
Weiss, Hugo 662
Weiss, Luigi 662
Weisse, Michael 732
Weissel, Georg 459
Weldon, Frank 156, 696
Wells, Robert 169
Wesley, Charles 183, 323, 447,
 704
Wesley, Samuel 376
Wexelsen, Marie 385
Weyse, Christoph Ernst Friedrich
 227, 408
Wheeler, John 125, 509, 702
Whitefield, George 323
Widdicombe, Trevor 755
Wilhousky, Peter J. 123
Willcocks, David 681
Williams, Charles Lee 145
Williams, Ralph Vaughan
 see Vaughan Williams, Ralph
Williams, Ursula Vaughan
 see Vaughan Williams, Ursula
Willis, Richard Storrs 110,
 378, 762
Willson, Meredith 379
Wilson, Brian 446
Wilson, Harry Robert 676, 765
Winkworth, Catherine 279, 459,
 710, 730, 734, 766
Wirén, Noel 93, 330, 454, 495,
 519, 521
Wither, George 66, 98, 771
Witt, Christian Friedrich
 183, 544

Wolfe, Richard William 95, 162
Woodward, George Ratcliffe
 216, 249, 258, 259, 260, 312,
 367, 390, 425, 512, 533, 546,
 565, 574, 593, 598, 599, 670
Worde, Wynken de 101
Wordsworth, Christopher 649,
 669
Work, Frederick J. 297
Work, John W. 297

Yon, Pietro Alessandro 292
Young, Andrew 150
Young, John Freeman 681
Young, Percy M. 258, 743

Zeeman, Joan Javits 623
Zienko, Alice 231, 287, 455,
 779